Collected Works of David V. █████
Volume I

HOW TO PUT THE SUBCONSCIOUS MIND TO WORK

&

THE SILENCE: WHAT IT IS AND HOW TO USE IT

Collected Works of David V. Bush
Volume I

HOW TO PUT THE SUBCONSCIOUS MIND TO WORK

&

THE SILENCE: WHAT IT IS AND HOW TO USE IT

Printed in the United States of America and Australia.

Spastic Cat Press
www.SpasticCatPress.com

ISBN: 978-1-61203-975-6

Table of Contents

HOW TO PUT THE SUBCONSCIOUS MIND TO WORK

CONTENTS

PREFACE

The very great advance made in the science of mental healing during the last half of the nineteenth and the beginning of the twentieth century must be self-evident to the most superficial observer. However, both in conducting classes and in giving private counsel all authorities come sooner or later face to face with what I believe impresses every unprejudiced person in the line of mental healing, namely, the wide variety of cults and the large number of teachers and organizations, each one thinking he or it has discovered the one and only true method of mind healing. To my mind this condition is one of the biggest obstacles the whole movement of the power of the mind to heal has yet to overcome.

There can be no single person, no single organization which has sequestered all of the healing truth. To think otherwise is to be circumscribed by one's own narrow prejudices.

Anything is true that works. Call it what you may. Tabulate its manifestations in what fashion you will, designate it what you choose. It matters not what name you give it--if it works it is true.

On every side we see cults, organizations and teachers who claim they draw from the only fount of mental healing truth. This, alas, is reverting to type, going back to the prejudiced, bigoted, circumscribed methods of the dark ages.

That there may be made available to the public a set of books on mental healing which demonstrates the power of mind from every angle--showing that one method may be true for Smith, another for Jones, and a third for Brown-- is my object in presenting herewith various successful methods of healing. The desideratum, to my mind, in all healing, study and experience, is the development of a breadth of mind which will be nothing short of cosmic consciousness. In such a domain all will be able to worship at one shrine, enjoy peace of mind, fraternize with their fellows or commune with

God in any manner they choose, free from the dictates of any powers that be, untrammeled by the chains of prejudice of their own or others' forging.

Never will the world come into a cosmic consciousness-- the fatherhood of God and the brotherhood of man—until we are willing to acknowledge the good which is to be found in realms other than our own -- whether it be in mental healing, in religion or in the life of practical experience.

Hence, in dealing with the power of mind to heal, the purpose of this series is to present, all told, some twenty- eight different methods of healing as operated by different cults, teachers, religions, organizations and psychological centers, all of which have proved variously successful as they have been employed to meet the needs of various individuals.

David V. Bush

SUBCONSCIOUS MIND

Alarm Clock

The Subconscious is the most wonderful thing in the human mind, and perhaps in all the world we know; for it is the omnipotent part of man. A single illustration will suffice to show this transcendent quality.

Did you ever go to bed at night desiring to awaken at a certain hour in the morning! The time may be altogether different from your usual arising hour, but is it not a fact that whatever it is, you generally awaken exactly on the dot. It may be two o'clock, three o'clock, four o'clock, five o'clock, six o'clock, or any other o'clock; but in nine cases out of ten you open your eyes on time.

This involves an operation of the omniscient part of man. The subconscious mind knows everything though, of course, it must be properly directed. If you wish to awaken at five o'clock in the morning, and are not used to rising at that hour, your conscious mind gives a strong suggestion which the subconscious takes up, and as a result you actually do emerge from sleep at the right moment, though without visible or external cause. Notice the omniscient (all-knowing) part of this again. You do not have to take out your watch and say "eight hours from now will be five o'clock Standard Time--I shall get up at five o'clock." No, it doesn't make any difference whether it is two hours or five hours, whether it is eight minutes or 800 minutes. At the appointed time you will awaken. Just pause a moment and see what this means.

You awaken at the appointed time, and there you are.

Time Changes

Travel westward, if you will, where the time changes. You go to bed saying to yourself that you will awaken at five o'clock in the morning. You are traveling by sleeper on a fast express. You go to bed by Eastern Time, and while crossing the land enter the belt of Central Time, which is an hour slower; yet you awaken at literally five o'clock--not four o'clock, the absolute hour which would have been five for you had you remained in the Eastern belt; but the actual five o'clock of the new region, which is the Eastern six o'clock. Marvelous are the understandings and workings of the subconscious mind!

Upon giving this illustration in my campaigns, I have often been asked with some perplexity how is it that, if the subconscious mind is the omniscient and divine part of man, this sensitive medium may take up wrong suggestions, such as fear, worry, doubt, sorrow, fright, lack, limitation or poverty. The answer is very simple. All life is orderly and scientific, and works according to certain rules and regulations of nature. The same omniscient spirit which is within man is also within the acorn and the tree. The principle of life is God-Power. The God-Power in the acorn makes the oak; in you, it makes the man.

Divine In Man

There is a vast difference between the oak tree and man, just as there is a vast difference between the primitive savage and the great example of the divine in man as manifested by Jesus of Nazareth. All men have the divine in them. Jesus is the highest exemplification of this divinity but it would be absurd to say that because the primitive man is not the Christ, the God spirit is not within him. In fact, Scripture tells us that man was made in the image of God--that is, that the spirit within man rather than the mere flesh of his body is the image. God spirit is in all living creatures, but is manifested differently according to the planes on which they live.

But to return to the question of my perplexed auditors--if the spirit of man is omniscient, why does his subconscious mind receive wrong impressions, and why must he make conscious suggestions for their correction? The answer is really very simple. You see the God power in the oak and know that the oak's growth is the result of what God and the law of the tree can do. Similarly, the God power in man can accomplish as much as man and God can do.

In other words, the omniscient part of man must work in accordance with the natural laws of life. The spirit as within man is obviously different from the pure spirit as emancipated from all earthly trammels. Of the one we may expect only inclinations toward complete divinity; the other is pure divinity itself.

The butterfly has only those same potentialities within it which were once encased by the lowly cocoon. The same God power was at work with the life in the cocoon, as that which is at work in the well developed butterfly; but for a while that now gorgeous and active spirit was limited and made outwardly dull by the sluggish primitiveness of the cocoon environment. So with man.

Spirit Limited In The Flesh

The spirit in man is for the time being limited by the flesh . . . the cocoon of man, if you please. The same God spirit which presides in the individual, handicapped as it may be by the fleshly tabernacle, will some time leave the body and go into another and higher sphere of development, as the butterfly leaves the cocoon. And in that higher plane, where there is no limitation of the flesh, what may the spirit not be able to do? It may travel to distant lands and return in an instant, as our radio vibrations are sent out and caught by the aerials which link in fellowship all the homes of America from Boston to San Francisco. The spirit of man, when freed from the cocoon of the flesh, may have as little limitation as the pure essence of God himself.

So one should not become discouraged by the seeming paradox involved in the necessity of suggestion to a subconscious mind which is omniscient and divine. We have to suggest, because that is the way in which the process happens to work. The way to catch radio broadcastings is to have your aerial, and gather in the vibrations.

There may be millions of Universal radios vibrating through the Universal ether, but if you have no aerial and cannot listen in you do not know what is taking place. You catch the message by having your aerial and your radio machine, and without these you can never get it. It is the way it is done, that is all.

So, if we would have the subconscious mind work for us, we must recognize the way nature intended it to work. While it is encased in the cocoon of the fleshly tabernacle, it is amenable to suggestion; and this is the only way we are going to get it to work at such a stage, because this is the present way that God intended it to work. While it is limited by the flesh, we must work in the fleshly way. When it is freed from the flesh who may dream or prophesy what laws it will own or what heights it can reach. We are here now, and the way to get the omniscient part of us to perform the wonders of omnipotence, is to work according to the laws which God has laid down.

Omnipotent and Omniscient

Since the subconscious mind is both omnipotent (all-powerful) and omniscient (all-knowing), it knows everything which ought to be done for man's good; and if properly directed by suggestion will do it. It will find one's right environment, and lead one to his right vocation. It will select one's proper life mate, and attract abundance and happiness to him. Its omniscience gives it a thorough knowledge of man's cellular metabolism, glandular secretion, vascular, muscular and nervous activity, and indeed of all things pertaining to health and vitality; a knowledge which needs only the guidance of sincere and intelligent suggestion to make it the omnipotent corrective of every bodily inharmony.

In "Therapeutic Suggestion Applied," the author gives a splendid elucidation of the workings of the subconscious mind for health.

How It Works

The objective mind is the mind which results from organization, and it may be regarded as the function of the brain. It is the mind with which we do business; the mind that operates through the five physical senses. It comes, develops with, matures, and finally declines and dies with the physical body.

It controls, in a great measure, all voluntary motion. We call this the "brain mind." It is capable of reasoning both deductively and inductively.

The subjective mind is a distinct entity. It occupies the whole human body, and, when not opposed in any way, it has absolute control over all the functions, conditions and sensations of the body. While the objective mind has control over all of our voluntary functions and motions, the subjective mind controls all of the silent, involuntary and vegetative functions. Nutrition, waste, all secretions and excretions, the action of the heart in the circulation of the blood, the lungs in respiration or breathing, and all cell life, cell changes and development, are positively under the complete control of the subjective mind. This was the only mind animals had before the evolution of a brain; and it could not, nor can it yet, reason inductively, but its power of deductive reasoning is perfect. And more, it can see without the use of physical eyes. It perceives by intuition. It has the power to communicate with others without the aid of ordinary physical means. It can read the thoughts of others. It receives intelligence and transmits it to people at a distance. Distance offers no resistance against the successful missions of the subjective mind. We call this the "soul mind." It is the living soul.

Now, in proper, healthy or normal conditions of life, the objective mind and the subjective mind act in perfect harmony with each other. When this is the case, healthy and happy conditions always prevail. But, unfortunately perhaps, these two minds are not always permitted to act in perfect harmony with each other; this brings mental disturbances, excites physical wrongs, functional and organic diseases.

Happily, by a knowledge of and a strict obedience to the laws of life, the objective and subjective minds can be kept in harmony with each other; and, when they get out of harmony and disease and pain result, they can be brought into harmony again and perfect conditions of health restored, all by suggestion. By suggestion, we say. Yes, by suggestion! Let the reader keep the following paragraph before him, and be careful to properly understand it, and he will readily see how suggestion controls physical conditions, and how we can command mind forces for the relief and cure of disease.

While the subjective mind possesses the power of intuitive perception, which enables it to perceive (independently of reason, experience or previous education) the laws that pertain to our physical and mental harmony--good health --it is entirely incapable of inductive reasoning, and is constantly amenable to the power of suggestion for either good or evil by the conscious mind of the individual himself or that of another. Therefore, notwithstanding, the subconscious mind has, when not opposed in any way, absolute control over all the functions and sensations of the body, and is entirely capable of preserving their harmonious and healthful manifestations. It is also true that improper suggestions from the objective mind of the person himself, or from some other person, may divert the action of the subjective mind, and sickness and death may result.

On the other hand, in cases of sickness, proper suggestions made to the subjective mind of a patient, by his own objective mind, or by that of some other person, will as certainly result in healthful changes and complete relief from pain and disease.

Physical Changes

Now, a careful study of the above paragraph will enable anyone to fully understand how physical changes may be wrought by mental influences; how pain may be relieved and disease controlled by proper suggestions. If the subconscious mind has full control over all our bodily functions, which is absolutely true, and if we can reach the subconscious mind by suggestion, which is also true, then all that is required in order to give relief and cure disease is for us to present suitable ideas to the minds of our patients--thoughts that will result in the relief and cure of disease and the correction of vices--and our work is accomplished.

The Subconscious Mind and Its Power

J. D. Powers in "Mind Power Plus" follows the same line of reasoning, thus:

When doctors and psychologists speak of the effect of the mind on the body and the health of the body they are dealing with definite facts and with laws capable of scientific proof. For it is known now that the subconscious mind, which is at once the master of the body and the servant of consciousness, is the bridge between the body and the mind.

Or in other words the subconscious mind runs all the bodily machinery. You consciously eat your dinner, but fortunately for you, you have nothing to do with the digestion of it. An unseen chemist, who knows just what chemicals are needed for each kind of food, goes to work at once to convert the food you have given to him into a living body, into the building up of tissue, of muscle and nerve. So also your heart action is taken out of the control of your conscious mind and left to a mind that never sleeps, never tires, never goes off the job, never forgets for an instant, and you go to your work and lie down in perfect safety so far as the action of your heart is concerned. So also during the day and the night, year in and year out, the blood circulates in all parts of your body, your breathing apparatus never stops for an instant, the liver and the kidneys and the various glands of the body do their work under the eyes and the never-relaxing supervision of this unseen, and, for the most part, unknown overseer.

Any physician will tell you that constant thought about any part of the body never fails to send an over-supply of blood to that part; and of course that means congestion and pain. By sending messages directly to an organ through the nerve centers or by changing the circulation, the subconscious director of our bodies can make any part of us misbehave in a number of ways. All it needs is a suggestion of an interfering thought about an organ, such as the heart or the stomach or the liver. Or all you need to do is to get worrying about yourself; that is the same thing, and gets the same results in ill health.

In other words, hands off--or rather, minds off. Don't get ideas that make you think about your body. The surest way to disarrange any function of the body is to think about it, especially to worry about it, to be pessimistic or blue about it. It is a stout heart that will not change its beat with a frequent finger on the pulse, and a hearty stomach that will not "act up" if you get to thinking about it or fretting about what you eat.

So Say the Physicians

The medical profession has for a considerable time recognized that there is some hidden power in the human being which can effect a cure much more rapidly and permanently than any administered medicine.

Now let us see what more can be said in its favor. Dr. Mitchell Bruce writes :

"We are compelled to acknowledge a power of natural recovery inherent in the body--a similar statement has been made by writers on the principle of medicine in all ages. The body DOES possess a means and mechanism for modifying or neutralizing influences which it cannot directly overcome."

I believe, that a natural power of prevention and repair of disorder and disease has as real and as active an existence within us as have the ordinary functions of the organs themselves.

"Every thoughtful practitioner," says Dr. Wilkinson, "will acknowledge that when his therapeutic reserves are exhausted by far the most reliable consultant is the VIS MEDICATRIX NATURAE. To ignore the fact that she has already been in charge of the case for days, when we first approach with our mixtures and tabloids, is at least a mistake in medical ethics."

"The VIS MEDICATRIX NATURAE," he also says, "is a power, a vital resistance to disease."

"Whatever other theories we hold, we must recognize the VIS MEDICATRIX NATURAE in some shape or other," says Professor O. W. Holmes.

"Je le pansay et Dieu le guarit ("I dressed the wound and God healed it") is written by Ambroise Pare on the walls of the Ecole de Medecine at Paris. "Nature is the physician of disease," says Hippocrates. "Reason dictates that disease is nothing else but Nature's endeavours to thrust forth with all her might the morbific matter for the health of the patient" (Sydenham). "This is more true of the symptoms than of the disease itself."

This power now is recognized and understood by modern science to reside within the subconscious mind. It is the subconscious mind itself.

Some medical authorities endeavour to explain it in this fashion:

It may be asked how the subconscious mind can affect and modify these vital functions? To illustrate very simply what we mean, it is a well-known physiological law that the vasomotor nervous system is greatly influenced by the emotions. Those having had experience in the use of suggestive therapeutics know that the psychic centers govern very largely the vasomotor nerves, and, consequently the circulation and the secretions. This is the reason why pills made of bread crumbs or other harmless substances, with suggestions, have been capable of causing diarrhea; this explains why disagreeable psychic sensations or depressing emotions are able to stop or poison the milk of a nursing mother. Herein is found also the explanation why a tumor increases rapidly in size if the patient is constantly preoccupied in thought with it, also with the naturally attending thoughts that depress. So, also is the concentration of the mind on a particular part of the body capable of modifying the flow of blood to that part.

While another school of science expresses it thus:

We would call your attention here, at this point, to the fact that the bases of Mind Cure, Mental Healing, Mental Therapeutics (or by whatever names the various systems of mental cure of disease may be called) undoubtedly are to be found in the fact that the vital functions and processes of the body are really performed by mind operating along subconscious lines--by the Subconscious, in fact. This being realized, it is seen plainly that Mental Healing (in each or all of its forms) is not a case of the power of Mind over Matter, but rather that of the influence of one phase of the mind over another phase—a case of "Mind over Mind," in fact.

And so it is possible for the body to originate, and the mind to recognize, sensations which are not actually present; for instance, cancer of the foot can produce severe pain for months; cancer, foot, and all, may be amputated, and yet the patient may keep on recognizing pain as coming from the foot--recognizing it as in the foot, for weeks after the diseased member has been buried in some distant field.

And so various sensations of feeling--itching, pricking, burning--as well as sounds and voices, and sights and objects, may be aroused in the brain, while in reality they have no existence--they are merely illusions, sense delusions, or mental hallucinations. Sensations can produce ideas, and it should also be borne in mind that ideas can produce sensations.

All our feelings possess a natural language or expression. The smile of joy, the puckered features in pain, the stare of astonishment, the quivering of fear, the tones and glance of tenderness, the frown of anger--are all united in seemingly inseparable association with the states of feeling which they indicate. If a feeling arises without its appropriate sign or accompaniment, we account for the failure either by voluntary suppression, or by the faintness of the excitement, there being a certain degree of intensity requisite visibly to affect the bodily organs.

The physical sense impressions become sensations and feelings in the brain; and feelings may be described as a translation of the more purely physical impressions into nervous sensations that can be recognized by the mind. And so the fundamental basis of thought is found to be wholly physical, and the first step in thinking, conscious sensation, has its foundation in the special organs of sense connected with the body.

Another Way

Yet again must medicine approach the great questions of life, growth and health; expounding them, through a leading authority, in such words as these:

It has often been a mystery how the body thrives so well with so little oversight or care on the part of its owner.

No machine could be constructed, nor could any combination of solids or liquids in organic compounds regulate, control, counteract, help, hinder or arrange for the continual succession of differing events, foods, surroundings and conditions which are constantly affecting the body. And yet, in the midst of this ever-changing and varying succession of influences, the body holds on its course of growth, health, nutrition and self-maintenance with the most marvelous constancy.

We perceive, of course, clearly, that the best of qualities, --regulation, control, etc., etc.--are all mental qualities, and at the same time it is equally clear that by no self-examination can we say that we consciously exercise any of these mental powers over the organic processes of our bodies. One would think, then, that the conclusion is sufficiently simple and obvious--that they must be used unconsciously; in other words, it is, and can be nothing else than, unconscious mental powers that control, guide and govern the functions and organs of the body. Consider, for instance, the marvelous increase of smooth muscle in the uterus at term, and also its no less marvelous subsequent involution; observe, too, the compensating muscular increase of a damaged heart until the balance is restored and then it ceases, as does growth at a fixed period; consider in detail the repair of a broken bone. These actions are not mere properties of matter; they demand, and are the result of, a controlling mind.

The circulation does not go round as most text-books would lead us to believe, as the result merely of the action of a system of elastic tubes, connected with a self-acting force-pump. It is such views as these that degrade physiology and obscure the marvels of the body. The circulation never flows for two minutes in the same manner. In an instant, miles of capillaries are closed or opened up according to the ever-varying body needs, of which, consciously, we are entirely unaware. The blood supply of each organ is not mechanical, but is carefully regulated from minute to minute in health exactly according to its needs and activities, and when this ever fails, we at once recognize it as disease, and call it congestion and so forth. The very heart-beat itself is never constant, but varies pro rata with the amount of exercise, activity of vital functions, of conditions of temperature, etc., and even of emotions and other direct mental feelings.

The whole reproductive system is obviously under the sway and guidance of more than blind material forces. In short, when thoroughly analyzed, the action and regulation of no system of the body can be satisfactorily explained, without postulating an unconscious mental element; which does, if allowed, satisfactorily explain all the phenomena.

Mind is the builder; mind is supreme; it is "the hidden power that rules."

It has been variously designated as "the vital principle," "the principle of life," "the soul," "the communal soul, "the unconscious mind," "the subconscious mind," "the subliminal consciousness," "the subjective mind," etc., the designation being governed by the point of view from which the subject is treated. But no one, be he materialist or spiritualist, denies its existence, or that it is endowed with an intelligence commensurate with the functions it performs in organic life. Philosophers may differ in their views as to its origin, or its ultimate destiny, or its psychological significance outside of the functions it performs in keeping the machinery of life in motion; but no one denies its existence, its intelligence, or its power over the functions, sensations, and conditions of the body.

As a man thinketh in his heart, so is he. As the subconscious thinks, it's owner's condition is or should be, so that physical condition actually becomes in time.

The Most Wonderful of All

The subconscious mind is the most wonderful thing in man. The most wonderful of all things, but being sometimes misused, misguided and no end of suffering ensue. Just as the most excitable love sentimentalist may turn this sacred stream of love into the most loathsome and deadly river of poisonous hate, so can the "wrong use of the subconscious mind bring about most deleterious effects in the human body.

The most important thing for modern civilization is a proper understanding and operation of man's greatest gift--the Subconscious Mind.

Where is the Subconscious Mind?

The subconscious mind is everywhere, in every nook and corner, in every crevice and spot, in all space and in all time.

The subconscious mind is everywhere; the sub-conscious mind is the creative force of the universe, it is the eternal energy of God spirit.

The subconscious mind being everywhere, it is in every cell, every molecule, and every electron in the body of man. The tiniest "teentsie weentsie" particle of cell life in man contains the life of the subconscious; therefore, the subconscious mind is not only in the brain and in the head: it is everywhere, now and forever, in man and every living creature.

In Its Infancy

We must remember, in regard to this subconscious self, that we are just learning to use its powers. A hundred years ago, we had just as much electricity in earth and air as we have today. But we did not know how to use it. Now we do know how, and how marvelously we are using the power of electricity today! So with these powers of subconsciousness. We are beginning to understand and use them. We are just on the brink of further and fuller developments. But what we already know we must use in order to come to greater things.

These subconscious powers are largely latent forces. Many of us are using only a half or a third of our real equipment. We can call out the reserves of life--in these emergencies of depression or ill-health. We can release the pent-up energies for our bettering or restoration.

Dr. A. A. Lindsay, the famous suggestionist and author, in "Daily Life Psychology" offers the following suggestion:

Suggestion the Key

That suggestion should be the key to the action of the subconscious, that phase of mind within the individual that performs automatically and, often to the individual's objective phase of mind, unconsciously, is as reasonable as for temperature to be the key to the action of water when it is to become slow in its ethereal vibration and congeal as ice or rapid in its particle vibration and expand and manifest steam.

A suggestion is an image, thought, idea or working pattern introduced in the subconscious; the subconscious takes the architectural plan and creates forms and images in every phase of one's being and life to fulfill the appointments of the picture pattern.

The subconscious controls the motions of every cell of the body and will order each one into the position called for in the picture held in the subconscious. The subconscious controls the chemistry, the composition of the cell's body and will change the ethereal vibration of the constituent elements of the cell chemistry to fulfill the picture in the subconscious. The subconscious controls every organ and does so by controlling each cell of the organ, therefore, organs and systems become that which the soul expectancy (subconscious expectancy) calls for.

The subconscious phase of mind in the individual is the phase that communicates telepathically to another sub-conscious phase of mind, therefore, when a working plan is present in a subconscious phase of mind calling for fulfillments in other persons, or by them, the results to the lives of the persons involved are due to the pictures and expectancies in the soul of the individual or individuals; suggestion is the key to all of the subjective phenomena that have their source in the subjective because the soul has all potency for the individual's purposes and that which it believes (expects) it creates.

Many things that are not true are made to influence the individual in all of the phases of his being as if they were true; a thing is not true just because one believes it, but believing it, he may make it so. One may receive an untrue diagnosis calling for disease of certain description which may not exist at the time; accepting the image as if it were true, the subconscious proceeds to make cell changes to fulfill the in harmony in the architectural plan, the untrue diagnosis. That is how thinking may make a thing true which under law would not be true, the law of health. One may be ill but becoming convinced that he has taken the remedy his subconscious acts upon the image and impulse of healing and restores harmony; that is how thinking will make a thing true. This is far from making one accept the delusion of being well while he is diseased.

So we see that the Subconscious Mind in its vital activities is constantly at work building up, repairing, growing, nourishing, supporting and regulating the body, doing its best to throw off abnormal conditions, and seeking to do the best it can when these conditions cannot be removed. With its source pure and unpolluted the stream of vitality flows on unhindered, but when the poison of fear thought, adverse suggestion and false belief is poured into the source or spring from which the stream rises, it follows that the waters of life will no longer be pure and clear. Let us notice the general direction of the vital activities of the Subconscious Mind.

The normal individual expends every day energy enough to raise one ton thirty-three hundred feet or thirty-three hundred foot tons of energy, and nine-tenths of this amount of power is used to carry on the functions of the body, digestion, circulation, elimination, and the remaining manifestations of life. This wonderful expenditure of energy is under the direction of the subconscious mind which controls these functions and which is ever on the alert hour after hour, day after day, as long as life continues.--Terry Walter, M. D., in "The Handbook of Life."

So we see it is very plain how the body is made sick by poisonous chemicalization and how the subconscious mind which has control of all of the bodily functions and is In every cell of the body, can in turn, when it is directed by the conscious mind, change the chemicalization from poison to health when the patient crowds out the old kinks, images and pictures and puts in their place new ones.

In the beginning God created the heavens and the earth. IN THE BEGINNING CREATION IS TODAY. There never was a beginning and there never will be an ending. NOW is the beginning. TODAY IS THE DAY OF CREATION. It is going on today, a manifestation of God's spiritual power.

And finally, in "The Subconscious Power," by W. W. Atkinson and Edward E. Beals, this principle is further adduced:

Among the most fundamental activities of the Subconscious are those which are concerned with the vital processes of the physical body--the processes of life in the living organism. Although the fact is not generally recognized, it is an established scientific truth that the Sub- conscious controls, directs, institutes and conducts the vital processes of the body concerned with growth, nourishment and the general operation of the living organism.

The operation of the vital processes manifested in every organ of your body is conducted by the Subconscious.

Every organ, every part, even every cell, is under the control and direction of the Subconscious. The work of repair, replacement, digestion, assimilation and elimination, which is underway in your physical body, is performed by the Subconscious. In short, your entire vital activity is under the control and direction of your Subconscious, although your ordinary consciousness is not aware of this fact.

That all which is called Vital Force, the Healing Power of Nature, or the "Vis Medicatrix Naturae" is but a form, phase or aspect of subconscious mental action—of the work of the Subconscious--cannot be doubted even for a moment by those who have carefully investigated Nature's healing processes. These processes constitute what is known as "the curative efforts of Nature" or the "Vis Vita" by which term is indicated that certain curative or restorative principle of Nature which is implanted in every living, organized body, and which is constantly operative for its repair, preservation, health and well-being. Instances of the effective work of this great natural principle are seen in the respective processes manifest in cases where a finger or toe is lost by the man. Here, as a prominent medical authority has said, "Nature, unaided, will repair and fashion a stump equal to one at the hands of an eminent surgeon."

The convertibility of physical forces and the correlation of these with the vital forces, and the intricacy of that nexus between mental and bodily activity which cannot be analyzed, all lead upward to one and the same conclusion --that the source of all power is Mind.

Bacon says: "Life is not force; it is combining power. It is the product and presence of Mind."

UNFRIENDLY SUGGESTION

All Is Mind

God's universe is to every man exactly what his mind sees it to be. If the mind be free, and light, and joyous, the world is ablaze with sunlight, joy, and happiness, even though in appearance it be the darkest day of all the year. But if sorrow and despair have found lodgment there the world's delights and grand activities are huge mountains of dreariness in which is no fascination at all, but intensest weariness instead. Develop the mind by educational processes and the universe is no longer the shallow thing it was before, but a profound aggregate of cause and effect, of mysterious laws and forces, of deepest, grandest purposes and design. Instill lustful thoughts into it, and a world of animalism results. While if spiritual thoughts hold possession, and the mind endures as seeing Him who is invisible, the world's barren waste becomes a paradise again.

"Morbid mentality is death's advance agent, and if you persist in picturing calamity it may, indeed, come to pass."

A physician who for twenty-five years practiced medicine, gives this interesting illustration:

Even the doctor himself shakes his head when he comes, as if to say, you are not much longer for this world. The patient is obliged to submit to his surroundings, take whatever is given him; and, worse than all, has to listen to everything that is said of and about him. And if the patient happens to belong to a family in which some popular family disease has prevailed, such as consumption, asthma, apoplexy, paralysis, or rheumatism, this inheritance is held up before him or her, day in and day out.

Unfriendly suggestions of every kind should be avoided in all cases. If we cannot say something good or encouraging, something that will make people feel better, we should say nothing.

An internationally famous physician is on record as saying:

I, myself, have committed the same fault. A female attendant suffered with pains in the stomach. I diagnosed and treated her anxiously for gastric ulcer. For months she kept her bed, and gradually recovered with the stomach very sensitive for years. I have not now the slightest doubt that her long sickness was produced by over-anxious investigations and strict regimen.

We think many physicians as they read this will search their own memories and find recorded there more than one parallel case.

Where It Began

On every hand we see unfriendly suggestion dealt a smashing blow squarely between the eyes.

The curse pronounced upon our grandmother Eve operates as an ever-present suggestion to the mothers of Christendom that painful parturition is an inalienable inheritance; whereas among other races, this inevitable crisis in every normal woman's life is attended with comparatively little pain or inconvenience.

And So We Keep It Up

We hear more about germs and the mischief they do than about the suggestions which render people immune. We see scareheads and placards and billboards advertising the symptoms of disease and the ills from which people suffer, dangers of contagion, and need for physic at all crossroads of civilization.

If we spent one half as much printer's ink and one-tenth as much energy and one-hundredth part as much faith in creating a healthful atmosphere as we do in advertising the dangers of diseases besetting the human race, it wouldn't take long to shoo-fly diseases, disease germs and medicine kits out of the closets of the human family.

This unfriendly suggestion has been habitual from time immemorial down until the present day. Indeed, in heathen countries now, the suggestion of devils and imps of sickness and sorrow, and superstitious ravings about ill health, misfortune, poverty and death, stares man in the face everywhere.

But in our own country the suggestion of sickness is seen and heard at every crossroad of man's activity and experience. Warnings of this, that or the other sickness, of nose, throat, ear, eyes, smallpox and yellow fever, bronchitis and appendicitis, operations and amputations, patent medicine and quack serums, make up a major part of man's daily round of living. We come into the world in superstitious dread of sickness, we travel through this "veil of tears" between the two peaks of eternity, urged on to our dreadful end by ill suggestions of every kind on every hand, at every turn.

Fear--the suggestive fear of poverty and old age, of loss of leg, arm or ear, fear of failure, lack and limitation, fear of not getting married and fear of the divorce court after we are hooked up, fear of the circumstances and environment round about us! Fear of getting no business and after it grows fear that we can't take care of it! Fear of the devil, damnation, death and the judgment!

It is one roly-poly, whirly-gig, merry-go-round, ring-a-round-the-rosie of fear, from the time our eyes are opened to see the light of day until they are closed by the hands of another as if to cover the last long fear stare as we make our exit from this stage of life.

It has been supposed that one must pass through a round of children's diseases and other maladies of early and later life, culminating in the loss of faculties and in death, with all of the horrors and all of the pitfalls that average life may have.

It is asserted by physicians of experience that in cholera epidemics a large proportion--more than half--of the cases are the result of "fear," otherwise suggestion.

Suggestion and Death

Sir William Hamilton has mentioned the case of a row of billiard balls.

When one is struck the impetus is transmitted through all the row but only the last ball moves, the others remaining in their places.

Something like this seems often to occur in a train of thought, one idea immediately suggests another into consciousness--this suggestion passing through one or more ideas which do not themselves rise into consciousness. This point, that we are not conscious of the formation of groups, but only of a formed group, may throw light on the existence of unconscious judgments, unconscious reasonings and unconscious registrations of experience.

Referring to suggestion causing death, Dr. Alfred T. Schofield, the famous physician author, says in "The Force of Mind":

Only recently I heard of a case in the South of Scotland when two medical men were walking together, and one was saying that he could make a man ill by merely talking to him (I do not give the doctor's name for obvious reasons). The other doctor doubted this. So, seeing a laborer in a field, the first speaker went up to him, and, telling him he did not like his appearance, proceeded to diagnose some grave disease. The man was profoundly struck, left off work soon after, feeling very ill, took to his bed, and in a week died; no sufficient physical cause being found. This was of course a shocking misuse of the power, causing great grief at the time at the unexpected and fatal result.

Also: A gentleman known to me, seeing a friend with stricture of the gullet, soon experienced an increasing difficulty in swallowing, which ultimately was a cause of death.

Philip Zenner, in "Mind Cure and Other Essays", also agrees with other authorities about the influence of suggestion.

Suggestion of disease comes from many sources. Seeing its manifestations may give rise to the same symptoms. A case of St. Vitus dance in the schoolroom may give rise to an epidemic of the disease. There have been instances where the appearance of bizarre phenomena of this order has resulted in an epidemic throughout a whole land.

As one works over a problem, puts it aside unsolved and awakes in the morning with the solution in his mind, so suggestion of disease, received by the conscious--or possibly only partly conscious--mind, may be forgotten and yet continue its blighting effect subconsciously. Perhaps the suggestion does the more harm, because nothing is known of its presence.

Parents and Guardians

Not only does the human race collectively feel the steadily corrosive effect of unfriendly suggestion, but:

Parents and guardians may ruin children by giving them bad suggestions; they may not only make maniacs of them, but they may, by abuse and bad suggestions, make them profane, untruthful, wicked, and almost worthless.

By continually scolding and berating a child, telling it that it is mean, that it cannot do a good thing, it cannot tell the truth, it is worthless, that it never will be of any account, and that nobody likes it or cares for it, they are certainly building up a bad character, the very opposite of what they are trying to make.

If you want to make a boy bad, tell him he is mean and despised by all good people; but if you want him to be good, appeal to his pride. All boys have more or less good in them, and if we would develop this, we should frequently remind them of their good qualities and make them know that they have good hearts in them.

From the days of Socrates to the present time, there have been great sages, philosophers, sociologists, and psychologists who believe that criminality is more a matter of suggestion and environment than anything else.

The late Hugo Muensterburg, commenting upon this assumption is reported to have said:

The criminal is therefore never born as such. He is only born with a brain which is in some directions inefficient and which thus, under certain unfavorable conditions, will more easily come to criminal deeds than the normal brain.

With the idea of a stereotyped born criminal there disappears also the idea of a uniform treatment against criminal tendencies. That men are different in their power of resistance or in their power of efficiency or in their intellect or in their emotions, we have to accept as the fundamental condition with which every society starts. It would be absurd to remodel them artificially after a pattern. The result would be without value anyhow, inasmuch as our appreciation is relative. No character is perfect. The more the differences were reduced, the more we should become sensitive even for the smaller variations. All that society can do is, therefore, not to remodel the manifoldness of brains, but to shape the conditions of life in such a way that the weak and unstable brains also have a greater chance to live their lives without conflicts with the community.

The situation is different as soon as the particular surroundings have brought it about that such a brain with reduced powers has entered a criminal career. The thought of crime now becomes a sort of obsession or rather an autosuggestion. The way to this idea has become a path of least resistance, and as soon as such an unfortunate situation has settled itself, the chances are overwhelming that a criminal career has been started. If such eases should come early to suggestive treatment which really would close the channels of the antisocial autosuggestion, much harm might be averted. Yet again the liability of the brain to become antisocial would not have been removed, and thus not much would be secured unless such a person after the treatment could be kept under favorable conditions. With young boys who through unfortunate influence have caught a tendency, for instance, to steal, and where the fault does not yield to sympathetic reasoning and to punishment, an early hypnotic treatment might certainly be tried. I myself have seen promising results.

On Every Hand

Says an eminent authority:
Bad autosuggestion's occur involuntarily with all of us from time to time, and in many cases, alas! are all too frequent. The emotion which has special power in reinforcing them is the emotion of fear. These autosuggestions tend especially to exaggerate and to prolong ill-health of mind and body. In a certain proportion of cases they may perhaps be held responsible even for the initiation or production of such ill-health. It is therefore clear that in all cases of ill-health the inculcation of habits of good autosuggestion is most desirable, both to neutralize the previous bad autosuggestions, and also to give an additional uplift to the vital powers of the mind and body.

Hay Fever and Flowers

At the sight of roses or goldenrod many people promptly develop a congestion of the nasal mucus membrane with sneezing, watering of the eyes and profuse nasal secretions. It matters not if the flowers be artificial or real or it may be they associate hay fever with "the last week of June" and because they expect it they get it.

A young man had hay fever and was sure it was caused by inhaling the particles blown from the center of a daisy. Whenever he came near daisies his eyes swelled, tears ran, his nose discharged and he had a cough. Someone who understood the power of mind put a bunch of daisies in his room at night. "When he went to bed at night he was not near the regular periodicity for hay fever. When he wakened in the morning and saw the bouquet of daisies the old symptoms immediately returned. By the time he had made his toilet and ready to leave for business, his friend brought to his attention that these were not real daisies but artificial. This brought the counter suggestion with such suddenness and abruptness that he never had hay fever or the symptoms afterward.

Results of Wicked and Good Prayers

Tuke relates this incident:
Two boys were sent to a man's house for arum roots. He was away from home, but the boys went to the field and procured them; the owner, returning before they had left, pronounced the most dreadful imprecation upon one and both of them, threatening them with the agony of body equal to that arising from a heated spear or hook. The boys returned. One of them was shortly afterwards taken ill, and his friends concluded that it was the result of the malediction. He soon after died in dreadful agony.

Again--Erasmus Darwin relates the following:
A young farmer, in Warwickshire, finding his hedges broken and the sticks carried away during a frosty season, determined to watch for the thief. He lay under a hay stack, and at length an old woman, like a witch in a play, approached, and began to pull up the hedge; he waited till

she had tied up her bundle of sticks, and was carrying them off, that he might convict her of the theft, and then springing from his concealment he seized his prey with violent threats. After some altercations, in which her load was left upon the ground, she kneeled upon the bundle of sticks, and raising her arms to heaven beneath the bright moon, then at the full, spoke to the framer: "Heaven grant that thou never mayest know again the blessing to be warm." He complained of cold all the next day, and wore an overcoat, and in a few days another, and in a fortnight took to his bed, always saying nothing made him warm; he covered himself with very many blankets, and had a sieve over his face as he lay, and from this one insane idea he kept his bed about twenty years for fear of the cold air, till at length he died.

Curses

No thinking person would believe that these "curses" were the result of divine interposition. They were the direct results of wicked prayers which again proves the wonderful power of suggestion. In both instances the men thought the prayers--the curse--would follow them and because they expected it, it was the natural operation of the law of autosuggestion.

But the encouraging thing is that positive thoughts called blessings or prayers for success and health are more effective than wicked prayers.

"Thoughts are things," says Shakespeare, but good thoughts and positive thoughts are by far better things than wicked thoughts and negative thoughts.

Another Slant

In "Mental Medicine" by Oliver Huckel, we get another aspect of unfriendly suggestion, that of the person who will not be responsive or give in to unfriendly suggestion.

This is a phase of unfriendly suggestion which we all want to study, understand and conquer.

A volunteer in the recent Spanish-American war lay sick with typhoid fever in a Southern hospital. The physician passing through the ward on his tour of inspection noticed his weakened condition and said to the nurse in attendance. "That man can't live." The young man overheard the remark, and with what remaining strength he had cried out, "I will live!" The physician's remark aroused his antagonism and impelled an auto-suggestion contradictory to the physician's declaration. The determination to live started all the curative forces of his subconscious nature, and the ideal of life, "I will live," crowded out the expectation of death. He did live.

Power of Mind Over Body

Dr. Bernheim was about to treat a young woman who was afflicted with aphonia (loss of voice) with electricity. Before doing so he put his hand over the larynx and moved it up and down and said to her, "Now you can speak aloud." He told her to say "a." She said it and the aphonia disappeared.

A Catholic woman went to Dr. Hammond to consult with him about her sickness. He considered that she had an incurable disorder and he told her so. She turned away with a sigh. "Ah," she said, "if I only had some of the water of Lourdes, then I should be cured." It so happened that a friend had brought the Doctor a bottle of the genuine water, that he might chemically analyze it and find out its medicinal properties. He told her that he had some of the water and promised to give her some of it, provided she would first try a more potent remedy. Aqua Crotonis--Croton Acqueduct water. She said that it would not reach her case. (The suggestion of the water of Lourdes had complete control of her mind). He gave her a little bottle of Lourdes water, but labeled it Aqua Crotonis. She returned to his office no better. Then he gave her a vial of Croton water and labeled it "Water of Lourdes." She was completely cured.

It's After All of Us

As all of us are susceptible to unfriendly suggestion, so all of us are equally susceptible to friendly suggestion. That is the encouraging part of the study of psychology. When we turn our faces from all unfriendly suggestion toward the friendly, from the bad to the good, from the sick to the well, from the unhappy to the happy, we change our whole world.

This method of healing has been and will be performed by the power of mind.

Back of All

We have asserted elsewhere that there is only one law of healing and that this one law was operated by Jesus in many different ways. Take for instance, the story of the blind man in St. John, Chapter 9. Jesus, we are told spat on the ground, made a paste out of the clay, and anointed the blind man's eyes then told him to go and wash in the Pool of Siloam. Note how the man's healing power within was aroused and stimulated by the act and the suggestion.

Of course, there was no healing power in the clay that was used, nor was there healing power in the spittle, but the suggestion of the clay, augmented by the reputation of Jesus, stimulated a faith within the man to such an extent that the healing took place.

After the clay was made and put upon the blind man's eyes, it became dry and sticky--I suppose similar to that "mud stuff" the barbers use in giving a mud massage. The longer the clay stays on the face, the more drawing effect it seems to have. It seems to crack and crackle on the face, and as it does this, pulls the skin and annoys the subject (one mud massage was enough for me). I suppose as this mud began to cake and draw the eyes of the man, he went through the streets with his mind deeply aroused to the fact that he wanted to get the mud off. So as he rubbed his eyes and brought his mind to the weak spot, circulation increased; this created a warm sensation; aroused a vibration, and by the time he reached the Pool of Siloam, and without soap or towel washed this sticky, dry, clinging mud from his eyes, the healing power within was so aroused that the man "went on his way rejoicing"--seeing.

Do not forget that, in addition to the suggestion of the mud and the reputation of Jesus, a command from the greatest teacher of the ages was given to the blind person--"Go wash in the Pool of Siloam."

Biblical Days

The same law of suggestion is apparent in the leper whom Jesus cleansed by telling him to go show himself to the Priest and make an offering as prescribed by Moses, as a testimony.

The Priest in this capacity acted as quarantine or health officer, and to get by him was some job. No one else could have instilled the confidence into the leper to even attempt to get by this quarantine board. But Jesus' reputation had so grown, and the leper was so anxious to be healed, that a great faith was established in him when Jesus said--"Be thou clean." And as he went, he was healed.

Jesus understood how healing was done, but you remember he told his disciples on one occasion, that he had many things to tell them that they could not yet hear. Jesus did not tell everything he knew. That he healed was enough for them in their day and in their state of consciousness. If he had attempted to explain from a scientific or psychological standpoint how the healing was effected, those primitive, superstitious, unlearned people could not have understood and would have gone away disappointed or doubting.

Long before we made a science of the power of mind to heal, primitive peoples and superstitious folk believed in it and employed it.

Pvrrhus, king of Epirus, had the power of assuaging colic and affections of the spleen by laying the patients on their backs and passing his great toe over them. The Emperor Vespasian cured nervous affections, lameness, and blindness, solely by the laying on of his hands (Suelin, Vita Yespas).

According to Coelius Spartianus, Hadrian cured those afflicted with dropsy by touching them with the points of his fingers, and himself recovered from a violent fever by similar treatment. King Olaf healed Egill on the spot by merely laying his hands upon him and singing proverbs (Edda, p. 216). The kings of England and France cured diseases of the throat (goitre) by touch. It is said that the pious Edward the Confessor, and in France that Philip the First, were the first who possessed the power. The formula used on such occasions was, "Le roi te touche, allez et guerrisses," so that the word was connected with the act of touching—physical contact. In England the disease was called the King's Evil; and in France the power was retained until within the memory of men now living.

Among the German princes this curative power was ascribed to the Counts of Hapsburg, and they were also able to cure stammering by a kiss. Pliny says, "There are men whose whole bodies are possessed of medicinal properties, as the Marsi, the Psyli, and others, who cure the bite of serpents merely by the touch." In later times the Salmadores and Ensalmadores of Spain became very celebrated, who healed almost all diseases by prayer, laying on of hands, and by the breath. In Ireland, Valentine Great-rakes cured at first king's evil by laying on of hands; later, fever, wounds, tumors, gout, and at length all diseases. In the seventeenth century the gardener Levret and the notorious Streeper performed cures in London by stroking with the hand. In a similar manner cures were performed by Michael Medina, and the child of Salamanca; also Marcellus Empiricus (Sprengel, Gesch. der Med., part ii. p. 179). Eichter, an innkeeper at Eoyen, in Silicia, cured, in the years of 1817-18, many thousands of sick persons in the open fields, by touching them with his hands. Under the Popes, laying on of the hands was called Chirothesy. Diepenbroek wrote two treatises on it; and, according to Lampe, four-and-thirty Chirothetists were declared to be holy.

Basis of "Miraculous"

In the "International Science Series," Binet, in an article entitled, "Animal Magnetism", refers to this.

Those who undertake miraculous cures ... do not deny the existence of disease, but assert that it may be cured by supernatural power. They act by means of suggestion and by gradually inculcating the idea that the disease is curable, until the subject accepts it. The cure is sometimes effected by the suggestion, and when it is said to be by saving faith, the expression is rigorously scientific. These miracles should no longer be denied, but we should understand their genesis, and learn to imitate them. These are therefore no imaginary diseases, but are diseases due to the imagination, and accompanied by real functional disturbances. Such disturbances may be developed under the influence of spontaneous (unconscious), accidental, or deliberate (conscious) suggestion, and they may be cured under the influence of another suggestion of equal intensity working in an inverse direction. The moral treatment ought not therefore to consist in denying the existence of the disease, but in asserting that it is susceptible of cure, that the cure has actually begun, and will soon be completed.

Would You Believe It?

The skin of a rabbit's stomach tied around a baby's neck to give it painless cutting of the teeth;

put a live toad in the mouth to cure whooping cough; dangle frog legs back of the ears to cure any form of excessive bleeding; fasten your clothes with pins that have been stuck into a frog to cure rheumatism; carry a potato in the pocket to cure rheumatism; a wife who has a cold should sneeze in her husband's shoe; one with a colic should hold a live duck to the parts--the colic will cease and the duck will die.

As examples of cures by faith in the personal power of man we may cite the case of the power of the touch of kings to cure sickness. Dr. Carpenter tells us, concerning Charles II: " Some of the principal surgeons of the day certified that the cures were so numerous and rapid that they could not be attributed to any natural cause."

A very curious case of the belief in the person is in the person of Dr. Tuke himself, and in connection with the extremely prosaic and apparently organic disease of "warts." Having heard of "wart cures" by faith, and being at an asylum on an official tour (where, of course, he was the great person, and, in the eyes of the poor inmates, possibly almost divine), he happened to see several afflicted with warts, and he solemnly predicted to the sufferers by what day each wart would have disappeared. He quite forgot the circumstance, but, on his next round, was agreeably surprised by the hearty thanks of his patients, who had been cured so near the time predicted that his fame as a "wart-curer' was firmly established.

Suggestions lodged in that mind can effect a complete change, morally and physically. If mankind could become in spirit "as a little child," trusting in God implicitly, the greatest power would be utilized in the establishment of health and equilibrium, and the results would be untold in comfort, sanity, and blessing. For instance, here is one who is suffering from worry, fear, and the vexations of life. How can he get rid of these things and relieve this suffering? Let him go to a quiet room or place, twice a day, lie down and relax every muscle, assume complete indifference to those things which worry him and the functions of the body, and quietly accept what God, through this law of demand and supply, can give. In a few days he will find a great change in his feelings, and the sufferings will pass away and life will look bright and promising. Infinite wisdom has established that law; and its utilization by those who are worried and fearful will secure amazing results in a short time.

The reader may ask how this is secured. The explanation is not far to seek. The physical system has been on a severe strain, owing to depressing effects of worry and fear, and has come almost to the point of breaking. Its nervous equilibrium has been greatly disturbed and the depressed condition has affected the heart action, the digestion, and the vital functions. When the person becomes quiescent, and relaxes the muscles by an act of the will and persistent passivity, the nerves have a chance to regain their normal, healthful action, all the functions of the body commence to work naturally, the health is restored, and the unreasonableness of fretting, fearing, and worrying becomes so apparent that the afflicted one sees the foolishness of that course of life and gives it up. The real reason for the change is found in the possibility of recovery by using the laws that God has placed within our reach, and thus securing the coveted health and power for all that we want and ought to do. The subliminal life is the connecting link between man and God, and by obeying His laws one's life is put in contact with Infinite resources and all that God is able and willing to give. Here is the secret of all the cures of disease and the foundation for the possibility of a joyful existence, happiness, and eternal life.

Suggestion is the method of securing what God gives, and the mind is the agent through which these gifts are received. This is not a matter of theory, but a fact. If anyone who is sick or who desires to be kept well will have stated periods of relaxation, open-mindedness, and faith, he can prove the beneficial and unvarying result of this method.

The necessity of study of suggestion and autosuggestion has been so strongly emphasized by

H. C. Sheppard, in "Psychology made Practical" that we quote here in full:

Suggestion is a meaningful word and is becoming more meaningful with the advance of psychology. To illustrate a complication in the way it is often wrongly applied, yet not too far fetched for the reader to see the point:

It will be helpful for the student to consider well and think out for himself and draw conclusions from cases paralleling or similar to the following--Suppose a man dominated (but not admitting it--that is, subconsciously dominated) by the impression and evidence of dishonesty. Presume such a man applying strong suggestions to himself for success. He does this consistently, systematically and progressively, never once touching upon an equally strong suggestion for honesty. What will occur? Will the man experience success? He surely will! But it will be a DISHONEST success! It may be so dishonest a success that some feature of it may come under observation of the authorities, and he and his whole success may next find themselves in the penitentiary. This, under analogical analysis, may be of inestimable enlightenment in application on less extreme, but at the same time, much more important considerations valuable to the student.

From observation and comparison of results following application of progressive suggestion by various persons, there is one recommendation which logically forms itself and is fitting to all. We hope and strongly advise that it be not carelessly ignored.

THE BASIC ASPIRATION AND UNDERTONING SUGGESTION THROUGHOUT ENDEAVORS OF THIS NATURE SHOULD BE FOR THE DEVELOPMENT OF HONEST AND ROUNDED CHARACTER IN PURSUIT OF THE ALTRUISTIC MASTER IDEAL.

The predominant mental impression in the subconscious mind determines one's temperament and the temperament determines the manner in which we react toward the events of life. The neighbor to the right, let us fancy, has brooded over this, that or the other until the predominant impression with him is one of gloom. A prolonged, dreary rain sets in. He groans, sighs and mourns, blaming everything but the thing he should blame and transform—his own gloomy disposition. That is the manner of his reaction. This reaction, of course, is a weightier reimpression and serves to add to his already enlarged gloom. Gloom has become temperament or character. A comet is seen, or he dreams a dream, or an enemy speaks injuriously of him, and with a heavier groan than usual he gets him a rope and seeks a lofty rafter in the old barn. The comet or the scandal does not prompt the act; his own character drives him to suicide.

Complex

So the predominant mental impression carried by the subconscious mind may not or need not always be simple. It seldom is. It is usually complex. It may be Gloom and Crookedness. It may be Gloom and Honesty. It may be Cheerfulness, and Trickery and Daring; Cheerfulness-- Trickery--Cowardice; Cheerfulness -- Honesty -- Cowardice; Cheerfulness--Honesty--Daring, and so on. Make one out to fit your own case; see wherein it can be advantageously changed, then proceed conscientiously to change it, as your study even thus far should enable you to do so. If you cannot make out your own diagnosis, prevail through some acquaintance to have your worst enemy make it for you. Do you think it would be far off? Is your diagnosis of the one you dislike so far from the mark?

The legitimate and proper labor to which knowledge and application of psychology should be put is to help discard the weak or destructive traits, even if they are to be torn away with pain. Thereafter Suggestion should be applied to build over the innate constellation of thought and tendency into a predominating mental impression worthwhile. If the old, undesired weaknesses and tendencies seem natural, then by analysis and Suggestion something better can be made just as natural. Held in mind that with this should go the realization that such mental reconstruction must lead to an effective, achieving personality and a cultivation of a feeling of identity with a sublime ideal.

In that way there is put into operation the Law of Constructive Suggestion which underlies all broad, clean thinking and right living. The aura becomes bright, and with a clean magnetism advertises the character of the spirit within.

In "Mental Medicine" the author supplements the former author's point of view:

Two questions have been asked by speculative philosophers of all the ages, neither of which could ever be satisfactorily answered prior to the discovery of the law of suggestion. The first is, Why are the lower animals so much more healthy than the human race? The second is, Why does man grow weaker as he grows wiser? Both these questions have been answered more or less satisfactorily from various standpoints, but it is now safe to say that the law of suggestion reveals the prime factor in the solution of both problems.

In the first place, the lower animals, owing to their lack of intelligence, are entirely exempt from the influence of suggestions adverse to health. The same is true of idiots and of many insane persons, and for the same reason. In neither case can adverse suggestions reach the subjective mind, owing to the limited intelligence of the objective. Hence "nature," as the world loosely defines that mysterious energy within which keeps us alive, is left free and untrammeled to follow its natural trend, which is always toward health and the conservation of the vital forces.

On the other hand, man, whose objective mind is capable of receiving and assimilating impressions from innumerable sources, is the constant prey of suggestions adverse to health; and the most significant feature of it is that, the more numerous are the sources from which man receives his impressions, the greater are the dangers which beset his pathway through life. In other words, the history of the world shows that as the sources of information multiply, the diseases of mankind increase in number and prevalence; and this in spite of man's increased knowledge of medicine, sanitation, and hygiene. This fact alone points unmistakably to a psychological cause; and to those who have followed my remarks thus far it will be obvious that popular ignorance of the law of suggestion is responsible. For if suggestion is a therapeutic agency as effective and universal as we found it to be, it follows that suggestions adverse to health must be equally potent in the other direction.

This view of the case will be confirmed if we find that suggestions adverse to health are as common and as prevalent and as virulent, so to speak, as the diseases themselves. That is to say, we may expect to find that the increase of such suggestions, and the facilities for imparting them to the public, are proportioned to the increase in the number of diseases which afflict mankind; and this, as a matter of fact, is precisely what we do find. Beginning with the lower animals and idiots, neither of whom are capable of receiving either a therapeutic suggestion or one adverse to health, and ascending through all the grades of human intelligence, we find that this ratio prevails. It follows that as in these days, books and newspapers furnish facilities greater than ever before existed for imparting suggestions to those who read them, we may expect to find that books and newspapers are the prime sources of the suggestions, good or bad, which dominate mankind of the present day. Now, it cannot be denied that the press, especially the newspaper, leads the van in the world's material and intellectual progress; but it is equally true that the newspaper, as a means of promoting or promulgating psychological knowledge, has thus far proved a dismal failure.

This is not the fault of the newspaper, per se; but it arises from the fact that the average newspaper man shows the prevailing ignorance of the fundamental principles of psychology, especially of the new psychology.

I shall not stop to dwell upon the fact that the new psychology, in the hands of ignorance, readily lends itself to the uses of newspaper sensationalism, for that is not the worst feature of the situation. It matters little that the newspaper has succeeded in frightening its readers into an insane prejudice against hypnotism, for popular prejudice against that psychological agency is not without its value in guarding the public against the possible evils of hypnotism in the hands of ignorance and charlatanism. But the case assumes a serious aspect when we consider the newspaper as an agency for the promulgation of suggestions adverse to public health; and the fact that it is done unintentionally and in ignorance of the law of suggestion serves but to enhance the gravity of the situation.

The first and most obvious agency through which the newspaper assists in the promulgation of suggestions adverse to health is the patent-medicine advertisement. Everybody is familiar with the patent-medicine man's insidious ways and with what preternatural cunning he insinuates ideas of ill health into the minds of his readers.

If his medicine is not a panacea for all the ills that flesh is heir to, he usually selects some disease that is quite common--say, dyspepsia, or liver complaint, or kidney trouble, or impure blood--and then proceeds to tell us that all other diseases arise from the particular disease which he has selected for a base of operations. He then proceeds to dilate upon the fatal character of his selection, and usually appends a long list of "symptoms" by which any one can know that he is a victim. The list is always extensive enough to include every conceivable sensation that is at all uncomfortable, so that few healthy persons escape, and none who are watchful for pathological "symptoms" in themselves can possibly count their cases outside of the fatal category. Fortunately for the patent medicine business, the latter class is very numerous. In fact, there are few persons who cannot, by persistent "introspection," evoke any particular "symptom" that has been suggested.

The tendency to do so is one of the serious difficulties encountered by the students of pathology in our medical colleges; and before the law of suggestion was understood by the faculties, many students were compelled to abandon their studies because of their irresistible tendency to "imagine," and eventually to experience, every symptom of the diseases they were called upon to study. Some, indeed, of the more persistent, paid the penalty of death by diseases brought on by the suggestions borne in upon them by their studies. I personally know one physician, a graduate of a regular medical college, whose usefulness has often been seriously impaired in critical cases by the fact that he almost invariably "took on the conditions" of the patient while at the bedside, especially if the patient experienced any great amount of pain,--cases of parturition forming no exception to the rule. Husbands have been known to suffer equally with their wives in such cases, and instances are not uncommon where the husband suffers all the pangs of "morning sickness" during the pregnancy of the wife. In one case the husband was personally known to the author. His first experience occurred while he was temporarily absent from home, and it continued for two weeks before he re- turned. In the meantime he consulted an eminent physician who happened to be familiar with the phenomenon, having met with several such cases in the course of his practice.

He recognized the symptoms at once; but the fact of the absence of the husband from home when he was first attacked puzzled him, for telepathy was not then recognized as a possible factor in such cases by physicians of the old school. Nevertheless, the doctor was so sure of the significance of the symptoms that he urged a comparison of notes when the husband returned home; "for," said he, "what mysterious bond of psychological sympathy may exist between husband and wife, no one can tell." A comparison of experiences proved the correctness of the doctor's diagnosis; for the husband's and wife's sufferings were found to have been coincident as to time and character, day by day, from the beginning.

Just as we may be affected consciously or unconsciously by unfriendly suggestion so we can much more readily be affected by a "friendly" or positive suggestion.

This is taken up elsewhere under "Suggestion and Autosuggestion."

To Sum Up How to Counteract

Hudson recapitulates thus in the Law of Mental Medicine:

1. Avoid all suggestions, from extraneous sources, which are adverse to health.

2. If such suggestions are forced upon you, meet them by counter suggestions affirmative of your own immunity from the suggested diseases.

3. Inhibit all conversation at the table adverse to the quality of the food set before you, especially as to its supposed indigestibility.

4. Never refuse to give a child the food it desires on the ground of its hurtfulness. If you are too stingy to give him what he wants, say so. But, as you value the health of your child, never suggest that the food he eats is liable to "make him sick,"--first, because you know you are lying, and, secondly, because he will find it out some day, and despise you for it.

5. Talk hopefully to the chronic invalid, for his sake; and for your own sake, when you leave him, thank God that you are immune from his diseases.

6. Think health and talk health on all suitable occasions, remembering that under the law of suggestion health may be made contagious as well as disease.

7. Finally, meet the first symptom of disease with a vigorous and persistent auto-suggestion of your immunity from disease or of your ability to throw it off. When you go to bed at night, direct your subjective mind to employ itself during your sleep in restoring normal conditions, strongly affirming its ability to do so; and when you rise in the morning, assume the attitude, in mind and body, of restored health and vigor. Should these prophylactic efforts fail to produce the desired effect, and should disease come upon you in spite of them, it is not the fault of the system. It is because you are not well grounded in the conditions precedent to success. Mental remedies are dependent for success upon mental conditions, just as physical remedies are dependent for their efficacy upon physical conditions.

Just as many a man has become sick by reason of adverse suggestion so in the same way sick people become well by positive and helpful suggestions which reach the subconscious.

As an illustration a famous physician tells the following incident which occurred during the great war.

During the war, those of us who had the opportunity of seeing nerve cases near the firing-line met innumerable examples of functional nerve illness (i.e., illness involving no detectable organic or structural change in the nervous system) initiated by bad auto-suggestion. One of my soldier-patients was guarding an ammunition dump, when the dump was blown up by bombs from a German aeroplane. The man, in a state of intense fear, began to run away. Trembling at the knees, he fell down, and at this moment the idea crossed his mind that he was paralyzed. He then found that his legs actually were paralyzed, and as he had been hit by fragments of earth, he attributed his condition to this.

On examination of him at the casualty clearing station I found no signs of organic injury of his nervous system, and therefore dragged him out of bed and urged him to walk, assuring him with the utmost confidence that he would certainly be able to do so. This suggestion neutralized his original bad auto-suggestion, and within a few minutes he had completely regained the power over his legs. Even in such a simple case as this, however, there was an additional mental factor, viz., the wish to become a casualty and so get away from the danger area. In other cases this wish often played a more prominent part in the production of symptoms, although in a subconscious form, i.e., not clearly present in the patient's main consciousness. It played a still more prominent part in fixing the symptoms if the soldier reached the base or England untreated.

The various mental factors at work in producing shell-shock were especially easy to disentangle in early cases, before the lapse of time had consolidated the illness and complicated it with the effects of meditation, false theorizing, and the subconscious working of other motives and desires in the patient's mind.

CURE ALL

Epilepsy

Epilepsy is one of the diseases of which we know very little. To say that all Epilepsy is caused by suggestion may not be supported by some authorities, but I believe that nearly all authorities now accept the theory that there are at least certain kinds of Epilepsy which are psychic--mental.

Gowers has described psycho-epileptic attacks, the symptoms consisting principally of periodic attacks of intense fear or of intense depression, usually beginning and ending suddenly, but of more or less protracted duration.

Coriat, in "ABNORMAL PSYCHOLOGY" supports this theory. The purely psychic character of the attacks is shown in their origin in anxiety or other emotions, the complete or abortive persistence of the anxiety in the attacks, the cleavage of the personality, their automatic character, and the possibility of their artificial reproduction or the artificial synthesis of the lost memory for the attack.

When the attacks consist merely of periodic anxiety and depression, they can frequently be reproduced at will by allowing the mind to dwell upon the attacks and can even be prevented by directing the mind along other channels. The feeling of depersonalization, of unreality, the possibility of artificial reproduction of the attacks and of the artificial recovery of the amnesic period, shows that we are probably dealing with a process of mental dissociation.

If this be true, and it is as reasonable as any other theory which has yet been adduced to explain epileptic attacks, we see where psychology may be the key to solve the whole situation.

Many people in our classes who have been sufferers from Epilepsy have been greatly benefited by mental treatment. Oliver Sabin tells of a man who had been a victim of epilepsy for over forty years but when there came into his mind the realization of the truth that he was the image and likeness of God, that he lived and moved and had his being in the God-consciousness, and therefore was perfect as God is perfect, the epilepsy never again made its appearance. Yes, epilepsy can be healed.

Epilepsy Can Be Cured

One of the greatest mental healers in America, was, over twenty years ago, given up by some of the best physicians in the country, with the diagnosis that his malady would lead either to death or insanity. He is still living and, in his own language, "I am not a dead one, and if I am insane, I am enjoying it." He has not had an epileptic seizure for a quarter of a century.

Into one of Henry Victor Morgan's meetings there entered a young lady who had been an epileptic for years. She had heard the story of someone else who had been healed of epilepsy and was so thrilled with the thought that healing could be effected by mind and that she could be normal like others, that she took the statement exactly as it was given in the healing meeting that day and went out cured. She has not had a seizure since.

Yes, many people are healed of epilepsy. We may not know the particular thing that has caused it, but we do know that mind treatments can heal.

The young lady mentioned above was healed and never had a second treatment, however, if one is not healed so quickly, the following method of treatment will be of great service.

That people have been cured of epilepsy is no longer a question. Many have been. The best suggestion we can offer you is that you practice the silence and charge the subconscious mind faithfully each night upon retiring with this affirmation (also take the affirmation when you hold the silence).

All the organs of my body are functioning normally. I am a son of the Divine, perfect in Spirit, mind and body. I am at one with the Universal Spirit of God and just as there is no imperfection in the Father, neither is there any in me. I am well, whole and perfect, strong and harmonious.

If you will hold this thought as mentioned above at least four times a day, five to fifteen minutes at each period, and then again as you drop off to sleep, using the method of charging the subconscious mind as outlined in this volume and Practical Psychology and Sex Life, Volume 3 in this series under chapters 2, 3, 4, 5, 6, 7, 8 and 9, you can get your mind so that your seizures will not be so frequent. The main thing is to have your mind thoroughly occupied with the affirmation or formula we gave you above (or other formulae), a few days before your customary seizures. When you have passed one or two of your ordinary periods for the paroxysms you will feel much encouraged. This will give you more strength to continue holding this thought we have given you, most faithfully a few days and hours before the expected time. This in time will crowd out the subconscious thought of epilepsy, making you well.

It will not be long before you will have passed the time for seizure the second time and probably the third time for a seizure, then again it will come back. This is to be expected but be not discouraged; know that if you have been able to delay one seizure each week, that you will have that same power again and in time have perfect control.

The Reason

Probably, for some reason or other, there is deeply imbedded in the subconscious mind the idea that at certain times the seizures are going to return. Every time that so-and-so happens, so-and-so will follow.

To make the opposite suggestion strong enough and often enough is to effect a healing, while, as we mention above, some are healed instantaneously.

Perhaps not all epileptics are responsive to mental healing and yet that may be due to the fact that we have not learned the last little letter in the alphabet of healing. Possibly, therefore, all cases of epilepsy can be healed. Surely it is worthwhile to make the effort. There is a large percentage of cures to the credit of suggestion. Some who have practiced this method believe that every case of epilepsy can be cured in the young before forty years of age is reached. In view of the fact that many have been healed even after that age we need not give up trying just because we have not yet learned a one hundred per cent healing.

The late Hugo Munsterberg, M. D., for a number of years Professor in Harvard University, was successful in curing certain kinds of diseases by hypnotism. If every other method fails, we should not hesitate in recommending that this method might prove successful with certain subjects, if treated by a reputable practitioner of hypnosis. To verify this method we give below an illustration by Professor Munsterberg.

Another Way

A young woman afflicted with epilepsy was brought up in the belief that she had only from time to time fainting attacks from overwork, and with them secondarily neurasthenic symptoms, especially spells of depression colored by a constant fear of the next fainting. She had heard voices all her life and they frightened her in an intolerable way. I produced a very slight hypnotic state. I concentrated my effort entirely on suggestions which were to give her new interest in life, and diminished the emotional character of the voices without even trying to make them disappear. I proceeded for several months. The young woman herself believed that the fainting attacks came less frequently afterwards; yet I am inclined to think that that is an illusion. But there was no doubt that her whole personality became almost a different one with the new share in the world.

The epilepsy remained probably unchanged but all the superadded emotions were annihilated and she felt an entirely new courage which allowed her to control herself between her regular attacks. She had been unable to undertake any regular work before for a long while, but all that improved. More than a year afterward, she wrote me: "I have really worked most of the time this past winter and spring and I think I can see a steady though slow gain. I am reading quite a little and doing it for the most part easily. To be sure I have, after I have read, hard times with the voices but their character is usually less determined and fearful than formerly. Several times I have thought I must come again to you but each time I have started again to fight it out for my-self, but now, as I am gaining, I can better estimate the great help your influence was to me at a juncture when everything seemed so hopeless and helpless."

Even in slight psychasthenic disturbances, the psychotherapeutic influence is not always suc-cessful, especially if there is no time for full treatment. But it is very interesting to see how even in such cases the symptom is somehow changing, almost breaking to pieces. It becomes clear that a protracted effort in the same direction would destroy the trouble completely. Typical is a case like the following.

An elderly woman has been troubled her lifelong by a disproportionate fear of thunderstorms with almost hysterical symptoms. As she had no other complaint, I hardly found it worthwhile to enter into a systematic treatment and could not expect much of a change from a short treat-ment, considering that her hysteric response had lasted through half a century. As she begged for some treatment, I brought her into a drowsy state and told her that she would in future enjoy the thunderstorms as noble expressions of nature. The whole procedure took a few minutes. Yet after some summer months she wrote me a letter which clearly indicated this characteristic compromise between the habitual dread and the reinforced counter idea. "I have the same sick dread at the sight of thunder clouds that I have always had, but I seem to have gotten somehow a most desperate determination to control my fear. I have done this to the extent of keeping my eyes open and looking at the storm. Is that hypnotism or pride?"

Insanity Also

We have had enough evidence now by the practice of mental therapeutics to know that insanity can be cured. Insanity may be healed also by music.

There is a doctor who does not want his name known because he would be ostracized by his profession, but who tells me that he has healed many a person from insanity by talking directly to the subconscious mind. The patient may seem to be listless and paying no attention to what the doctor says. That does not discourage the experimenter. He continues to talk in a construc-tive, positive, health bringing, normally constituted way to the subconscious mind of the indi-vidual. Sometimes weeks afterward he will see the same patients (he's working in a big State Insane Hospital) when they will speak to him in a normal way and say they knew everything he was telling them when he was talking to their subconscious and yet they could not answer, or they seemed to be speechless.

It is the same thing in healing insanity as any other kind of weakness or sickness, namely, reach the subconscious by a counter suggestion. Crowd out the old thoughts and images with the new.

One of the particularly evil suggestions of the day is implanted in wide spread medical dicta relative to venereal diseases, especially syphilis, which is said to be detected by the blood test.

Of all of the discouraging things I ever met in my practice, the most pronounced examples (psychologically speaking) have been good, normal young women who have contracted syphilis from their husbands, have had blood tests made month after month, with the awful news, periodically imparted to them, that they are no better.

George Starr White, M. D., has written a most illuminating treatise, "The Blood Test Fallacy" in which he shows that blood tests are absolutely erroneous and that there is nothing to them. We have records of people who have been healed of blood poisoning, without any recurrence in any way whatsoever for fifteen years and more.

To tell a person that he or she is infected with the most loathsome and horrible of scourges and then to continue to inform the sufferer that he or she is getting no better (because blood tests indicate no improvement) is about as deadly a suggestion as imagination could conceive.

Don't believe everything that you hear.

The Blood Test Fallacy

For many years the medical profession has been taught, and they, in turn, have taught the laity, that "pure blood means health." How often we hear it said that "the blood tells."

Inasmuch as great truths are taught by similes, I shall introduce one here: In a certain village there are one hundred inhabited houses. The water supply is carried through a common main to all these houses. A sewer system takes away the liquid refuse from these houses. Would you judge the character of any one of those inhabitants by the water-supply pipe, or by the outflow of the sewer ? The water might be contaminated that goes to those houses, but the inmates might be educated enough to so change that water as to make it safe to use. One house might pour quantities of alkali into the sewer, but another might pour in enough acid refuse to neutralize the alkali of the other. In short, no one would think of judging the character of the inhabitants in a village by the water supply, nor by the sewer outflow.

In all life--be it animal or vegetable--there is a "liquid tissue" which acts as a carrier of food to all parts and also acts as a carrier of detritus, or worn out tissues, to be cast out.

The sap of the tree carries the life-giving particles, be they gaseous or solid, to every part of the tree and fruit. It also carries off, for final disposal, that which is not wanted by the tree. Would you imagine that the sap of a tree would tell that a limb was dead, or that some fungus had attacked the bark of the tree or the fruit? No, it will not.

The blood of any animal--red blood or white blood-- carries food to all parts of the body and carries away the waste particles. The fluid that carries the food is called arterial fluid, while that which picks up and carries away the waste is called venus fluid.

In warm-blooded, and in some cold-blooded animals, the food-carrying fluid is red and called arterial, or oxygenated blood, while the waste-carrying fluid is blue and called venus, or deoxygenated blood.

This blood is a tissue just as much as muscle and bone are tissues. It is a part of the "community" and like the water pipe in a community, carries something in for the "families" to use, and like the sewer, carries out of the "families" what is not wanted.

From time immemorial there has appeared to be something mysterious about red blood. Had the "old philosophers" reasoned from the standpoint of evolution, they would have discovered that the juice of plants and the sap of trees and the white blood of some animals and the red blood of other animals, are all for the same purpose and act about the same. Because the blood was red and represented life, as it were, the erroneous idea arose that "pure blood means health."

An animal may have any kind of disease and still not have it show in the blood. The blood itself can be diseased, and because of its inability to carry on its work make all other parts of the body sick, but an arm or a leg or any part of the body can be diseased and the blood not show it at all.

I have often seen the blood of persons dying from various diseases tested and show nothing abnormal, except, maybe, a lack of red cells, the carriers of food, and an increase of "white cells," the carriers of waste material. By certain standard laboratory tests, the blood may even indicate disease when this action resulted simply from some temporary change in the blood itself, dependent upon the demands made upon it.

Now I expect those who have not investigated the subject, or those who have not made it a business to study laboratory methods of all kinds, to say that such statements as the above cannot be true. I am prepared to say that I know they are true.

I have sent, or had sent, samples of blood from persons afflicted with known diseases, to State and Government laboratories as well as to the best known private laboratories, all using so-called ethical and standard methods of testing, and received no two reports alike. The reports are always more often contrary to the clinical findings than corresponding to them.

Here is the crucial test: Let the blood be sent to any board-of-health laboratory, state or city-- and no symptoms of any kind be given, and the reports will be a revelation to the sender. If the symptoms are given, be they correct or not, the reports will usually be in keeping with the report sent.

I have squandered hundreds of dollars on laboratories throughout the United States to make sure that I was correct in this and now I know that I am correct!

I have had personal training in all modern laboratory work and I know that I know what I say when I state that there is no test of the blood that will tell what ails the person from whom that blood was taken, unless the disease be of the blood itself!

I have talked "confidentially" with the heads of the best laboratories in the land and they have told me the same thing, but added, that inasmuch as their work was that of testing, they had to use the recognized, standard, ethical methods. They also would state, if closely questioned, that they usually reported to suit the sender, for to be at variance with the sender would likely make them lose his patronage. This is human nature. There is no use in trying to side step that factor, even if the blood would tell. But the blood cannot tell!

The brain or nervous system sends out a call for certain food and the blood brings it, if it can be had, or can be manufactured for it in the system. The blood then picks up what waste it can and carries it off with whatever it may pick up along the way and sets it free through the various channels provided for it in the system.

Nature has a way of walling off all localized diseased tissues if given a chance. While that process is going on the "builders'" are very busy and call for materials that they would not otherwise need. Certain portions of the blood contents might be depleted for a short time, but the blood always seeks its equilibrium. Depletion can take place from numerous causes, therefore no test is reliable for that. The waste-carriers in the blood may be overworked from some localized disease, but the blood is so eager to equalize its load that it is impossible to tell by a blood analysis just what the blood is doing in carrying away debris.

Here is what any one can prove and settle all controversy : Take blood from any person not living rightly and it will have a certain test. Change the habits of that individual for a day, if no more, and then test again. The "blood picture" will be entirely changed. If a person overeat, the blood has to work as hard to take away the excess as if it had to carry away from a diseased part in the breast, arm or leg.

The blood of one who breathes only a fifth of his capacity will have an entirely different test than that of one who breathes three-fifths of his capacity.

Many a person has gone to a sudden grave because some laboratory reported that his "blood test" indicated that he had some incurable disease. Many a family has been broken up because some laboratory has reported from the "blood test" that one or the other of the pair had syphilis. Many a doctor has given treatments that have ruined the patient's health because the laboratory had reported wrongly from the "blood test."

This state of affairs will not cease, in a general way, till the prominent medical men understand that the blood does not tell. When doctors understand that the person in toto must be diagnosed and not the blood tissue only, our methods of diagnosis will rapidly improve. Investigators are working on the wrong track. They are wasting valuable time and countless thousands of lives.

One of the most popular methods of medical faking at the present time, is to test "energies from the blood," then "find" every horrible disease known and tell the victim that they can guarantee a cure in a certain length of time for a certain sum of money. Had the gullible public not been fooled into thinking that "the blood tells" there would not be so many fake "blood-testing systems" in vogue.

Regarding "energies from living tissues," I have written and talked about my findings after over forty years of careful investigation.

Live, red, arterial blood gives off an energy the same as the live, arterial sap in trees; while the energy from venus, or blue blood, while it is in the circulation, gives off energy the same as that from venus sap in the leaves of plants. After any blood is drawn it is venus, or deoxygenated blood. It is dead, hence it has the same energy as the air in the room or vessel that it is kept in. Dead material of any kind has lost its vital force, therefore it gives off no characteristic energy. Only vital force gives off energy! It is on the same plan as the water in a kettle--it gives off no steam till it is heated, then the amount of steam is in direct ratio to the amount of heat applied.

The State of California, always up and coming, is leading the van in education along this line. The State bought enough pamphlets entitled "The Fallacy of Blood Test" by Dr. White to send one to every voter in the State. The danger of circularizing foolish and absurd claims about blood tests is certainly apparent after you have read the foregoing by Dr. White.

Diagnosis May Be Wrong

Tumors of all sorts are simulated with a fidelity that is absolutely startling, and skilled doctors are constantly being deceived. They may occur in any part of the body, but are most common in the breast and abdomen. In the breast severe pain is complained of, and a hard mass may be felt, which, however, disappears if the hand be laid flat upon the part. Not so, however, with those in the abdomen. Patients with these perverted nerve centers have an unconscious power of either contracting part of a single abdominal muscle so rigidly that it forms a hard, round, solid swelling, plainly perceptible; or they can spasmodically contract the digestive canal at two points so as to imprison between them a largely distended portion which, being filled with flatus and partly movable and easily felt in the abdominal cavity, is exactly like an abdominal tumor. If the person be thin and the tumor be pressed down or resting on the abdominal aorta, the pulsations from the blood-vessel are so perfectly communicated to the false tumor that it is believed to be an aneurysm.

I was told by one of our best known physicians that fifty cases had been sent in to the hospital of this form of pulsating tumor, as abdominal aneurism; all of them, previous to admission, having been examined and certified to be such by medical men; and yet, on further examination, every one of them turned out to be of hysterical, and not local, origin. The only way in which they can, in many cases, be found out, is by anesthetizing the patient, when the tumor generally disappears, but, of course, returns immediately the patient regains consciousness. I remember in hospital practice one special case of this sort under my care of a woman whose whole abdomen was greatly distended by a supposed tumor of enormous size. Under chloroform it at once disappeared, but on regaining consciousness there it was as large as ever. The woman was not, therefore, "cured," and it was no comfort to her to know that when she was unconscious the swelling was not there; all she wished was to be relieved of it.

I therefore put her under chloroform again, and, while unconscious, tightly bound her round with plaster-of-Paris bandages that I allowed to set as hard as stone before she regained consciousness. This time, of course, she could not expand, and the "tumor" was gone. She was delighted we had "removed" it; and after keeping the bandage on three weeks, it was taken off, and the woman left, most thankful to be relieved of her distressing complaint.

The late George C. Pitzer, M. D. who was actively engaged in the practice of medicine with drugs as well as by suggestion for forty-two years says he has:

Cured by suggestion scores of people of organic diseases, as well as nervous troubles, where other means, such as medicines, electricity, etc., had entirely failed. I say I have cured scores of such cases by suggestion alone. I have cured people by suggestion that I could not even help with medicines.

It ill becomes, therefore, the medical man who recognizes in these cases that it is the mind that cures, to decry any form of faith cure, however little its process may be understood by him in detail. We have seen that the powers of the conscious mind over the body are well-nigh immeasurable; and knowing, as we now do, that our old division into functional and organic diseases is merely the expression of our ignorance, and that all diseases, even hysterical, involve organic disturbance somewhere, we are prepared to believe that faith and other unorthodox cures, putting into operation such a powerful agent as the unconscious mind, or, if you prefer the formula, "the forces of nature" are not necessarily limited to so-called functional diseases at all.

That certain kinds of nervous diseases--functional disorders can be cured by mind, has been long accepted by many in the medical profession. Moreover, as we have already seen by the testimony given above, many are now admitting the same thing in connection with organic diseases, or at least are remaining discreetly on the fence. They are not yet definitely "agin" it or for it, but several are open minded and advanced enough to give the subject a thorough and conscientious study. One of the most outstanding studies along this line was conducted at the shrine of Lourdes in France.

Tens of thousands of people have been healed purely by mental suggestion after visiting the Lourdes Spring, France. Physicians became interested in the "miraculous" power which seemed to move within the waters of the great spring and examined patients before they had their healing and after. The record says that of 8,000 patients who were carefully watched by the medical profession there were something over 1,000 who were healed of functional diseases and over 7,000 of organic diseases. This leads us to conclude, without a peradventure of a doubt, that mind can heal organic as well as functional diseases.

In the early day of this mental science movement which is now gripping the civilized world, there were some of the skeptics gradually converted to the idea of the power of mind over the body and admitted that certain forms of nervous diseases might be healed. While there are skepticism's in some quarters about the kinds of diseases to be treated by mental therapeutics I believe most of the leaders in mind cure treat all kinds of diseases, acute or chronic, with success.

And it does not matter the age of the person. Small children and adults are cured with equal degree of success. Patients with organic and functional ailments are treated with equal success. The mental therapeutist need turn no one away.

Advanced mental scientists also, I think, will try not to maintain too great an extreme. We would not say that suggestion will cure every case of sickness, functional or organic, because it will not.

Not because it cannot, but because the human element sometimes enters into the situation to such an extent that the patient is unready or in some way unable to get en rapport with the healer or the natural laws.

But when the patient conforms to all the natural laws of living, as outlined in this series, becoming in thorough harmony--rapport--with his healer and his God; then he may claim that everything which man and God can do can be done, and that the same power which made man can surely keep him well.

There is no limit to the power of mind in healing.

ORGANIC AND FUNCTIONAL DISEASES

What They Are

Medical Science classifies diseases into two general groups, functional and organic. Functional diseases are due to temporary disturbances of function--diseases in which there is no actual loss of tissue. Organic diseases are those in which an actual destruction of bodily tissue has occurred, such as tuberculosis, cancer and blood diseases.

Metaphysicians Are Sure

Whether organic diseases yield to mental methods of treatment or not, still remains a matter of controversy among medical men. But inasmuch as the subconscious mind builds all organs and all living tissue, the metaphysician has no doubt about the matter at all. He remembers that the power of growth and repair are inherent in all living organisms, that the harmonies of exercise of this function are presided over by the subconscious mind, and that consequently it is just as easy for the subconscious mind to build areas of new tissue into old tissue as to build new tissue in the first place.

When we bear in mind that the loss of tissue in organic disease is dead tissue within the body it takes no stretch of imagination to see how the old dead tissues may be sloughed off and new tissue rebuilt by mind. For instance, in the case of cancer, it's an abnormal growth, poisonous tissue. Mind brings the cancer to a focus, breaks it and it is sloughed off one way or another through the system, or perhaps there is other organic trouble such as a waste kidney or a kidney diseased. Mind can just as well dissolve and slough off the waste kidney and remake a new kidney as it could slough off any dead and rotten tissue and build new.

We rebuild our bodies every eleven months. We are making new tissue continually. To replace the old with new is not miraculous. In fact, it is to be expected. Hence, the great difference of opinion between medical authorities about organic diseases and functional diseases need not bother the metaphysician or psychologist. Mind here does its natural work in conjunction with natural laws the same as in healing functional diseases.

Another famous physician also gives some light on the matter of organic and functional diseases:

It has been found that a great number of physical disorders, which heretofore have been considered purely of an organic or a chronic functional character, are merely physical reflexes of a neuroi.

Besides this, as L. E. Emerson, himself a physician, comments in "Nervousness."

May Make a Mistake

But it is also to be noted that while organic diseases may be mistaken for functional and the patient suffer accordingly, in a great many more cases, probably, the mistake is the other way about, and functional diseases are believed to be organic. Indeed, I am told by physicians with very extensive practices that a large proportion of the cases they see and treat are functional.

This is due to a blind, instinctive fear on the part of the patient; fear for his life, perhaps, or fear of possible pain, when he perceives some sign that in his ignorance he may attribute to some dreaded disease. For instance, I know of a patient who discovered, on drawing a deep breath, a lump in his chest which frightened him very much. He thought of cancer, of surgical operations, of possible agony' and death, and he became almost nauseated with fear. But he pulled himself together and went to a physician who assured him that it was nothing but the end of his breast-bone, and instantly all fear left him.

The importance of this illustration lies in the fact that it makes clear the difference between the real meaning of a symptom and the attitude the patient takes towards his symptom. The whole trouble in this case was functional, due to ignorance and fear, and the patient was cured by psychotherapy; in plain words, taught a little more about himself, by one in whom he believed. The case also illustrates the importance of facing a situation and settling a question which may be due entirely to fear and ignorance, and not due to any inherent or organic disease or deformity.

It has been nearly a quarter of a century ago since Dr. George N. Beard, one of the most eminent specialists in America, who was a Professor in the University of New York, made some elaborate experiments in one of the large public institutions of the metropolis to determine the power of the mind--and more especially the patient's mind--over physical conditions, or as he puts it,

In order to determine, as accurately as possible, how far it is possible to cure disease by mental influence alone.

In these experiments, which were kept up for many weeks, no medicine of any real value was used, but simply what are called placebos, to act upon the minds of the patients, and induce them to believe that they were taking or doing something that would surely cure them. A favorite device was to tell the patients that they would get well at a certain day and hour. I would say: "Take this, and you will be well on Thursday afternoon at three o'clock." "Take a drop of this mixture just as you are half through dinner, and in half an hour your pain will leave you." In the majority of the cases, though not, of course, in all, these predictions were literally fulfilled. The patients did get well on the time appointed, and many and profuse were the thanks that I received for my success.

In these experiments were proved absolutely and beyond all question, that it was possible to relieve in this way, not only imaginary functional troubles, but also genuine and organic diseases, although the results were more certain and more permanent in functional than in organic disease. It had previously been denied by physicians that organic diseases could be affected through the mind.

What astonished me most was the permanency of the cures in many of the cases. They not only got better, but they kept better, and in some instances, recovered entirely.

Again quoting Dr. Schofield:

Believing as we do that the old division into functional and organic diseases is merely the expression of our ignorance and that all diseases, even hysterical, probably involve organic disturbance somewhere, we may believe that mental cures are not limited to so-called functional diseases at all.

And A. A. Lindsay, M. D., in "Healing and Culture," gives added weight to the position of those who credit the power of mind over organic diseases.

I feel confident that my extensive accounts of diseases involving organic changes will create attitudes of the correct sort in the minds of people who may have accepted certain erroneous teachings that only imaginary or at most, imaginary and nervous disorders can be treated successfully by drugless methods. I might well say, there are no diseases that do not involve imagery, for no forms exist that do not first have a mind picture; I can also correctly declare, that there is no disease that does not involve the nerves--all things of the body are controlled through nerve centers and nerves.

With such an explanation, I am willing to concur in the idea, only nervous disorders exist; I would not consent to the limitation involved in a classification of disease, as organic, functional and nervous. The truth literally and best stated would be, all disease is organic, all disease is nervous and all disease involves imagery. All chronic disease is psychical; this places us on the proper basis for suggestive treatment.

There is no disorder which makes impression only upon a certain organ or tissue; it may be most emphatic in one part but the entire being becomes different with every change in any part of him. If medicine were a science and could heal a certain organ; it would not cure the man; something must act upon the power that is present in every cell in order to bring harmony to the entire being.

Therefore, to us the phrase, "Organic disease" is obscure, for if functional disease may after all be organic at the bottom, a fortiori there can be no organic disease without some derangement of function.

It Matters Not to Mind Healers

It may seem startling to some of the ordinary medical men who do not keep apace with the hour, that some of the leading reputable physicians have come to the recognition that so-called organic diseases are often not organic but functional reflexes.

So you see mental therapeutists do not always believe everything they hear and surely but a small percentage of that which they see. One generation of doctors claims organic diseases. The next generation disbelieves this, and says that what we thought was organic is only functional reflexes and disturbances and any profession that has made as many mistakes throughout the ages as has the medical profession, dating back from the early priesthood in Egypt coming down through the dark ages to witch burning periods of early modern times, it's a profession that has formed such a habit of mistakes that it is reasonable to believe that all of the mistakes have not yet been made.

CONSTRUCTIVE SUGGESTION

Scientific Law Underlying All Life

Just as there are exact laws and formulae in mathematics, physiology and chemistry, so there are exact formulae and laws governing the mind and body and when we know, understand and work in harmony with these laws, we come face to face with the marvelous and almost unbelievable power and possibilities inherent in every human being.

Hoffman says, in "Psychology and Common Life":

In days gone by, disease was treated by external applications, as plasters, poultices, cupping, etc. Later medicines were administered through the stomach, then by hypodermic injections: but in the time to come, the wise physician will apply treatment to the brain, the central power house of the body.

J. W. Frings says:

Thought is that which changes the form and arrangements of the grey matter of the brain. It is a real force capable of doing work--and doing it.

And Maudsley also says:

The connection of mind and body is such that a given state of mind tends to echo itself at once in the body.

Memories of Sickness

When we raise the question, what bearing has the subconscious mind upon disease, we open up the most interesting and illuminating phase of mind healing.

Down in the depths of the subconscious may be memories of sickness, of troubles, of misfortunes, of sorrows, of loss of sexual desire, of love, ambitions unfulfilled, negative thoughts of a varied kind which are causing sickness, yet all unconsciously to the conscious mind. All habits are rooted in the subconscious. Any sickness, whether it has come into being by contagion, fright, panic, negative thought, unrealized ambitions or misfortunes may become a habit. This habit of sickness may be of an intermittent, periodical or chronic character--the subconscious habit.

The ideas, for instance, belonging to a fright complex, which originally were accompanied by palpitation of the heart, tremor, perspiration, muscular weakness, etc., when reproduced in memory are again accompanied by all these physiological reactions.

If this be true, all of the medicines in Christendom, all of the pills in the Pharmacopoeia, all of the prescriptions in this place or Hades cannot make a person well.

If thinking troubles, fright, fear, panic, sex, unrealized ambition, or any negative thought has first caused sickness, and this sickness has become a habit (subconscious), there is only one way to heal it, that is, by first crowding out the old sick habit in the subconscious mind, by "holding the thought" opposite to that which caused the sickness. Or conform to hygienic laws such as proper eating, regular exercise and deep breathing. Form new acquaintances, new social relationships, take up new kinds of reading (along mental science lines), in short change your environment in every particular helping to make a permanent change in your mental processes so that the habit of sickness will be crowded out by the habit of health.

Thought Has A "Feeling Tone"

It is well understood now in the realm of psychology that all intense esthetic emotions and feelings are accompanied by an increase of the vital functions, while on the contrary, certain depressed emotions and feelings are accompanied by a decrease of the vital functions.

It is also generally recognized that most, if not all, ideas have a feeling tone attached to them. Therefore, our emotions and our ideas both, with their feeling tones, either stimulate or decrease the vital functions of the organs of the body.

It has been observed in hypnotic subjects, for example, that where, for any reason, depressive memories and such idea-complexes enter and remain in the mind of the hypnotized subject, no matter what suggestions were given, the patient upon awaking becomes or remains correspondingly depressed.

In the same way in our conscious state, either consciously or unconsciously, we reach the under stratum of mind--the unconscious or subjective --with our emotions and ideas, which in turn react upon the physical condition of the body. This we see is the principle. On the one hand, we have the development of that which tends to lessen the vitality of the body and produce sickness, if our thoughts are negative, gloomy, and depressed; while on the other hand there is the development of invigoration, health, strength and courage, according to how our emotions, feelings and ideas are brought into the conscious field of the individual, or to the extent that these same emotions, ideas and feelings may remain submerged in the subconscious.

By entertaining any emotional state, negative conditions or ideas which have their feeling tone, we make so definite an impression upon the subconscious mind that this mental attitude becomes a habit. For example, one who begins today to worry a little, and next week has another streak of worry, and the week after that takes on another fit of it, and the week following basks in it again, finally forms a habit of worrying. Any other emotional state, negative thinking or inharmonious condition which we dwell upon from time to time likewise becomes a habit. This reaches the subconscious mind and then becomes fixed, so you see we get "fixed" in worry, "fixed" in negative thinking, "fixed" in inharmonious conditions, and we are "fixed" to stay inasmuch as the subconscious mind is the seat of habit, unless we take up a counter suggestion and reach the subconscious mind by some other positive, healthful, constructive attitude.

The wrong habit in the subconscious mind may have been caused by fatigue, overwork, emotion, unhealthy ideas, self-pity, self-examination, erroneous beliefs in and apprehension of disease, with all the depressive emotional tones that go with such states, or by habits of introspection and concentration of the mind on the functions of the body, etc. These thoughts produce sickness. THE SICKNESS LIKEWISE BECOMES A HABIT, then we have to reeducate the subjective mind to overcome its habit of sick thinking. The main principle is to substitute healthy for unhealthy conditions.

Not So Hard

The therapeutic process is the association, through education of health ideas and stimuli that adapt the individual to his environment. There seems to be some difference of opinion among authorities on mental therapeutics as to the best method of procedure in such cases. Some seem to think that it requires a great deal of skill, a vast amount of time, prodigious study and scrutiny of the patient's mind, feelings, habits, etc. My own opinion is that this is not a difficult procedure (I mean the reeducation of the subconscious mind) but a very simple one. Therein I believe is the key to our uncommon success in healing.

The psychology of it is apparent. If you believe a thing is hard, it will be hard. If you think it is prodigious, you will be expecting mountains hard to remove. In my extensive teaching, I have discovered that intricacies of the mind, although profound, are yet simple and easy to understand. The average proportion of people healed in our classes is over 90 per cent. That is, they give their testimony to the effect that they have had demonstrations during our classes. I am sure that this is the case because we make the thing so simple and so easy to understand. Our patients are not expecting trouble "complexes." They are not anticipating unsurmountable obstacles. They are not persuaded that they have the unpardonable sin of sickness. They expect a healing, and they get what they expect. We make it so plain and so simple that the reeducation of the mind is gently effected and they correspondingly respond.

We proceed to ask them as outlined in "Psychoanalysis-Kinks in the Mind" what has caused their sickness. One of four reasons is usually given. When the person affirms it was a fright, a scare, a worry, misfortune, failure, love affair, repressed emotion or ambition, dream or physic condition, the main spring of the trouble is touched, the bottom on the health door of the conscious mind is pressed, and the old obsession of sickness is crowded out by a counter-suggestion. I marvel that we have made such a prodigious job out of mental healing. That healing may take place readily in many kinds of sickness in certain individuals is not to be wondered at when we consider that constructive and positive thoughts have so much more force and power than negative, destructive and inharmonious thoughts. To discover one or more of the four reasons why you are sick, and then to take a positive counter suggestion, a constructive opposite suggestion to the negative thought, is so powerful an antidote to the negative, that the expected healing is evident and easy to understand.

Wax Cylinder

We may liken such impressions made upon the subconscious mind to the impressions left on the wax cylinder of a dictaphone or phonograph-- those impressions keep repeating and repeating themselves automatically while certain stimuli prevail. Change the stimuli and you change the trend of thought. The changed trend of thought then reacts upon the physical condition to introduce a normal state and dispel an abnormal sick state.

An Illustration

It is well known by those familiar with the manifestations of hypnotism that a hypnotized subject will continue doing whatever he has been told to do until he is released by the same power which induced the suggestion. For instance, if the operator tells a hypnotic subject that his back itches he will continue to scratch his back until released; or if told to make a speech, to laugh, or to cry, he will scrupulously obey orders. If a suggestion has been passed on to the subconscious mind by the little sentinel at the "trap door," although the suggestion be wholly wrong, the subconscious mind holds tenaciously on to that suggestion, picture or image which has reached it, by reason of any one or more of the "four reasons" why people are sick, and remains until, in one way or another, a counter suggestion is sent which takes the place of the wrong one there.

In practicing this method of substituting in the habit corridors of the subconscious mind another counter suggestion, we reach the same goal, namely, that of uprooting the old habit and in its place planting the new.

"When an idea becomes uppermost in the human intellect, when a certain notion becomes set in the mind, there are only two ways of removing it. One is by suggestion, and the other is by the development of the opposite ideas by a process of reeducation.

All Healing Suggestion

A suggestion is, we might say at first, an idea which has a power in our mind to suppress the opposite idea. A suggestion is an idea which in itself is not different from other ideas, but the way in which it takes possession of the mind reduces the chances of any opposite ideas; it inhibits them. So all healing is accomplished by suggestion.

It has at last been demonstrated beyond a doubt that we can, by properly directing a patient's thoughts, resist the progress of morbid mental activities, that all negative, inharmonious suppressed thoughts can be radically changed and that remembrances of dreams and psychic, harmful images can be eradicated from the treasure chest of memory, which means that natural conditions of health can be completely restored.

Only One Thought

We have pointed out elsewhere that it is impossible for the conscious mind to entertain two contradictory thoughts at the same time and that our conscious mind determines the suggestion which shall reach the subconscious. Therefore, if a person should, for instance, support a continued worried mental attitude in the conscious mind, this in time may reach the subconscious and there become the predominating thought, with all kinds of sickness following.

As we take the counter suggestions--the antidotes--for the reasons which have caused our sickness--we shall not only reach the subconscious mind but we shall unconsciously affect the conscious mind for right thinking, positive thinking and constructive thinking.

Just as a person cannot pout and laugh at the same time, neither can the conscious mind suggest health or constructive and positive thinking without the conscious being feeling the effects of the suggestion. So, we see, the conscious and the subconscious are correlated and coordinated, each affecting the other.

Different Ways

Some need Suggestion couched in the mystical terms of some of the cults; others need it garbed in religious drapings, while others prefer some vague metaphysical theory which seems to explain the phenomena. Others still are repelled by any of the above forms, but respond readily to the suggestion of a physician administering "straight" suggestive treatment, without any religious, metaphysical, or mystical disguise. In all of these cases the real healing work is done by the Subconscious Mind of the patient himself, the various forms of Suggestion, serving merely to awaken and rouse into activity the latent forces of nature.

The Four Reasons Why Most People Are Sick

Success in healing by suggestion depends upon the principle that the subconscious mind holds tenaciously to someone predominating thought and, since it always holds the strongest idea presented to it, its hold upon this idea is released only when another is given in its place. Any idea will be given up by the subconscious mind when a stronger one is impressed upon it.

Most sickness has been brought into the body first, by trouble, sorrow, etc.; second, by negative thinking or emotional states; third, by suppressed ambition, desire, love; fourth, by dream or psychic picturing. The subconscious therefore will abandon the old ideas and grasp the new ones --the opposite thoughts, the antidotes--and will begin to work them out in the body, just as soon as the suggestion of health, harmony, growth, peace, love and joy becomes the predominating thought crowding out the old idea of trouble, negation, suppression or dreams. Says Prof. William James:

Habits of all sorts are simply the result of the repetition of an action. Physical habits result from repeating a physical act. Mental habits result in the same manner. Any physical habit can be changed by choosing an act opposite to that which created the wrong habit, and by steadily repeating this act until the new habit replaces the old one. And mental habits can be replaced by choosing a different idea and dwelling upon it until it becomes the habit of the mind to think the new way. Pain, sickness, weakness, unhappiness, and poverty, are all mental habits. So are their opposites. A man's state of consciousness when he has twenty dollars in his pocket is radically different from what it is when he has two pennies in his pocket. Every state of consciousness attracts its own kind. Being well is a habit. So is every other desirable condition. Getting the habit is our task.

Since the conscious mind can entertain but one predominating thought at a time, and it cannot hold two mutually contradictory ideas at once, the one thought or idea to which the will holds the attention of the conscious mind as an affirmation, opens the little "trap door" of the conscious mind and passes into the subconscious this uppermost thought.

Talking to the Subconscious Mind

Intelligent affirmation (suggestion)—thinking intelligently and strongly of the thing desired, soon becomes the predominant thought in the subconscious mind. This predominant thought becomes the pattern or blueprint which in time is materialized--inwardly and objectively--into the reality of the picture or blueprint of the predominating thought. In other words, whatever we think of oftenest and most strongly, we get. To have health and keep it, health must become a predominating thought. The way to put the subconscious mind to work, is to work on a predominant thought, and thus materialize the thing desired by affirmations, either silently or orally by one's self or in the company of others.

People who do not understand the law of the subconscious mind sometimes get but slight results from affirmations because they think that positive thoughts for health, such as "I am well, whole and complete" are a lie. But, as I say, one does not always understand the law of the subconscious. It does not reason. It does not argue. It hangs tenaciously to the thought suggested to it and when you give a positive formula for health, you are giving the most direct command to the subconscious mind to get busy on your blueprint of health. You thus become your own health architect to build strength, life, vitality and health into every cell of your being.

Webster's dictionary says that a lie is "a criminal falsehood, an intentional violation of the truth." When you take a positive suggestion or formula for health, you are suggesting that the spirit within--the God-life--the great "I am" is well, whole and complete, which is absolutely correct. The spirit of man does not become sick. It is his body. We, therefore, talk directly, forcibly and positively to this well spirit (the subconscious mind) which in turn communicates the health thought to every cell of the body. This is itself intelligence which reacts and is made by the thought which the subconscious mind sends to it.

Changing the Complex

The very act of bringing to the light of consciousness the repressed ideas or the implanted obsession, when the patient's mind is unkinked, gives him an insight into the meaning of his trouble. We let him see new points of view, we introduce fresh ideas and feelings into his complexes. In short, we reimpregnate and thus reeducate the subconscious mind. This in itself has wonderful therapeutic value as will be remembered if you recall how the mind is inextricably interwoven with the conscious and the subconscious and how the subconscious mind controls the functionings of all of the organs and senses of the body. It is apparent on the face of the matter that the mental attitude of patients suffering from any kind of disease which has been produced by wrong thinking, must be changed, new groups of complexes must be formed and this is done almost automatically when we once discover what caused the sickness.

The patient then sees life from another plane ; he regards his condition in a new light and his sickness from another angle and by taking counter suggestions -- opposite thoughts -- new as-sociations and groups of complexes are called into play and the process of rehabilitation and health restoration is a simple, scientific and workable hypothesis.

Bear in mind that the subconscious mind will do anything it is given to do. It will recharge the body with health, vigor, strength--make one all over--as well as alter one's attitude toward life en-tirely. The subconscious mind will change failure into success, despondency into joy, depression into happiness, futility into achievement; hence the injunction Paul gives us in Philippians 4:8 is truly psychological. Finally, brethren, whatsoever things are true, whatsoever things are honest, whatsoever things are just, whatsoever things are pure, whatsoever things are lovely, whatsoever things are of good report; if there be any virtue, and if there be any praise, think on these things.

This, in a word, is psychology. To think only of good things until the subconscious mind is obsessed with the good and so crowds out the bad.

Think of those things until the habit of thought has been changed.

Suggestion controls the world, and 'All things are ready, if our minds be so.'

Thought and Brain Formation

Professor Elmer Gates, of Washington, has demonstrated this physiologically in his studies of brain formation. He tells us that every thought produces a slight molecular change in the substance of the brain, and the repetition of the same sort of thought causes a repetition of the same molecular action until at last a veritable channel is formed in the brain substance, which can only be eradicated by a reverse process of thought. In this way "grooves of thought" are very literal things, and when once established the vibrations of the cosmic currents flow automati-cally through them and thus react upon the mind by a process the reverse of that by which our voluntary and intentional indrawing from the invisible is affected. In this way are formed what we call "habits," and hence the importance of controlling our thinking and guarding it against undesirable ideas.

But on the other hand this reactionary process may be used to confirm good and life-giving modes of thought as Paul pointed out above so that by a knowledge of its laws we may enlist even the physical body itself in the building up of that perfectly whole personality, the attainment of which is the aim and object of our studies.

So by taking a thought, the opposite to the one or more which has caused our sickness, we not only supercede the old with the new (open the "little trap door" to let out the old thought) and by affirmations (suggestions), but we, by these affirmations make new grooves of thought, forming new thought habits, thought habits of health -- and then health we have.

Or again as Scripture says:

"Be ye transformed by the renewing of your mind."

We thus seek to change radically the patient's habit of thought by rousing new mental activities in his brain which shall do away with the old and misdirected thoughts, establish new ones and thus restore perfect conditions of health.

When the antidote is given--the counter suggestion to the one or more kinks in the mind-- and is followed by encouraging, hopeful thoughts more frequently than unfriendly and depressing thoughts, conditions of health are sure to be restored.

It is the repetition of suitable suggestions under proper conditions that relieves pain and cures disease.

Another Way

Another word which could be used to express the same idea is "erase." Whatever the mind has produced, it can eliminate. Whatever has been written upon the subconscious mental slate can be erased, wiped out; the mental sponge which does the erasing and wiping away is the counter suggestion passed on to it by the conscious mind, aided by any other agency which stimulates the conscious mind--the sentinel at the gate--to open the little trap door and let in the new thought.

A rather homely, yet understandable expression is "painted over," meaning, of course, that the old, wrong thought is painted over by the new counter suggestion.

Albert T. Schofield, M. D., in "The Unconscious Mind" illustrates this thought in the following manner:

The thought of an acid fruit will fill the mouth with water.

A successful way of stopping discordant street music is to suck a lemon within full view of a German band.

Dr. Murchison says there is good evidence that nerve influence may not only cause functional derangement, but also cure structural disease of the liver.

A man who was very sea-sick lost a valuable set of artificial teeth overboard, and was instantly cured.

If the thoughts are actively directed to the intestinal canal, as by bread pills, it will produce strong peristaltic action. Vomiting occurs from mental causes, apart from organic brain disease. Bad news will produce nausea; emotion also, or seeing another person vomit, or certain smells or ideas, or thoughts about a sea voyage, etc., or the thought that an emetic has been taken.

The thought of food produces a copious flow of gastric juice in the stomach and saliva in the mouth.

And Edward Carpenter substantiates this:

It should be as easy to expel an obnoxious thought from your mind as it is to shake a stone out of your shoe; and till a man can do that it is just nonsense to talk about his ascendancy over nature, and all the rest of it.

Mental Purge

One of the first things prescribed in physical treatment is a purge. It should also be about the first thing in mental treatment. The mental purge may be called a counter thought or suggestion. It separates the mind from false beliefs. The counter suggestion crowds out the false belief, the wrong thought, and purges the subconscious mind of the false beliefs. Then the action of God takes place.

From the earliest times, cheerfulness--a merry heart--has been recognized as possessing positive therapeutic power. Solomon must have understood the psychology and physiology of faith and mental purge when he wrote the following passages :

Faith

A merry heart maketh a cheerful countenance: but by sorrow of the heart the spirit is broken. (Prov. XV:1S.)

He that is of a merry heart hath a continual feast. {Prov. XV:15.)

The spirit of a man will sustain his infirmity; but a wounded spirit, who can bear? (Prov. XVIII:1b.)

Be not hasty in thy spirit to be angry: for anger resteth in the bosom of fools. (Eccl. VII:9.)

It Can Be Done

The path to a health consciousness is to get the strong, positive idea of UNITY and live under the law of similars.

This can be done. One may not be successful at the first attempt. A week may not see much change, a month may pass before improvement is noted. I have known people who have tenaciously hung on to their healing thought for a year before they derived much benefit, but they succeeded at last!

Begin at once to affirm with all the health and strength of the universe and stick to it in the face of all the opposing negative thought vibrations generated within yourselves or thrown into your mind by others. No matter how fast negative thoughts crowd in upon the mind treading upon the heels of their predecessors, they can be crowded out by a strong positive affirmation of health, happiness and success.

One or more of the "four reasons" why people are sick, will we have seen, eventually succeed in polluting the whole trend of thought, will tincture or inoculate the mind with sick thoughts which in turn depress the whole physical system, and we are sick.

When we take a counter thought or suggestion --antidote--we crowd out the polluting sick thought. Our suggestion then acts as a powerful and all-embracing idea which "sweeps through the mind with absolute conviction and utterly vanquishes every opposing thought. This is exactly the sort of intellectual house-cleaning that takes place when one's mind is converted to a new way of thinking."

This counter suggestion or antidote is augmented by magnetic and electrical healing, persuasion, hereto suggestion and silent treatment, which all act as stimulants to arouse the activity of health thoughts in the subconscious mind and health is restored.

There is no doubt that our thinking raises or lowers the rate of our vibration. And each disease has its own rate of vibration.

Natural Law

To some to be healed by vibration may appear miraculous but of course it is the natural operation of a common mental and physical law of vibration. A superstitious or religious belief that the Lord spoke and it was done, or, a bigoted idea of the miraculous power of God could have produced the same effect. Anything, be it rabbit's foot or goose quille, the King's garment or a magic wand, which, by thinking stimulates enough faith to tap the reserve power in the subconscious, could have effected a healing just as well and it would have been an operation of a natural law--the natural law of belief and faith that the healing would take place. But in all healings the natural operation of certain laws which always bring certain results implies surely a loftier conception of God and his laws to the thinking person than the superstitious conclusion that God, the miraculous and divine spoke and it was done.

The truth is that all law is divine and all law is God's law, so God becomes nearer and dearer and the conception of Him more clear cut, intelligent and reasonable when we recognize that all things performed in nature conform to and are the result of law and order.

All appeal to the supernatural, to the miraculous or mysterious is misleading--all healing is in accordance with natural laws.

"We know that each word has its rate of vibration, hence every thought has its particular vibratory rate. The positive thought always has a rate of vibration higher than the negative; the health thought a rate of vibration higher than the sick; the cheerful thought a vibratory sensation higher than the discouraged. Hence the moment a person takes a positive, constructive, hopeful, health-giving affirmation, the higher rate of vibration within the individual begins at once. It may at first be imperceptible, but it begins just the same. It will not be noticed or felt for some time, but it has begun, nevertheless.

This higher rate of vibration will unconsciously reach the subconscious mind to change the old habit of sickness into the new habit of health.

To illustrate: sit loungingly in a chair and repeat seven times to yourself in a monotone, "gloomy, downcast and sorrowful." Then sit quiet for a few moments, letting the body become more slovenly in its posture while you repeat seven times again, "gloomy, downcast and sorrowful," still in monotone. Continue to sit slovenly in the chair a few moments and repeat the same thing again, then straighten up in your chair, supporting your body by the spinal column.

Do not lean against the back of the chair, let the head tilt upward, let the hands rest gently in the lap, palms upward, and repeat the positive words, "cheer, courage, happiness." Say them seven times in a spirit of fervor and a tone of confidence, then relax in your chair any way you please for a few moments. Once again take your upright healthful, cheerful position and repeat seven times the words, "cheer, courage, happiness." After which you may again relax, then take your position as mentioned above and repeat the same words seven times again. After you have carried this out faithfully you are bound to feel a higher rate of vibration in the words of "cheer, courage and happiness" than you felt in the "gloomy, downcast, sorrowful."

Dr. Wm. Sadler tells of a friend who would, upon seeing a reptile, almost have a spasm. We induced this fear-ridden person to go with us one day to a certain drug store in San Francisco where some ten or fifteen living snakes were on exhibition in the front window. It was a difficult ordeal for our friend; but the watching of these reptiles for three-quarters of an hour was sufficient effectually to cure that horrible dread of creeping and crawling things, and so that this person has ever since been able to look at snakes without experiencing the least sensation of fear or feeling of terror."

Thus affirmation--holding a thought -- changes the current of our thinking. We may, by right thinking--holding a thought--change the mental, social and physical conditions about us and in us. "Holding a thought" is as scientific, practical and healing as the law which controls the ebb and flow of the tides.

And Morton Prince suggests:

A new setting with strong effects may be artificially created so that the perception acquires another equally strong meaning and interest.

The second way theoretically would be to bring into consciousness the setting and the past experiences of which the setting is a sifted residuum, and reform it by introducing new elements, including new emotions and feelings. In this way the old setting and point of view would become transformed and a new point of view substituted which would give a new meaning to the perception.

"Sidetrackability" is the name which someone has given the condition of those nervous, erratic people whose energies are being diverted from a legitimate and natural source into abnormal and harmful channels.

Should a person notice any of these nervous energy leaks he should instantly treat himself to overcome these little sidetracked abilities. This can easily be done. Take a positive thought the opposite to what nervous habits you may have and keep repeating the thought until you crowd out the old with the new.

Various Kinds of Suggestion

Drunkards have often been reformed by the religious appeal alone, as may be seen by a visit to the Bowery Mission, or any similar institution working among the submerged; or by reading Begbie's Twice Born Men. They have often been cured by suggestion alone, as many physicians and experimental psychologists can testify.

Any kind of an experience, action, or thought which may change the current of one's thinking acts as a suggestion and may be taken up by the subconscious mind to form new habits of thinking and living. Therefore Scriptural quotations and religious services are two of the strongest means of suggestion for health success and happiness that we have. The less intellectual or cultured the person the lower the type of religious enthusiasm necessary for purposes of suggestion. The higher the intellectual development and the more cultured the individual, the more reasonable must be the religious appeal as a suggestion.

If we learn instantly to take an antidote—opposite, positive and constructive thought--to the unfriendly suggestion and teach our children so to do (training children in habits of right thinking is of far greater importance than many parents even suspect) we shall prevent much, if not all of these "four reasons" why people are sick from getting hold of us and thus forestall most of the ills that flesh is heir to.

Burglars

I give the following illustration as a sample that one may always be ready to sweep the mind clear of any kind of "unfriendly" suggestion which may possess one, from fright, fear, panic, accident or "habit" of thought. I know that while keeping in tune with the laws of life nothing can harm me. "No evil can come nigh my dwelling." I follow a hunch as nearly to the letter as possible. I know that if ever I were threatened with disaster, trouble or misfortune, I should have a warning.

Someone who knew that I was taking to my room each night a considerable sum of money had planned to burglarize me. I have always said that if a burglar did get into my house he may, as far as I am concerned take anything I have. He is the type of man against whom I should never try to defend myself single-handed--I mean, the burglar with weapons. I am, however, of the muscular type, I can scrap if I have to. Instinct on one occasion overruled my better judgment, but still I was protected by the law in which I so firmly believe--"no harm can come nigh my dwelling."

I had a hunch one night that I was to be held up. So I turned over all of the money I had, consisting of a few thousand dollars to someone else and made my way alone to my room. Sure enough, my hunch was right. I awoke to find a man stealthily creeping about the room at the foot of my bed. He evidently had learned where I had been putting my money at night. It wasn't there; all the money I had in the room was on the bureau, about 40 cents in a little cheap 10c pocket book and about $60.00 in a wallet, these two lay side by side.

When I awoke to see a stranger in my room I instinctively followed the characteristics of my type, although I had nothing to lose and no weapons at hand, I climbed out of bed and asked him what he wanted. He stood erect, silent, in a posture of defiance, but didn't answer. Again I asked him what he wanted and reached down by the head of the bed for the only weapon at hand, an old shoe, as I did this he flashed a gun. I had said I would never attempt to scrap with a burglar if he took me unawares, yet I was doing the very thing I said I wouldn't do. The fire-works of a gun can travel faster and with more deadly effect than an old shoe in the hands of a scared stiff "muscular" but--"no harm can come nigh my dwelling." This was my thought.

Of course thoughts are things and thoughts shape the destiny of our lives. Thought changes our environment as well as our physical condition. When I was looking into the barrel of the burglar's repeater, I confess that I shook like a maple leaf in the frosty air, and wasn't quite sure that my shoe could be well directed, hence I resorted to the only method of self-preservation I could think of on the spur of the moment—my voice, and when the gun was leveled at my "cocoa " and my arm shivered so that my shoe would certainly go amiss if I let fly. I let out an unearthly yell that I had never heard before,

St. Patrick never heard before, Gabriel never heard before, and I am sure the burglar never heard before, I evidently scared him more than I was scared myself, for with the first shriek I shrieked the burglar made for the window, leaped through the open space and was gone.

I will confess that I was scared as bad as he, if not worse. I had goose pimples all over, cold perspiration squirted out of me like running water from a broken garden hose, and I turned on the light to let him know I was still alive, should he have a thought about returning. When the light flashed on it was revealed to me that only one of my pocket books was gone--the ten-cent one with 40 cents enclosed. Thus again proving the law in which I believe, that intuition and hunch will always protect us.

For two weeks afterwards I would feel cold shivers chase themselves up and down my spinal column, my flesh turn into goose pimples, and cold perspiration squirt from my skin. Unconsciously the experience with the burglar cropped up again and again.

When the nameless visitor hopped out of the window, followed by the bang of my shoe, I began to work my psychology. Never such a fright, such a fear and such a shock I never had before. Knowing that in time of fright or panic the subconscious mind may become obsessed by the horror of the scene, I immediately began suggesting to myself something like the following--"all things are in divine order, peace, power and plenty are mine, I rest at peace in infinite love."

This was about 3:00 o'clock in the morning and needless to say there was no more sleep in my bed chamber that night, nor on the other hand, was any ill effect to follow. I simply repeated my thought and held my affirmation for goodness knows how long, but it was long enough and, furthermore, kept me good company for the rest of the night to prevent any wrong suggestion having been taken up by the subconscious mind.

Whenever anything of any character in any way disturbs the mind always be prepared to hold a strong counter suggestion, and "no ill can come nigh thy dwelling."

The Same Method Works For All

It must be recognized not only that disease of divers kinds may be healed by suggestion but also that the chief value in suggestive therapeutics will eventually be found to consist in the almost unlimited power which it gives one to protect himself against contracting disease.

To do that it is only necessary to hold one's self in the mental attitude of denying the power of disease to obtain mastery over him. When the patient recognizes the first symptoms of approaching illness, he should at once commence a vigorous course of therapeutic auto-suggestion.

He will find prevention much easier than cure; and by persistently following such a course he will soon discover that he possesses a perfect mastery over his own health.

Rejoice

Inasmuch as the natural condition of man (contrary to old-theological teachings) is to strive for moral and physical harmony, it is easier and takes less time to plant in the subconscious mind a positive and constructive thought than a negative or destructive one.

Therefore rejoice and be exceeding glad that when you desire to correct any kind of inharmony, the constructive forces of nature and God are on your side. It is easier to build than to tear down. It is easier to climb than to fall. It is easier to achieve than to fail--WHEN ONE FORMS A HABIT OF CONSTRUCTIVE BELIEF AND LIVING.

Remember that nothing is impossible for us, that we are part of the Divine, that the God given power resides in each individual.

F. W. Sears, M. P., in "How to Give Treatments," offers a splendid illustration of how the mind heals.

Sick Headache Cured

Having gotten that vision, that idea, and come into a full belief and understanding of the cause of our sickness and of this statement, "that nothing whatever is impossible for us," then we should get to work and displace in our thought world the vision, the idea that we have any disease, and place in its stead the vision or idea of perfect health.

For instance, let me give you a personal illustration that perhaps is more practical and will bring it closer home than anything else. For a number of years I had chronic sick headaches. The attacks occurred every ten days to two weeks. In the old thought world we would say I inherited them from my mother, who is still living at 75 and enduring hers. Her sister, who is also living at 86, has had them all her life. It is evident I came into this incarnation with a well-defined idea of sick headache stamped upon the cells of my physical body, and that consciousness was one of the things which related me with my parentage and environment in this incarnation. I carried that idea, that vision, that image of sick headache until about fifteen years ago.

As the years went by the sick headache consciousness became more firmly fixed and deeply imbedded in my physical cells and my headaches increased correspondingly in intensity and severity. On the occasion of my last attack I woke up in the morning with my head feeling as though a thousand tons was pressing down on it; I had so much nausea at my stomach that I could not raise my head from the pillow. I said to myself, "I will be well. I will put into practice these things I have learned, I will fill my thought world with thoughts of health and fill it so full that there will be no room left for disease. I will cure myself of sick headaches; now is the time for me to begin putting into practice, into practical application, the things I know; I will get up," and I did so.

Then I began to affirm--"The All-Health energy of the universe is pouring into my head; I am free, free from sickness; I am free from all aches and pains and all nausea; I am perfect health,"--and many other similar affirmations. The idea in making these affirmations is to materialize, to emphasize in words as well as in thought, the vision of the thing we want in order that the image may be stamped upon the intelligence of the atoms or cells of the body; also that through the vibrations we create in our bodies by these affirmations, we may relate with the currents in which the All-Health energy is found.

I kept up the affirmations, and I also made some denials that I was not sick. At that time I found denials were of some help to me, and we frequently do find that to be the case. I made the affirmations and denials again and again every few minutes during the day; in fact not fifteen minutes went by without my making them and declaring my freedom from disease.

The result was that by five o'clock in the evening I could think of my head without the ache being there, and of my stomach without the nausea; but my head was just as sore as though it had been pounded with a club.

Deep Breathing Helps

The change in the vibrations of my head was caused by the affirmations and also by the deep breathing which I did. I inhaled long, slow, deep breaths, and with each inhalation I affirmed that "I was breathing in the health energy of the universe now." The making of these affirmations continuously and persistently all day long, although I felt I could not hold up my head, increased the vibrations of the atoms of my body and finally resulted in the headache stopping and the nausea disappearing. I ate quite a hearty dinner, not having eaten anything all day and then went to an entertainment in the evening, after which I danced for a couple of hours, ate ice cream and cake--and have never had any sick headache since.

Twice since then the headache started to come back, but before it got hold I began the same method of treatment, making my affirmations and deep breathing, and it did not last more than fifteen minutes either time, and although that was fifteen years ago, I have never had a sick headache from that day to this.

Eyes Cured

Now as to my eyes. My trouble was astigmatism and I had to have special lenses made for each eye. When I broke a lens I was in misery until a new one was made. I wore glasses continuously for more than twenty years, and during the last few years of that period I had to have the lenses changed every three to six months, but laid them down finally on May 1, 1906, and have not had them on since. Before taking them off permanently I treated myself for at least a year in order to develop the consciousness which would permit me to get along without them.

How?

When treating myself I would put my hand over my eyes many times a day and make this affirmation: "My eyes are strong and well and my sight is perfect. My eyes are strong and well and my sight is perfect." No matter how at variance with that statement my eyes actually felt, I kept that thought constantly before their cell intelligence for a year before I finally laid down my glasses. I used to begin treating them when I first arose in the morning.

At such time I would find that my eyes were pretty clear and I would go without my glasses as long as I could, perhaps fifteen minutes, and then later on, leave them off for half an hour, gradually extending the time I did without them until through such extension and the development of the consciousness I was working with all the time, I created the conditions which enabled me to lay them down completely.

Baldness Cured

The next thing I went to work on was my head, which was as bald and shiny as a billiard ball.

It is true I haven't a very heavy head of hair at the present time, but I have hair. I did not have the overwhelming desire for hair that I had for perfect eyesight. I did want my eyesight because I have always used my eyes so much, and I wanted to continue to use them, but the hair I didn't care so much about. The only thing that ever made me want to grow it was the fact that in the study of my history in this and former incarnations, I saw that baldness was the result of negative energy which I had heretofore generated the same as my defective eyesight, and so I wanted to antidote that now. I knew there was no time when it could be displaced as easily as the present time, because the longer we let these things run on, the more fixed does the habit become, and I wanted to get rid of the habit of registering any negative energy in my life.

I went to work in more or less of a half-hearted way because everyone said--"Why you can't grow hair on a door knob," and "I never knew of it having been grown on a bald head before." I used to loosen the scalp through massage, and at the same time affirm that "My hair is growing thick and heavy on top of my head, I have a thick, heavy growth of hair now."

I used every method I thought might help until I got the hair started. Every morning I loosened the scalp with my fingers and stimulated it with a stiff hair brush. Occasionally I applied a little ointment to soften the scalp, after having shampooed my head with some good tar soap. I did this because everything and every method we can use to help restore us to a normal harmonious relationship, is constructive.

On everything else but my bald head my consciousness was strong enough to actualize my vision of perfect health and harmony, but when it came to the bald head it took a whole lot more development, a stronger and more powerful realization than I had then to "get the vision" of a heavy head of hair on it, and as I had no one to "cheer me up" and help me raise my vibrations, but had to "go it alone," I therefore used whatever things would give me even the slightest bit of encouragement or the smallest ray of hope. In that way I began to develop the consciousness which has finally produced what hair I have.

I have a picture of myself which was taken when I was a boy and had a fine head of hair. In trying to "get the vision" of hair on top of my head I would hold that picture before me and try to imagine (image) myself with a head of hair like that now; it was not until about a year ago that I was able to get such a vision but I finally succeeded.

Many attempt these treatments and fail because they are not persistent enough. Many times we expect to change a habit of years, perhaps of incarnations, in a few days or a week or two, but in our present state of consciousness that is impossible. We can develop a consciousness which will enable us to change anything in the "twinkling of an eye," but until we do develop it, we have to go more slowly.

Everything begins and ends in our thought world, and until we have changed our habit of thinking we cannot change its effects on the intelligence of the cells of our bodies, because the physical cells and the atoms of our environment reflect the kind of energy we generate in our thought world.

You see, thought is so dynamic and forceful that when you take an affirmation, you are taking something that will work. That is the nature of affirmations. If the thought you hold expresses your desire or ideal, and if you express that affirmation or ideal with conviction and with persistence it will work. One of the main things to remember in all suggestion and in all affirmations is that one must never give up--must never say die.

SUGGESTION

How

We believe that where the environment is right and the work is faithfully and wisely done, suggestion by affirmation will cure more people, no matter what the disease, than any other method now in use.

The Soul is fed by Affirmation as the body is by bread.

--Victor Hugo.

Psychologically it does not matter what fundamental principle your affirmation springs from provided you believe it and find it therapeutically workable.

We have seen in the preceding pages that a suggestion is an image, thought, idea, or working pattern, introduced or passed on to the subconscious mind.

An Example

Inoculate and permeate your mind with the idea you can keep well by affirmation provided you use it. This is the shortest road to health, yet there are many people who in process of time are healed though without having absolute faith in their healing. Any thought which is repeated whether Poll Parrot like or with due regard to its significance will in time change the current of one's thinking. The safer, surer and better way is, of course, to saturate the mind with the idea that you can be healed and kept well by the power of mind.

Read the following affirmation slowly, then read it again and again like this:

I Think Life.

I Think Health.

I Think Strength.

I Think Vitality.

I Am in Tune with Infinite Spirit.

I Breathe Life. I Feel Life.

I Breathe Health. I Feel Health.

I Breathe Strength. I Feel Strength.

I Breathe Vitality. I Feel Vitality.

I Am in Tune with Infinite Spirit. I Am in Tune with Infinite Spirit.

I Am Life.

I Am Health.

I Am Strength.

I Am Vitality.

I Am in Tune with Infinite Spirit.

Keep repeating it and repeating it, until you form not only a mental image of the way the affirmation looks, but memorize it. The deeper the conviction you have that the mind can heal, the quicker the healing you are striving for. But if you cannot at first absolutely believe that the mind can heal, keep repeating your affirmation just the same. This should be done many times during the day until it becomes a subconscious habit in the chambers of memory. By constant repetition of proper affirmations one may virtually make a groove in his consciousness until he finally becomes that which he tells himself he will become.

Affirming should be done at intervals during the day as often as possible only the affirmer should not repeat his affirmation until he is fatigued. The affirmations may be taken when you are on long walks, while riding on the street car, or even at work; in fact, odd moments may be very profitably occupied in repeating affirmations.

If you are not thoroughly convinced that mind will heal, keep taking your affirmations nevertheless with as much concentration as possible. Of course, the more sincere the belief you put into your formulae, the quicker you may expect to be healed.

Throughout this volume we present more affirmations. Look through this book until you find one or more that seem to fit your case and temperament. Learn these affirmations, and repeat them as directed above.

How to Think About Yourself

Here is a rule of life which all should observe. When you are talking about yourself never say anything concerning your own self, your surroundings, your affairs, your hopes or aspirations, your family or your friends, except that which you expect to be materialized and realized.

Always believe and think about things as you desire them to be. You wish health? Then affirm health, think health, feel health, breathe health, live health.

Do you want success? Then think success, feel success, breathe success, live success.

Do you want abundance? Then affirm abundance, think abundance, feel abundance, breathe abundance, live abundance.

Do you want friendship, love or happiness? Then affirm friendship, love, happiness; think friendship, love, happiness; feel friendship, love, happiness; breathe friendship, love, happiness; live friendship, love, happiness.

Think only of those things which you desire for your success, health and happiness; for what you think, you get.

Let me emphasize here that any thought held, even though half-heartedly or automatically, will in time, change the current of one's thinking or mental habit (but a positive manner, a resolute volition will enhance the intensity of the affirmation and bring about quicker results). Henry Harrison Brown has well said: The President of a divinity school told his students that they were to pray when the time came to pray whether they felt like praying or not; to keep on praying till they did feel like it; and then to continue because they felt like it. This same rule is for you. Say.... "I feel better!" whether you do or not. Keep on saying it till you do feel better, and then keep it up because you feel better.

There is one Affirmation that expresses this, and will create the mental condition that reflects health of body. That Affirmation is....I AM HAPPY. Happiness is the mental cause; Health is the bodily effect. Therefore keep happy. Abolish all sadness, sorrow, fear, unhappiness of all forms by saying.... I AM HAPPY!

But this is hard to do when you feel ill and miserable! True! But it is not so hard as to still complain and suffer. Choose between the two. You always have the power of choice. Which shall it be? "Choose ye this day whom ye serve." Life or death? 'Health or disease? Happiness or unhappiness? You alone are to decide. It is hard to submit to doctors, nurses and pain. Is not Affirmation pleasanter and easier? Habits can be created along these lines as easily as in the others, and habit makes anything easy. Mental habits of health easily keep you well. Affirmation-cure compared to the old method is as play to drudgery. Affirmation is the stopping of all resistance, is the giving up of all antagonism, the cessation of all struggle and the throwing of all responsibility upon Life, while you enjoy results. The Power that is not the conscious self does the work. The Power that built the body rebuilds it.

"We have mentioned elsewhere that not only may the thought become a subconscious habit, but conditions and environment or physical sensations may be registered in the subconscious mind so as to form a habit. Therefore, one should live under such conditions as to bring about advantageous changes in his social, physical and mental environment for an unfavorable environment is a handicap to one's health, success and happiness.

Religious People

If a person is religiously or spiritually inclined, the first thing that should be attempted by one who is seeking to change his environment or mental attitude is to direct one's mind in the way of understanding things based upon the love, wisdom and goodness of God. Realize these vital truths: that His Presence is everywhere--God is omnipresent; that He is all-powerful--God is omnipotent; that He is all wise--God is omniscient. He therefore knows all things and understands all things.

Are not two sparrows sold for a farthing? And one of them shall not fall to the ground without your Father. Fear ye not therefore, ye are of more value than many sparrows.--Matthew 10: 29-31.

And yet all people are religiously minded. They may not have subscribed to a particular creed, cannot, perhaps, repeat certain dogmas, do not even attend church. But we are religious animals, all of us, and if a person is limited in any way through poverty, sickness, lack or limitation, the first step in casting out fear of these things is an intellectual understanding, a reasonable conception of God, as a God of love; and that this same God is so identified with our lives that He is in touch with our every act, with every throb of our hearts.

Perfect love casteth out fear. God is love. Hence the love of God casts out all fear of poverty, lack, fear of failure, trouble, sorrow or sickness. If we can teach ourselves and others to love that which we fear, then fear passes away automatically. So the biggest thing in the conquest of fear is to have the right conception of God as a God of love.

It is well to remember that all suggestion and affirmation should be taken in the present tense. Now we have that which we desire. This makes a stronger, more positive appeal and vastly enhances the power of the affirmation.

This is the first step in casting out Fear by an intellectual love, and as we realize that that same God is so identified with our lives and is bringing us continual benefits and so enables us to enter into His life for comfort and health, there arises the other side of Love, born of comfort and care and the qualities that enter into them, and this we call the emotional side of Love. This furnishes the patient with the thought of a complete truth. We cast out Fear by embracing and dwelling upon the boundless love of God which dwells in us, which is an intellectual conception and an emotional impulse. This method is applicable, no matter whether the agent of fear be a person, or thing, or some indeterminate and imaginary object. Simply teach the patient to love that which he fears and the fear passes away.

Meditation

Any affirmation is most efficacious in time of quiet meditation. To meditate is to pray. To meditate is to affirm. To meditate is to enhance the desire of your heart. To meditate is to get that which you want. Nearly all great and successful business men have their quiet hour for meditation, relaxation and renewing mind and body.

One may take more than one affirmation at a time, but it is always better for you to follow a fixed rule in your affirming. Do not use more than one at a time unless both carry the same thought. The subconscious mind will not work on two contrary thoughts, at the same time. Therefore, to get the best results, therapeutically, spiritually and mentally, work upon only one subject or one desire at one time. Unify your affirmations of health while you are thinking health; on success, while you are thinking success; on happiness while you are thinking happiness, etc. Let your mind be centered on the unifying affirmations along one line at a time.

By this I do not mean that you can only hold a thought for one thing only until that has been accomplished. It takes some of us twenty years to reach our goal of success and achievement. During these twenty years we can affirm for health, happiness and other things, but should not affirm more than one thing at one time. For instance, one may go to bed at night (by the way, the best time to take your affirmations is upon retiring) and give the subconscious mind the suggestion of health. All night long the subconscious mind is remaking the body. As one begins the day, he may suggest abundance and success. Not only will the subconscious mind take up this thought, but vibrations for success and abundance will be sent out into universal space.

Later in the day one may hold the thought for happiness or love. Away go the thoughts which one has suggested into the universal ether to lodge in the consciousness of those who can bring into your life the happiness and love you desire. During all of this time the cells of the body, which have taken the suggestion from the subconscious mind of health, have been remaking themselves.

One may thus take many affirmations for many things, at different times, but should always center upon the one thing at hand (be it health, success or happiness), at the given time.

Each Word Has Own Vibration

As we mentioned elsewhere, each word has its particular vibratory rate, although there are certain words and sentences which have a stronger influence upon some people than upon others, owing to the individual's own rate of vibration, so these affirmations are given simply for convenience, and as examples. If you do not find in this volume the formulae that grip the soul, make some affirmations of your own. Each life craves its own expression and in experimenting with words, sentences and formulae which have the rate of vibration to give you the best results, you are also developing your own inherent God-given views and impressions.

Doubtless there are others who get more benefit from taking the affirmations herein outlined. There can be no hard and fast rule laid down in Psychology or Metaphysics. Each person is a law unto himself, each person should have the privilege of living his own life in his own way. Find that way which is the best for you and live it. Similarly, find the affirmations or formulae which are best for you to use; then use them.

"Holding a Thought"

Whatever affirmations or formulae you decide upon, hold them in the conscious mind with enough intensity--free from stress or strain, with passive attention--until you are thinking of the positive instead of the negative. This has been done by hundreds of thousands before you and can be done by you.

Many a person prevents his own healing, or demonstration for success, prosperity or either by auto-suggestion or by hetero-suggestion by being too anxious.

Be not overanxious.

That is the essential reason for one's learning how to relax. It is in this relaxed condition, when the mind is free, cleared of all negative rubbish, tangled thought currents and confused contentions that the demonstration takes place.

When we are overanxious we are clogging the natural healing channel. We are putting driftwood in it. We are piling up debris, obstructing the source flow of the power to bring about a demonstration.

Unclamp

It is when we relax, let go, unclamp, that the healing spirit of the Infinite works its most wonderful demonstrations.

If we are overanxious we are straining and pressing the mind to such acute tension that the healing spirit of God cannot perform its function.

In one of my public demonstrations, when I gave an invitation for those who were desirous of being healed to come on to the stage, among many others a blind man was led forward for healing. I was attracted to him the first night he stepped upon the stage. The second or third night I was resolved to give him a public demonstration, although I had the feeling that a successful issue would not take place that moment. Nevertheless, I knew by my hunch that by demonstrating on this blind man I was doing the right thing. When the healing treatment was over and I asked him to open his eyes and tell us if he could see, the lids flew up and the eyes moved, but he could not say there was light.

He broke down and burst out crying, but told me the apparent failure was not my fault. He knew that he was too anxious. The next night he was on the stage again, and the night following, when he was able to make his way to the stage without any assistance. Light had come. Within three weeks his sight returned.

The night I treated him publicly on the stage he told me it was not my fault that he didn't see. He said, "I know that I was too anxious."

That tense, taut anxiety prevented his healing that night, but he didn't give up. He learned to relax, learned to let go and trust the ever healing spirit of the Infinite so that, as already mentioned, his sight returned.

In preparing the mind for healing and getting ready for demonstration, be sure not to be overanxious.

Take Your Choice

Choose any affirmation, as we have mentioned, or other thoughts which have power to cure (you may be able to make up some even better than any which have yet been published), and let the thought drop through "the little trap door," into the subconscious mind. Then forget it and turn your attention to the affairs which belong to the moment.

By forgetting it, I mean for you to take your thought, your affirmation, and then relax. Do not try to remember that you have taken this affirmation--"forget it." The science of this is very plain. You have probably tried to recall a name or an address or some experience of the past, and the more you have concentrated upon it and endeavored to bring it back to conscious memory, the more it seemed to evade you. After your vain effort to recall it, you have given it up, forgotten it. But, in a little while, lo, and behold! the little thing which you could not recall when you tried, bobs up in mind!

After you have taken these affirmations, let them rest--forget 'em.

Your affirmations thus dropped into the subconscious act as a post-hypnotic suggestion does and, while you are attending to the duties of everyday, the thought dropped into the subconscious directs the soul in its body building.

Of all single causes of sickness now, fear and selfishness, I suppose, would head the list. Selfishness has the power to contract, the same as fear. Selfishness contracts not only all the organs of the body, interfering with circulation, respiration and natural functioning of the internal organs, but it also contracts the mind, as though somebody had stepped on the mental hose, and while this selfish spirit is manifested the compression is increased so that it will be impossible for the influx of the spirit to come.

That is the reason, as I have mentioned elsewhere in this series, that I have all my patients and classes relax and hold a thought for universal health, success, abundance and harmony. The chief duty of a person who is selfish is to find some way in which he can live more for others or can get hold of the idea of service to the world or get his mind off himself. This will open the organism to the influx of the healing power.

Empty the Mind

Above everything else, before one begins to "hold a thought," he must empty his mind from all negative thinking of every description, and chuck into the waste heap of forgetfulness, every vestige of selfishness. A person cannot demonstrate health or anything else with any degree of success if he is all tied up in a knot by selfishness.

The influx of the spirit cannot reach the center of his being. When one is selfish his whole body is tense and filled with physical kinks like a kinked garden hose, through which the water cannot run. Chuck out selfishness and step off your garden hose because, just as the water cannot make its way freely through a hose that is kinked, neither can the spirit of healing flow freely through a body that is kinked and controlled by a mind filled with kinks. Kick the kinks out of your mind before you "hold a thought." Especially kick the "selfishness" out before you attempt affirming.

The word "affirmation" means "to make firm." To get the best results repeat your affirmations with firmness, not tenseness, but in a spirit of actually meaning what you say, so as to stamp them upon your subconscious. Of course, this form of treatment and the employment of any affirmation or formula to achieve health and success can be modified according to conditions.

And do not let us in the early stages of an attempt at healing be too dogmatic and thereby discourage a person who is just learning the A B C's of mental healing. Be chary of saying "you must have faith." Faith is not strictly necessary, although a preliminary faith induced by a consideration of the imminently reasonable nature of the process is an undoubted advantage.

But I come back to what I believe is the quickest, surest way of taking an affirmation, namely:

Down to Business

It should be taken with strength, courage, positiveness, backed by the spirit of assurance and faith that what you are demonstrating for you shall have. In fact, make your affirmation a demand. The more emphatic you are in demanding of the subconscious mind that it perform certain acts, the quicker will be the results.

I have shown elsewhere that the subconscious mind is like a servant or a soldier who likes to be commanded.

Each affirmation is better if a prefix such as the following is used: "My subconscious mind, I desire and command you to give me health, strength, power"--or whatever you may be asking.

Or, "my subconscious mind, I desire and know that every organ of my body shall function normally; that you shall attend to every detail of my domestic, vocational and social affairs."

If you want success, demand success. Demand it with your whole heart and soul and with the utmost confidence. If you want health demand health, likewise with your whole heart and soul, power and confidence. The following is a splendid affirmation:

I am a center of power-creation. I receive power from the universal fund of creative forces. As such a center of power-transmission, I demand that degree of success to which my endowment, my thought and my efforts entitle me. I am sure to succeed in my ambition! My demand is certain to be realized!

Some teachers recommend that the "thought be held" twenty times a day--use your own judgment.

Generally speaking, the man who takes these affirmations audibly ought to "talk up" to himself ; that is, he ought to take them with such firmness and determination that they bring about the desired effects. Let him, in short, talk to his subconscious mind just as if he were talking to a long lost brother. The more emphasis and the more spirit put behind the words the sooner will the demonstration follow.

Cleanse Your Mind

Cleanse your mind and keep it clean; forgive every one and bless every situation; hold only positive thoughts--of success, health and happiness; love everybody and forget the past; offer daily thanksgiving and gratitude; give of your means, your time, your talent, your energy and blessings; think and maintain constructive and harmonious thoughts; be cheerful, merciful and kind; in short--

Think Right!

Think right, read and study, saturate your mind with mental science teachings, and you will not revert.

No doubt the sickness you suffer from has been caused by wrong thinking. Such wrong thinking has become an obsession in the subconscious mind. To have a demonstration you must get some thought into the subconscious other than that which is there now. It is there whether you are conscious of it or not. To effect a cure, take one or more of the affirmations without stress or strain, without doubt or worry.

Just before dropping off to sleep at night, repeat it several times. With some persons it should be repeated many, many times, without stress, without worry, without strain. As you awake in the morning repeat this several times again and during the day. To get the best results you should set aside ten to twenty minutes a day in a quiet place, without any interruption, repeating and concentrating on your formula. Besides taking it at night just as you drop off to sleep, you should repeat it at least four times during the day.

Affirmations or formulae--no matter what you may desire to demonstrate, whether health, success or prosperity--should be accompanied by a regular routine of reading.

Then the reader should by all means make a study of the Silence, what it is and how to use it.

Make these statements faithfully and free from all doubt or hesitation. The more doubt the patient has the more liable is the unconscious auto-suggestion to counteract the thought that is being held.

If necessary, meditate upon each word for some little time. By this means an inner light sometimes unfolds into the affirmer's consciousness.

It is particularly true that the idea contained in the affirmation is more firmly and quickly impressed upon the subconscious in the Silence-- although repetition, even without any effort to enter the Silence, will bring good results. It is especially effective to make the affirmation at moments when the desire for the thing affirmed is especially strong. The fervor with which affirmations are made at such moments, gives added power to the projection of the thought upon the universal ether. Furthermore, the thought is thus more deeply impressed upon the subconscious.

Repeat the affirmation many times each day without stress or strain--free from worry and anxiety--until your entire consciousness vibrates to the affirmation. Crowd out all negative thoughts by constantly affirming the positive.

The affirmations given in this book are intended to suggest to you those which are most effective. It is assumed that you will modify them in any way necessary to fit them to your particular requirements.

To realize for yourself, the statements should be expressed in the language of "I," "me," "my," and "mine." To realize for another, the language should be changed to "you" and "yours." For example: I am spirit, life spirit is now flowing through me freely and I am well, whole and complete.

For Others

(We often get much better results in healing others by speaking directly to them in the second person and even using their own names.)

God is spirit, you, John Doe, are life. Life spirit is now flowing through you freely, and you are well, whole and complete.

You are filled with the abundant, ever present life of Spirit. It flows through you freely, cleansing, healing, purifying and vitalizing every part. You are one in this life, and in it you are every whit whole.

For Oneself

I am filled with the abundant, ever present life of spirit. It flows through me freely, cleansing, healing, purifying and vitalizing every part. I am one in this life, and in it I am every whit whole.

Orally or Silently

This may be given orally or silently. With some people suggestions have much more force than silent thoughts. If the healer is sitting by the patient and using audible suggestions—that is, giving his formulae aloud, it will often lend much more weight and will give the patient an opportunity to interrupt or ask questions, put him more at ease and inspire him with greater confidence in what is going on, thus stimulating his faith for healing.

But the healer's images, impulses and affirmations may be conveyed by telepathy to one who does not even understand the operator's psychological vocabulary.

Conduct

Remember then, and doubly remember, that conduct and conscious feeling impress the mind even more powerfully than any affirmation you may make in words. The Scriptures say, "A merry heart doeth good like a medicine." Cheerfulness is better than medicine. A person with a morbid mind can never be healed by mind cure. Therefore, cultivate cheerfulness and joyousness, affirm that you are happy and follow your affirming for happiness by the conduct of happiness.

Joyful emotions send the blood pounding pell mell through the body, with health in its train, and bring strength and power to every part of the being. Therefore, before taking any affirmation, or holding any thought, one's mental attitude must be tuned up to the pitch of the healing vibration, helped by cheerfulness. This is true of affirming; exceptions to the rule are often seen by magnetic or vibratory methods of healing.

Conform to Laws of Life

These affirmations cover a multitude of sins but other things must be taken into consideration--harmonious living with all of the laws of life.

There are certain limitations to what the mind does in our healing because that is the law. If a headache comes from over-eating, it's over-eating that caused the headache and a correction of eating will be the healing of the headache. This is so obvious that to the thinking person it's not necessary to be repeated or expounded.

For instance, our finger nails grow but we use a file, knife or clip to cut them. We don't charge our subconscious mind to file our finger nails nor do we expect our conscious mind to clip them off.

All the affirmations in Christendom or Kingdom Come will not do as much to keep one's body clean as good old soap and water. It is therefore not enough to affirm health, success or happiness. The "thought held," the affirmations, must be backed up by conforming to mental and hygienic laws--cleanse the mind. By cleaning the mind we mean, as mentioned in Volume III of this series, that you must get all negative and inharmonious thoughts swept out of the chambers of mental imagery. We cannot charge our subconscious mind to make us well if we are disobeying physical, mental and hygienic laws.

In holding a thought for health, never limit the thought to a particular organ. It may be well to take your affirmation that the liver is working well, harmoniously and perfectly in every respect, but always end the treatment (whether it be self treatment or treatment given to someone else) with the idea that the whole body is well, whole and complete. It is just as easy to heal the whole body as it is to heal one organ.

To Recapitulate

We have found out now by this time that most of our sickness comes from a kink in the mind--some mental disturbance, conscious or unconscious, which has long existed as a subconscious condition. The method of healing such sickness should begin

First. With trying to uproot the old ideas and put in their place new ones. We are to endeavor to crowd out the old thoughts with new thoughts. When this is done the healing commences.

Second. These opposite thoughts which we shall give to the subconscious mind—suggestions --are calculated also to arouse dormant cells to the performance of their proper functions.

Third. We take these new thoughts, usually the opposite of the ones which have produced the sickness, so that we may place entirely new impressions in the mind of the patient.

These thoughts or ideas we call affirmations or formulae. To repeat ideas and thoughts hostile to those which have caused our sickness is to crowd out the old sick thoughts and to usher in new.

These thoughts we call suggestions. That is, we direct the conscious mind to pass on to the subconscious mind suggestions designed to counteract those we have been entertaining. When we can make these suggestions strong enough to reach and control the subconscious, our healing is affected. Any other demonstration than health is effected the same way.

These suggestions when given to someone else, should be delivered in monotone. This is not absolutely necessary but the monotone has a soothing effect and is a comfortable, easy-going form of expression which is inclined to produce a state of quiet and repose in the mind of the patient.

These affirmations or formulae may be taken as self treatment. In such case we call it autosuggestion--suggestion to one's self. Most anyone who has reached the psychological point necessary previous to being healed and who will be persistent in taking the affirmations or formulae given below can heal himself. To do that, the best results are obtainable in some such manner as this:

My subconscious mind, I desire and command you to make me well, whole, harmonious and complete.

Or you may repeat any other health formula which you may make yourself or select from those found elsewhere in this volume. It is always better to preface your affirmations with these words,

"My subconscious mind, I desire and command you to," etc.

Suggestion And Autosuggestion

In a home where inharmony exists (or where parties to a business relationship are at daggers' points), it is very necessary to correct the conditions. Do not allow yourself to consent to inharmony but hold the thought of harmony, growth, love, business, position, God, and all that is good. One constructive thinking person can change the mental attitude and the mental atmosphere in home, business or society. It will help you if you choose beautiful harmonies for the eyes to gaze upon habitually, music for your hearing and wholesome, constructive thoughts for your meditations.

If others conspire to bring about inharmony, do you silently persist in your meditations, and hold the thought mentioned above?

In all demonstrating one should be free from negative thinking, fear, worry and inharmonies of every description. Especially is this true if one is to demonstrate health.

The hardest thing in the world is for the patient to be willing enough and patient enough to face his shortcomings, and then determine that he will conquer them. May we supplement what has already been said along this line by urging the patient not to be diffident in recognizing his bad qualities. The Scripture says," There is none good but one, that is, God." Matthew 19:17. The big man is the one who will face his problems as they are, and then with resolute determination resolve to overcome the deficiencies. "He that is slow to anger is better than the mighty; and, he that ruleth his spirit than he that taketh a city." Proverbs 16:32.

But in doing this be sure not to condemn oneself or to pity oneself. It is enough to recognize one or more of the four reasons which have made you sick; now get busy and shoo them out. Self-love, self-pity, self-condemnation, are the most virulent, insidious and subtle forms of selfishness. Jesus did not deny the presence of the devils. Had he done that the devils might have been pleased. He "perceived" them, and commanded them to be gone.

This having been done, let him adhere to the instructions outlined in this volume.

Relaxed and Passive

Before the thought is given or the formula suggested, the patient should be as relaxed and in as passive a state as possible. He should let go all strain and tension. With a certain type of patient it may be better to have his eyes closed and to let his mind drift, his thoughts falling into pleasant recollections and pleasurable anticipations, without, however, his trying to think of anything in any special way.

This quiet attitude should be maintained for probably fifteen to twenty minutes, while the practitioner gives a silent treatment.

There is no certain or stated length of time. It all depends upon the case, the conditions, the individual patient and the healer.

In a receptive and passive state, we have a general access to the subconscious that has been wrongly impressed. By taking a counter suggestion we remove the error, plant and cultivate a new habit until we are able to manifest anew.

Brain Cells Quiet

Before you take any affirmation ponder well on these words of wisdom:

The best condition or state for administration of Suggestion to oneself, or to one's own subconscious mind, is obtained when the body is relaxed and brain cell activity quieted.

Now, command in so many words, amplifying or elaborating according to your own need:

I declare and command that this plan, this ideal, this mental picture by me in mind delineated, be fulfilled amply and fully, according to my Soul Need, which I vouch it to be; that it be physically manifest and a possession of my personality!

A real Need is a Vacuum which Nature abhors and which she fills without delay. Poverty or disease comes only to those who by act, attitude, thought or any other form of Suggestion, have (unconsciously, perhaps) created a Soul Need within themselves for just such conditions.

Readjustment of Needs can be made by Suggestion. Embody the Suggestion in a Command, impregnate it with feeling and realization that it must be fulfilled. You are reinforced in such endeavor by universal laws of creation, which rest on the same factor of predominating mental impression. There can be no failure.

The Lord said: "Let there be Light, and there was light." The same book tells us that we were Created in His image. Does man, the miniature of Deity, contain also a miniature created power? Even one instance of successful regaining of health by Suggestion (creation), invoking the growth of new body or brain cells, is evidence that man does contain the ability to create all the conditions and factors of his existence. Even one instance showing that upon change in realization and consciousness there has followed change in circumstance and environment for the reason would be evidence. Psychology tabulates thousands of such instances.

If the attention is distracted by noises of any kind, a little cotton placed in the ears may prove of service. The better way, of course, is to practice holding one's attention so that the mind will always be under control and thus oblivious to all sounds and noises.

The physical body should be relaxed; the mind should be passive.

Either physical or mental strain is an impediment to one's reaching the inner forces of one's being. Be relaxed in mind and body before putting the subconscious mind to work or before taking your affirmations.

Before he holds a thought, that is, before he takes an affirmation, a very good plan is for the patient in this relaxed condition to picture in the mind that which he desires.

This, as we have already learned, is called visualizing. Some who are good at visualizing find it difficult to hold a thought--the extra words seem to distract from that which they desire to accomplish. Therefore, if you find that it is difficult for you to remember the exact words of a formula or affirmation, hold the thought which you desire in your own way, but, before this, endeavor to picture that which you desire.

If it be health that you wish, picture or visualize yourself enjoying perfect health. The completeness and detailed visualizing or imagery will determine greatly the completeness of your eventual physical realization of the desire you are holding in mind.

If it be abundance or prosperity you desire, picture yourself as doing the things necessary to bring about a normal condition so that you will have abundance and prosperity. Imagine and "see" yourself prosperous in your vocation, surrounded by creature comforts, living in an environment congenial to your being. Visualize yourself surrounded by prosperity and abundance, see yourself in the environment of opulence, imagine all the things your heart desires. Do not limit your picture, make it big, and above everything else, do not be timid or fearful that you are asking and trying to realize too much. Make your demands without doubt or worry, stress or strain.

No Doubt. No Worry

If you are doubtful in your picturing, if you are fearful in your imagery, if you are worried while "seeing," these negative states of mind, your unfavorable mental attitude, may act as a sort of counter suggestion which may not only delay but may prevent entirely the things which you are trying to bring into crystallization.

I say before holding a thought to picture that which you want is the most effective way to bring about a demonstration of whatever you desire.

When you are having this visualization or picturing, the attention must formulate your desire while you are still holding your picture (if you are going to use the method of affirmation and suggestion). Fix the attention of the mind on the spoken suggestion or affirmation about to be implanted.

During all of this time the subject will unconsciously be relaxing in mind and body more and more. The muscles and nerves will become more relaxed and the mind will take on a more complete state of passivity, after one has held the thought. If you have not noticed this, be sure for the future that you have had,

First, relaxation of body.

Second, passivity of brain cell action.

Third, imagery or picturing that which you desire.

Fourth, actually taking words or an affirmation.

Fifth, that you let the mind be as blank as possible (after you have held your thought), that you remain passive in mind and body as long as you can without being conscious of what you are doing.

Sixth, that having gone through these necessary steps you know the operation is complete and feel assured that you have planted a suggestion according to the laws of suggestion. Then be at rest. Be not anxious about results. You have done your part, "nature will and must do the rest. You cannot do nature's part. You can, however, spoil nature's work by trying, by anxiety or greed, for quick results."

Under the conditions above cited, the patient is in a quiet, passive, receptive condition; he is ready for any friendly suggestion that we may make; and earnest, honest, persistent efforts under these conditions will absolutely bring the desired condition sought, if such results be within the bounds of possibility.

Position

Dr. Worcester indeed introduces a saving sentence of great import, namely, "When our minds are in a state of peace, and our hearts open and receptive to all good influence, I believe that the Spirit of God enters into us and a power not our own takes possession of us."

We have mentioned elsewhere that the best time to implant a thought in the subconscious mind is before retiring at night, just before dropping off to sleep or just as one awakes in the morning.

There is a way station in consciousness between the waking and deep sleeping states which is the most pregnant psychological moment of all. This "moment" may last a fraction of a second, as is sometimes seen in somnambulism, or it may last for the entire portion of the usual sleep period.

This is called the "Hypnagogic State."

To charge the subconscious mind before going to sleep one may use the system or method mentioned above.

If at such times you think of the thing you most desire, that desire will sink deeply into your subconsciousness, and a whole train of ideas and emotions will be set to work to realize that desire, without any conscious effort on your part. This desire may be health or any material object. Here we have arrived at a law that is of vital importance.

Do not undress hurriedly and retire in a rush. Retire slowly, contemplatively, relaxed in mind and body--in a state of spiritual poise and mental equilibrium.

Breathing and Affirmations

Elsewhere we have shown the importance of deep breathing when we take our affirmations.

Full, regular breathing with mental affirmations will cast out fear, the blues and other diseases, and will attract absolutely anything desired. This should be used in self healing as well as in healing others.

"I am" has been called the " great affirmative."

I believe it is the consensus of opinion of not only modern teachers of mental science, but the old philosophers and sages throughout the centuries, that "I am" is the greatest of all affirmations.

"I am" is the all-inclusive affirmation "which expresses unity and the thought of limitless expression."

Someone has said...

It is the perception of Individuality; the declaration of Selfhood; the proclamation of Humanity; the line of distinction between brute and Man; the warrant of individual Immortality; the assertion of Free Will and Personal Liberty; the Affirmation of Mastery of Fate through Conscious Choice. I AM is the all-inclusive Affirmation which expresses Unity and the thought of limitless Expression. I am ... What? Whatever I choose to be, for I am an expression of Infinity; I am an incarnation of Divine Life; I am an incarnation of Omnipotence; I am an expression of Omniscience; I am a manifestation of Omnipresent Life. This being true, it follows that I AM WHATEVER I AFFIRM I AM, because I am an expression of Infinity, and Infinity is limitless.

Henry Harrison Brown in " Self Healing Through Suggestion," suggests another method to use to practice the law of suggestion upon retiring.

Exercises Recommended

Upon retiring, lie upon your back and breathe deeply and think ... I AM DRAWING LIFE FROM THE INFINITE RESERVOIR. O, HOW BEAUTIFUL. HOW GOOD IT IS, TO LIVE! Upon awakening, do the same. Imagine that you are breathing from the GREAT I AM, and preparing for the day. Rejoice in the sense of being. Say ... I AM! While dressing, rejoice. Look at your body and see it in imagination as you wish it to be. Tell it is growing into a perfect representation of the Ideal body you have already built. Pet your body while at bath and while dressing, as a mother pets her babe. Love it as God manifest in the flesh. Love and appreciate it as the objective instrumentality of the Ego you are. Every portion of it is divine, and all parts sacred to Love and Truth. So love it, and so FEEL to it, for it is your FEELING that affects it. Awaken these FEELINGS of Life, Health, and Happiness by Affirmations. Though you feel the opposite of the Affirmation, affirm, and keep on affirming until you do feel. When you FEEL what you affirm, you are cured.

Allow no business thought to intrude while preparing for the night or for the day. Conscious efforts in Truth at these hours tell immediately upon the body. Hold these morning and evening seasons sacred to Life. Devote them to such uses and Life will reward you. Retire with happy thoughts. Begin the day with them, and your body will show the gladness of life.

It is recommended that upon retiring each night, you take some Affirmation as your companion. Choose one that fits your case. Go to sleep with it. On awakening choose one for the day. Soon a habit will be formed of thinking during the day along lines thus chosen. Practice alone will bring this condition, therefore . . . practice . . . and, Practice...and, PRACTICE, until in realization you no longer need to practice, for you are ONE with your Ideal.

The following affirmations are also taken from the same book, "Self Healing Through Suggestion," by Henry Harrison Brown.

Put the following Affirmations into your own language and use them as advised:

Healing Affirmations

All life is one. There is naught but life. In the one life I have my being. I am life. The one life is infinite. In that infinity is my constant supply. Life manifests in me normally. I am health. My body is the manifestation of my spirit. Spirit is perfect. I direct the manifestation of myself as spirit by my thought. I now manifest the perfection of the divine spirit of which I am.

Thought is creative. I have no fear-thoughts. Pleasant thoughts build up my health. I think only pleasant thoughts. I think happy thoughts. To mind all things are possible. Thoughts of perfection create health of body. Nothing checks the flow of life in me. In thoughts of health I am healthful. In happy thoughts I am happy.

All my thoughts rise from love of the good, the beautiful and the true.

All former conditions created by fear-thoughts I have put aside. I have only love-thoughts. I am well and happy.

I resign my body to the one in whom I live and move and who finds his self-conscious expression in me.

In perfect faith I live in the consciousness of the omnipresent life and am well.

The infinite one supplies all my needs.

The one who lives in me, through me, and around me, is my silent partner. He cares for me.

My silent partner, through my ideal, supplies me with all I need for health and happiness.

I leave all to him while I enjoy the health and happiness that is mine.

Suggestion

Mrs. Clara H. Scott, in her "Truth Songs," gives one of the most helpful Affirmations. You can sing it, hum it, say it, think it, recite it, to yourself. Do this feelingly until you DO feel it. Learn to make it a constant thought companion. You can hold it silently in mind. Through use, its Truth heals you:

God is life! That Life surrounds me
In that Life I safely dwell!
'Tis above, beneath, within me!
That Life is mine, and all is well!

When you grow into seeing everything from this point of view, health is constant.

Or Try This

Should you prefer, you can substitute "I" for God; thus ... I AM LIFE. You can also for "Life" use Love, or Truth, or Power, or any chosen word. By singing you are enabled the sooner to drop it into the Subconscious.

For the help and inspiration of those who have been raised in the Christian Church, "Unity" of Kansas City, uses the two following prayers, one for health and one for prosperity. If so desired they can be substituted for other affirmations.

Healing Prayer

Jesus Christ is now here, raising me to his consciousness of Truth, and the Truth has made me free from sin, sickness and disease. In trust and relaxation in mind and body, every function does its perfect work, and I am healed.

Prosperity Prayer

Jesus Christ is now here, raising me to his consciousness of Truth, and the Truth has made me free from all anxiety about finances. Fully trusting God as my resource, I have all sufficiency in all things.

Or

My mind and affairs are Divinely adjusted, and I am at peace in the consciousness that I have all-sufficiency in all things.

God is love and fills the universe and there is nothing beside Him.

Remember the great Master himself has said:

Therefore I say unto you, All things whatsoever ye pray and ask for, believe that ye have received them, and ye shall have them.--Mark XI: 24 (R. V.)

THE "PRESENT"

The following lines from Dr. Sheldon Leavitt, M.D., have a direct bearing upon the setting up of the strong Present, of which I have already spoken in this series.

The present tense crystallizes possibilities. In "I am" and "It is" are wrapped great possibilities. There is a wealth of satisfaction to be found in being able to say, in all faith, "I am well, I am strong, I am happy." Assurance like this crystallizes into tangibility, the things for which otherwise we are perpetually longing. It is a giant hand reaching out into the future and bringing to our feet what has long eluded us. Faith then proves a wonder worker. It stands sponsor for us under all the trying conditions of life. When desire rises within us for some great good upon which to build a useful and happy life, the Present tense of faith at once brings it within our grasp.

In this connection, Henry Harrison Brown again says:

Through Affirmation you make connection between the Engineer of Life, which is the Conscious I AM, and the power, which is the Soul. Your thought, expressed in the Affirmation, expresses your conviction of Truth. This conviction directs the outward expression of the Soul. For Soul can only manifest that which the Conscious I AM declares is Truth. Thus in your choice of Affirmation lies your power to control your Life. You are to say that which you wish to be expressed in your body. You are to control your thoughts, so that you will think nothing you do not wish to manifest in your body. Impress this thought deeply upon your consciousness ... I AM THAT WHICH I THINK I AM!

Other Times for Affirming

While it is now definitely known that suggestion with a curative object reaches the subconscious self more easily when sleep is near:

And while the most important time to take these affirmations and formulae is just as one drops off into sleep at night and as he first awakens in the morning:

This should not prevent the patient from taking his silence, his healing affirmations and formulae at other times during the day;--one supplements the other.

Helping Ourselves and Others

"My subconscious mind, I desire and command you to send vibrations of success, health and happiness to all the world,"

Or,

Name specifically someone whom you want to help or (the following is the thought we hold at our noon day healing classes before we attempt any healing demonstrations for ourselves), "health, abundance and harmony for the whole wide world."

I teach my classes that the very first thing necessary for one's own healing is to have the spirit of thanksgiving and gratitude for themselves, and the spirit of helpfulness toward others--to bless everything in their lives.

This is following the injunction of Jesus, who tells his followers that before taking a gift

But seek ye first the kingdom of God, and his righteousness; and all these things shall be added unto you.--Math. 6: 33.

But besides this philosophic angle there is a practical side, namely, by holding a thought for other people it is a great assistance in helping one to get his mind away from his own troubles, and very often that is the one thing needed to effect a healing, either a physical healing or a healing of the pocket book.

Form the habit of talking to the subconscious mind, first, to help others and, second, to help yourself.

Make this a daily habit.

Make it a weekly habit.

Make it a yearly habit.

Then by and by everything will be adjusted properly for the individual while, in the meantime, the subconscious mind is automatically directing all of the affairs of one's existence.

To get the best results you should set aside ten to twenty minutes a day in a quiet place without any interruption, repeating and concentrating on your formula. Besides taking it at night just as you drop off to sleep, you should repeat it at least four times during the day.

"Day by day, in every way, I am getting better and better." Coue has his patients repeat this immortal formula of his twenty times a day.

Another time when commands may be sent to the subconscious mind is just before or after periods of intense application, when the mind for an instant is "VACANT," as we say, and not under the control of any strong idea. By introducing thoughts and commands about our desires we readily impress them upon our subconscious mind.

Form the habit of talking to your subconscious mind just before dropping off to sleep, the first thing as you awake in the morning, and at stated periods during the day. Nothing can be more conducive to success, health and happiness than this.

In time you will automatically be talking to the subconscious mind--in other words, you will have formed the habit and the subconscious mind will be working for your good by this unconscious (to your conscious mind) habit which you have taught the subconscious mind to perform.

If you have reached that state where you desire nothing for yourself, you may, while talking to the subconscious mind before retiring, upon awaking in the morning and during the day, send out healing vibrations for others, prosperity thoughts for the world, happy formulae for everyone, such as

My subconscious mind I desire and command you to send out vibrations of healing, success and happiness to the whole wide world and (here use name or names of those you want particularly to help).

AUTOSUGGESTION

What It Is

A suggestion is an intimation, hint, idea, thought or something similar, conveyed either through the physical senses--hearing, seeing, smelling, touching, tasting--or direct from mind to mind--that is, telepathically. An autosuggestion, of course, is a suggestion to one's self by one's self.

The suggestion of environment--that of Autosuggestion is with most people frequently stronger than any other.

Talking to One's Self

With most people, autosuggestion is clearly stronger than any other. It is a case "sez I to myself, sez I." It is a means by which we may treat ourselves. When we learn the art of Autosuggestion, we can almost perfectly control our own conditions. Everybody can at least to a certain degree influence himself for good. The faculty for developing and accepting autosuggestion, is readily cultivated. It is like everything else--Practice makes Perfect.

Those who fail in autosuggestion, fail partially or totally because they do not do the work well.

That is why we strongly urge those who do not make a success of autosuggestion to employ the services of some practitioner who will lend needed help to get the sub-conscious mind to do work the conscious desires.

It is not enough to give ourselves a passing thought now and then, just a little time snatched from other interests. It is the same as visualizing. It is the predominating thought which in the end prevails. Autosuggestion must be practiced regularly, with interest, fervor, and persistence.

If we expect to accomplish much by autosuggestion, we must give it our undivided attention at stated intervals and continue each effort for at least twenty minutes some authorities say, then longer, from thirty minutes to one hour each day in cases where the conditions require immediate and radical changes.

The length of time, however, will depend somewhat upon individual temperament, the type of the subject.

"Where people thus earnestly engage to employ autosuggestion, and keep it up, persevere in it from day to day, from week to week, or even from month to month, they can absolutely overcome any adverse condition or habit where a cure is yet possible by any known means on earth."

It is now generally accepted by academician psychologists that by autosuggestion we can make ourselves what we want to be. We can change our futures, our anatomy, our form and our appearance. We can relieve ourselves of pain, heal our diseases, and keep ourselves well. A great medical suggestionist tells us that: we can improve any or all of our mental faculties, cultivate ready memories, personal magnetism, and make ourselves brave and courageous; gain perfect control over our tastes, appetites and passions, and absolutely attain business and professional success in any direction that our tendencies lead us.

We only have to determine what we want to be, or what we want to do, then go at it in earnest, do the work regularly and continuously, and success is the reward of our efforts.

It is what we think we can do, and what we say to ourselves we can do that we can surely do.

Fremont said to himself, "I can find a path over the Rocky Mountains upon which a railroad can be built connecting the Atlantic and Pacific Coasts." The path was found and the road was built.

Napoleon said to himself, "I can cross the Alps," and Napoleon did cross the Alps.

Now the behavior and successes of these great men should be living examples for us. They should serve as powerful suggestions, and when great responsibilities face us, or when seemingly difficult tasks are placed before us, we should say to ourselves, "I can and I will cross the Alps," and then undertake the work in hand with the same zeal and determination that characterized Napoleon's march, and pursue it persistently to the end, and success is absolutely assured at whatever we may undertake.

Autosuggestion is talking to ourselves, and when we are talking to ourselves, we are talking to our subconscious mind. By the regular and persistent practice of talking to ourselves, we can perform marvelous things in our health, success and happiness and in shaping our destinies.

We can work out our salvation by talking to ourselves. As we mentioned in the chapter upon the subconscious mind, it is the omniscient and the omnipotent part of man. It works out our life's problems in such a marvelous way that, were we not intelligent and did we not understand what takes place, we should simply say that it transcends rational explanation.

The failure is converted into success, by autosuggestion. The sick are made well. The discouraged become buoyant and optimistic. The downcast and downhearted become hopeful and faithful. By autosuggestion he who has lost his grip again gets a hold on life and does more than he ever dreamed he could. The wonders of the power of autosuggestion have not yet half been told.

We can successfully promote great financial enterprises, forward banking, mining, railroad or other important interests, and as someone has said "organize benevolent, temperance, religious, and political associations, establish institutions of learning, and exploit profitable, legitimate enterprises of any kind--do anything that lies within the bounds of human possibility, all by simply holding to the thought, and persistently saying to ourselves, I can and I will!' "

And no matter where the stars may place us. That should not disturb us. While astrology is founded upon truth, and while the planets have their influence, it is more for good than bad, and we need not suffer from every chilly wind that blows. No, no; we can properly clothe ourselves, absolutely fortify ourselves against all unfriendly stellar influences, push all obstacles out of the way, and attain success in life, either in harmony with, or regardless of the stars. I say to myself, "I can," and I say to myself "I can and I will," and it is done and I am free--independent.

There is another side to autosuggestion, the negative or destructive.

In "Suggestion" the author takes up this side of autosuggestion.

But there is another side to auto-suggestion. While it may be used for good in many ways, and while its possibilities are almost unlimited for accomplishing good and great results, we may so persistently keep our minds upon one subject, and talk to ourselves about some one particular thing to such a degree of excess, that we become mono-maniacs--insane. Or we may indulge in adverse or unfriendly thoughts about ourselves and talk to ourselves about trifling infirmities, till we are worn out and really sick, incapacitated for anything. And if we go on in this way, we may break ourselves down, and actually die prematurely.

We may, by persistently talking to ourselves and our neighbors about our ailments, which at the first may be very simple, change innocent troubles to serious diseases. From the slightest symptoms, we may fix our minds upon what we fear it is going to be, and may so persistently think and talk to ourselves about it, picture in our minds the most serious conditions imaginable, till the dreaded disease is certainly materialized. In this way unfriendly auto-suggestion leads thousands of people to untimely graves. It is readily seen that in this way people may actually think and talk themselves to death.

People sometimes bring upon themselves sudden disaster by adverse or unfriendly auto-suggestions.

Playing with his friendly dog, a man is slightly bitten, merely scratched by the dog's tooth, but he is frightened, fears hydrophobia, begins to talk about it, pictures in his mind all of the horrors of one suffering from hydrophobia, will not be comforted, but continues to talk to himself about hydrophobia, and he persistently keeps the picture of hydrophobia before him till he actually has fits. The thoughts of hydrophobia, mind pictures continuously kept before the eyes, are finally materialized.

People occasionally kill themselves outright by autosuggestion. In fact we believe there are many cases of this kind if we only knew of them.

On April 1st, 1898, at eight o'clock p. m., I was called in haste to 4362 M. Avenue, St. Louis. Upon my arrival I found that I was at a church. When I entered the door I saw that the congregation was in great confusion, many of the people surrounding the platform, just in front of the pulpit, while others were moving about promiscuously. I pushed my way forward, and when I reached the platform, I found lying upon it one of my old friends and patrons, O. J. C, and upon a careful examination I pronounced him to be dead.

Mr. C. had been a member of a church organization denominated "The Four Fold Gospel Workers," who believe in the word of God (the Bible) in its entirety. Mr. C. had been a leader in this church, and was engaged in conducting the services of the evening at the time the following sad event occurred.

Mr. C. was a very devotional, earnest kind of a man, honest and faithful in every regard, and believed in the literal interpretation of the Scriptures. He had opened the services by requesting the audience to join him in singing the following verses:

One sweetly solemn thought
Comes to me o'er and o'er,
I'm nearer my home today, today,
Than I have been before.
Chorus.--Nearer my home, nearer my home,
Nearer my home today, today,
Than I have been before.
Nearer my Father's house,
Where many mansions be,
Nearer the great white throne today,
Nearer the crystal sea.
Chorus.--Nearer my home, nearer my home.
Nearer my home today, today,
Than I have been before.

After the singing of the above lines he quoted the following passages of scripture:

"But sanctify the Lord God in your hearts: and be ready always to give an answer to every man that asketh you a reason of the hope that is in you with meekness and fear." I Peter, chap. 3, verse 15.

1. "Hear ye, children, the instruction of a Father, and attend to know understanding."

2. "For I give you good doctrine, forsake ye not my law."

3. "For I was my Father's son, tender and only beloved in the sight of my mother."

4. "He taught me also, and said unto me, let thine heart retain my words; keep my commandments, and live." Prov. 4th.

Here Mr. C. stopped reading to comment upon the "life" referred to in the closing words of the last line of the reading. During this comment he touchingly referred to the death of his son, who had died some years previous. He described how the son had embraced him in his dying moments, and how he looked up into his face with such an expression of dependence and trust that none but a confiding child can imitate, and with his last breath exclaimed, "O, papa! O, papa, give me life, give me life!"

When Mr. C. had finished this narrative he, himself, while standing on the platform, in front of the pulpit, turned his eyes toward heaven, and exclaimed, "Give me life, give me life!" Just as he pronounced the words "give me life," the second time, he suddenly fell forward upon the platform, dead!

The song, the reading, the story of the dying boy, the powerful suggestions of a life beyond, the vivid idea of a literal home in heaven, as Mr. C. honestly understood it, his gaze fixed upon some particular heavenly apartment, possibly his son occupying a place in it, all taken together, were more than his mortal frame could bear. The power of thought--autosuggestion--separated his soul and body, and he was dead. Had he remained quietly at home on that eventful evening, he might have been living to this day, for he had not been ailing in any way--was not sick.

We had Mr. C.'s body well protected till we were quite certain that he was really dead. We did not permit any preparations of the body for burial till we were absolutely certain that life was extinct, lest somebody might say that Mr. C. was only in a trance.

But it is the friendly side of autosuggestion that interests us most, and one of the very best methods of using it is as follows:

No matter what we may need, let us carefully write out our wants in detail, covering everything that may be desirable for us to enjoy, and then fold the paper, put it in an envelope, and place it under our pillow every night.

All the night-time, while we are sound asleep, the thoughts, the suggestions, the prayers, as written upon the paper, are resting with our subconscious soul minds, and the results are always good. I'll say this is a good method of using autosuggestion, but it need not be used to the exclusion of the usual method of talking to ourselves at stated times--treating ourselves by autosuggestion.

Again, let us impress it upon the reader that auto-suggestion, to make it more perfectly successful, should be practiced regularly, at certain hours, and kept up persistently to the end--till we get what we want, never limiting ourselves to any time for attaining success.

Right here we would warn people against the habit of treating themselves all day long, constantly keeping their ailments or urgent wants before them. This is all wrong. We should have stated times for this work, and then do it and do it well, and then drop it and turn our attention away from ourselves, engage our minds in the social affairs or business matters of life, and go wherever duty calls us. At no time should we stop and regularly treat ourselves for anything during the busy business hours of the day, but we should wait till the proper time arranged for our treatment, and then devote ourselves wholly to the work. This need not hinder us, however, from being ever on the alert, by day and by night, to stoutly resist evil temptations that may come in our way, by quickly turning them aside and going on. It is the habit of constantly holding our frailties, ailments, or needs before us that we should strenuously avoid.

As stated elsewhere, we can, by autosuggestion, make of ourselves what we want to be. If we aspire to be lawyers, ministers, musicians, artists, politicians, statesmen, builders, mechanics, teachers, bankers, or financiers of any kind, we need only to prepare ourselves by acquiring the necessary education for the particular profession selected, and then daily look forward and see ourselves occupying the place or position desired, let nothing disturb or discourage us, or lead us off on by-ways, persistently move forward in straight lines, always and ever affirming and saying to ourselves, "I can cross the Alps," and "I will cross the Alps!"

In this way we may become eminent and useful at anything we undertake, and attain to any degree of success within the reach of human achievement.

It should be well remembered that in treating ourselves by auto-suggestion, we should always suggest what we want; and in talking to ourselves, as in making oral suggestions to others, we should express our wants in the simplest, plainest language at our command. No particular set formulas are required. A simple, earnest statement of our wants or needs is all sufficient for success.

Auto-suggestion is not alone useful where people depend upon it altogether, but we can turn it to good account in having people use it while we are treating them by personal or absent treatment.

Some people seem to lack confidence in their own efforts, especially when not encouraged or supported by outside help. In fact, nearly everybody can help others by suggestion more than they can help themselves by autosuggestion. This should not be so; and it is not true in any case where the patient has full confidence in his own efforts, and regularly, earnestly and persistently does the work.

Hugo Munsterberg, in "Psycho-Therapy" gives an interesting case in autosuggestion.

Graining Success

The writer is a young woman of twenty-four, whom I did not know personally. She wrote to me as follows: "I am a writer by profession and during the last year and a half have been connected with a leading magazine. In my work I was constantly associated with one man, the managing editor. This man exerted a very peculiar influence over me. With everyone else connected with the magazine, I was my natural self and at ease, but the minute this man came into the room I became an entirely different person, timid, nervous, and awkward, always placing myself and my work in a bad light. But under this man's influence, I did a great deal of literary work, my own and his, too. I felt that he willed me to do it. The effect of this influence was that I suffered constantly from deep fits of depression almost amounting to melancholia.

This lasted until last fall, when I felt that I should lose my mind if I stayed under his influence any longer. So I resigned my position and broke away. Then I felt like a person who, having a drug to stimulate him to do a certain amount of work, has that drug suddenly taken away, and without it I am unable to write at all ..." I wrote to the young lady that she could cure herself without hypnotism and without my personal participation. I urged her simply to speak to herself early in the morning and especially in the evening before going to sleep, and to say to herself that the man had never helped her at her work, but that she did it entirely of her own power, and that he never had any influence on it, and that she can write splendidly since she has left the place, and much better than before.

A few months later she came to Cambridge and thanked me for the complete success which the auto-suggestive treatment had secured. She was completely herself again and was fully successful in filling a literary position in which she had to write the editorials, the book reviews, the dramatic criticisms, and the social news. As a matter of course, such treatment had removed only the symptom. The over-suggestible constitution had not been and could not be changed. Thus it was not surprising that in the meantime, while her full literary strength had come back, she had developed some entirely different symptoms of bodily character which I had to remove by hypnotism.

Win. M. Brown, M. D., in "Suggestion and Mental Analysis" gives the point of view of a physician who has made a study of autosuggestion, namely:

The Best Way

An impression may be obtained from some writings that the longer the periods during which auto-suggestion is practiced, the better the effect. It is, however, much better in using auto-suggestion to get the state of mind for a very short time, for a minute or less, and not to attempt to keep this frame of mind for a longer time. The reason for this is that a short interval of time suffices to secure the state of mind, to establish contact with the subconscious and to implant the idea of the desired end.

The subconscious then, without further assistance from consciousness, goes on to realize the idea at its own leisure. In this way you take advantage of a normal suggestibility and are free from any danger. But if you try to prolong the state for several minutes, you run the risk of your own patients who suffer from depression have themselves told me that, although the suggestion may seem to work when they get treatment from me, when they seek to suggest to themselves, all the time a small voice is negating the idea they are striving to implant. This opposition is sometimes of more effect than the auto-suggestion, and the patient be- comes worse rather than better. In such circumstances, if you shorten the time spent in auto-suggestion, you secure a better result.

This Power Is Yours

The Academicians, and Psychologists are not alone in asserting that the mind can do anything it wills to do. We who are teaching the practical side of Psychology have demonstrated that we can disregard all kinds of environmental and hereditary handicaps. The mental deficient be- comes a genius, the unsuccessful, successful, the poverty-stricken, prosperous--all by the law of autosuggestion.

Lillian Whiting has put in poetical terms this same aspect of the power of autosuggestion.

Every morning one holds in his own hands the power to rise to newness of life and to shape conditions. The law by which this is done is as definite and as inevitable as the law of gravity. It is now time for the Newton of the spiritual world to arise and announce the Principles by which the Soul may formulate its conditions.

"Learn to trust yourself and use the powers you have. Say, 'I can and I will.' Do not say, 'I will try, but I know I will fail.' "

How

In making autosuggestions to yourself, the same as in suggestions to others, make your affirmation strong and complete rather than with an interrogation point after it, for this means doubt, and doubt and confusion will be the result.

Every affirmation or autosuggestion which is taken in an insincere way or chock full of doubt, takes a much longer time to effect results. In fact, the result may be negative, for the subconscious mind is quick in scenting uncertainty and doubt in oneself or another and if we were to continue talking to ourselves in a doubtful, insincere manner, the subconscious mind might take up the in-sincerity and the doubtful side of the affirming, rather than that which we really desire, the positive.

So, in our self-suggestion, one must, for best results, first be sincere; second, no doubting; third, in a spirit of conviction; and fourth, back it up by faith in what you are trying to demonstrate.

The surroundings for autosuggestion should be identical with those for suggestion, and heal-ing (as outlined in the foregoing and following chapters)--an undisturbed hour, and a quiet spot with cheerful surroundings and everything that will place the mind at rest, poised and serene. Some find the early morning hour best, others the evening hour, some at high noon, and others in the middle of the afternoon.

But the most successful time--that is when the subconscious mind is the easiest reached by autosuggestion, the same as suggestion, is just upon retiring or just before dropping off to sleep at night, and as one awakes in the morning.

Of course, there are various degrees of receptivity in different individuals at different times.

As there are exceptions to all rules, there may be exceptions to the time to practice autosuggestion, just as some take suggestion quickly and receive immediate results, while others are less susceptible to suggestion and benefits delayed.

Certain habits of thought and action make one more or less amenable to autosuggestion as well as to hereto-suggestion--more than one suggesting to another.

Place

Whatever place or quiet hour one has selected, he should assume an attitude of ease and relaxation. The best posture, ordinarily, is to sit In an easy chair, or recline in a morris chair or on a couch or bed. To get the best results, the same hour should be observed each day and kept for silence and autosuggestion.

By using the same chair or couch in the same surroundings, one builds up an "atmosphere" which is most beneficial, and wherever it is possible this program should regularly be followed.

Some say that one should not go to sleep while giving oneself autosuggestion, but I am convinced that if the body is tired and needs rest there could be no better way to drop off to sleep than by talking to oneself for that which he desires. I should not be understood, however, as saying that when one is tired or weary, autosuggestion gets in its best licks. No, when one is fresh and rested, filled with vigor, strength, is by all means the best time. But, should one feel weary, do not hesitate to drop off to sleep.

We are often asked how we should talk to ourselves, to which we always reply: Talk to the subconscious mind as you would to a person. Sometimes "boss" it, command it, compel it to do what you desire it to do.

One author says:

The more energy and intense earnestness you put into suggestion the better. At times you can profitably shout your affirmations and intensely will that they shall be obeyed.

More than one man has broken up severe attacks of disease by this method: even swearing has changed mental and physical conditions. We do not advocate this last suggestion, but only use it as an illustration to show what intense feeling can do.

To Bless or Curse

It follows that suggestion is of practical value to man in exact proportion to the uses which he makes of it. That is to say, he may make it a blessing or a curse, according to the uses for which it is employed. But use it he must, for it pervades the mental atmosphere as the sunlight of heaven pervades the solar system. He cannot escape it, for it is one of nature's all-pervasive forces and knows no variableness nor shadow of turning. Like every other law of nature, it is primarily for the highest benefit of mankind; but, like every other beneficent energy, it may destroy him if, either through ignorance or perversity, he fails to place himself in harmony with it.

There is another phase to autosuggestion, namely action. Upon this point, C. Franklin Leavitt, M.D., the eminent international Psychoanalyst, throws much practical light.

Your Biggest Fight

ACTION is, in fact, the most powerful autosuggestion of all. It is a sort of double-barreled suggestion. First comes the suggestion of the thought, then the suggestion of acting out the thought. ACTION is also tremendously important because of the fact that it brings a person's powers into exercise. And it is by USE of one's powers, as we all know, that one develops more power.

So make yourself act positive, confident, optimistic, serene and kindly, even though at first you may have to do this in a perfectly mechanical way; even though you may have no feeling about it whatever, even though you may have to go against feeling. When you feel like weeping, SMILE! When you feel like cringing, act BOLD! When you feel all of a turmoil, act CALM!

Of course a spontaneous smile--smiling because you feel like it--is more effective than a forced smile would be. Feeling always carries a lot of power along with it. But forced cheerfulness makes a real impression, too. It cannot fail to. In fact, if a certain mode of action is persisted in, the feelings to correspond will arrive of themselves in time. FEELINGS ARE BORN OF THOUGHTS AND ACTIONS.

If your thoughts should happen to change, your feelings would swing right along behind them, like Mary's little lamb behind Mary. You know it.

So if you want to change those feelings of worry, depression, unrest, resentment, etc., to feelings of poise, happiness, peace, confidence and love, stop acting the way you FEEL and get busy acting the way you would like to feel. You'll find it will work. In his little essay entitled "The Gospel of Relaxation," our friend Mr. James has something most significant to say on this very matter:

"There is ... no better known nor more generally useful precept in ... one's personal self-discipline, than that which bids us pay primary attention to what we DO and EXPRESS, and not to care too much for what we FEEL. If we only don't strike the blow or rip out with the complaining or insulting . . . our feelings themselves will presently be the calmer and better with no particular guidance from us on their own account . . . By regulating the action, we can regulate the feeling. To wrestle with a bad feeling only pins our attention on it and keeps it still fastened in the mind; whereas, if we act as if from some better feeling, the old bad feeling soon "folds its tent, like an Arab, and silently steals away."

Of course it is not one bit easy to act cheerful and calm and courageous when you feel perturbed and fearful and miserable. In fact, it is a very, very hard thing to do, for you will come up against a solid wall of resistance in the form of old, negative habits.

Your biggest fight, as you strive to develop your best self, will be just this--the fight with FEELING. FEELING is very powerful. The difference between it and THOUGHT would be hard to define, but let us have a try at it.

You can think that a certain scene is beautiful, but remain entirely untouched by it. Another day that same scene may move you to tears--it will make you feel something.

You may think that a man is cruel, in a perfectly impersonal way, just as you think it may rain or clear. Or you may feel it, and be impelled to murder.

FEELING, we may say, is THOUGHT warmed to white heat. FEELING gets you--it stirs you up and urges you powerfully toward action. It is very powerful, for either good or evil. Get the right feeling back of you and it will push you where you want to go, almost in spite of yourself. On the other hand, get the wrong feeling behind you, and you will be impelled irresistibly to ruin--unless your reason, your judgment and your will have been so trained that they can take charge of the situation. When feeling is on top you have a fight on your hands which will call out all of your reserves, I assure you. It will give you "a run for your money" every time.

We are all dominated by our feelings far more than we realize. The most that the best of us have done is to have achieved a certain outward control over such manifestations of feeling as temper, petulance, ugliness, impatience, etc. But how about such feelings as worry, tenseness, self-consciousness, pessimism, jealousy, intolerance, resentment, apprehension, etc.

Try to conquer all these in yourself; go at the thing in earnest and see what you are up against. FEELING leads you most authoritatively in the line of least resistance. We tend to do what we have been in the habit of doing. Did I say "Tend"? We are driven that way inexorably, and are certain so to act--unless we take matters into our own hands and firmly DETERMINE that we will not give way to FEELING.

You most be prepared for a siege. Besides being very powerful, FEELING is insidious in her attacks, crafty, deceptive and tremendously resourceful. She will confound your reason, paralyze your judgment and will distort your mental vision and influence you to act the way she wants you to in spite of yourself. And the worst of it is, she will do this to you over and over, for she is capable of going at the thing in a different way every time and will get you off your guard more than once. Be on the watch. Furnish yourself in advance with the strongest possible resolution that no matter what comes, you will act the way you have decided to act, and not the way you feel like acting.

Even with this resolution you will have many a fall, for you will be deceived, over-persuaded and over-powered.

But after a while you will get to know your assailant a little better and will thus be able to put up a better fight. You won't go down so easily, you'll get up more quickly. In time even a sudden attack, no matter how violent, will not be able to take you unawares, for you will have formed the habit of ruling your actions with your reason, your judgment and your will and these will leap to your rescue. Eventually you will get so you can look feeling in the face and say, "I am no longer in your power, but you in MINE!" And you will have one of the biggest victories--perhaps the biggest!-- a man can win. All the great teachers, throughout the ages, have taught that if a man desires to master environment, conditions, persons, circumstances, DESTINY—he must first of all master HIMSELF!

Same Spirit Always

In all autosuggestion, one must be sure that the same spirit of faith prevails as in other suggestion. In Mark 11:24, the great Teacher enjoins upon his disciples: "Therefore I say unto you, all things whatsoever ye pray and ask for, believe that ye have received them and ye shall have them."

It is a truism of applied psychology that the results you achieve following conscious effort will be commensurate with the real desire of your heart. Desire grows with hope. Autosuggestions of hope can be made, which will increase hope and desire in the conscious, as well as in the subconscious mind.

Too Much of a Good Thing

One should give his whole attention to autosuggestion at the time of talking to oneself. In other words, whatever you do, do with all your might. Solomon says, "The desire of the righteous shall be granted"; righteous here, being employed in the sense of earnestly seeking the truth. Bear in mind that which you demand. Keep your attention fixed on your autosuggestion. The more the mind is held in attention to the thought at hand, the quicker may one expect results. Then, after holding the mind at attention, taking the affirmation with firmness and confidence--forget it—let go--don't try to think of it anymore . Herein is the secret of autosuggestion. It is the touchstone of success or failure.

Many persons try to keep talking to themselves all day long and it cannot be done. They wear themselves out mentally and physically. They keep on repeating the same thing in such a fatigued, half-hearted manner, that their affirming acts as a counter suggestion to the subconscious mind. That is, the subconscious becomes befogged and bemuddled. It does not know which suggestion to take, that contained in the formal words which the patient is uttering, or the fatigued, worn-out mental attitude in which he is affirming.

A Few Don'ts

Do not allow others to undermine your faith in yourself, in God, and in the law of suggestion. Do not let others switch you from your main purpose, which should be to use autosuggestion for health, your greater success and your complete happiness. Do not permit, much less encourage, others to talk to you in a negative way. For the more you entertain the negative, discouraged, down-in-the-mouth thoughts of opposition which people may try to shoot into you, the harder it will be for you to continue in your work of self-help.

For instance, a youngster bumps his head and runs crying to his mother. She boo-hoos over him and says, "O, my dear, isn't it awful to have such a bump! Oh, my poor li'l tootsie wootsie." The more she tootsie wootsies him, the more the little tootsie wootsie cries--the trouble at hand is aggravated.

But suppose the youngster bumps his head even harder and runs to a psychological mother. She, instead of bemoaning the awful crack her scion received, kisses the sore spot with the suggestion that it is all right, "just a little bump, it won't hurt much, gone already, run along and play." The youngster tears out of the house, his crying turned to laughter, his tears diamonds sparkling in the sunshine.

Remember, we become like that which we think. Think therefore only of those things which you desire and which you want, and do not entertain opposite thoughts from anybody.

How to Overcome

Remember to carry out the analogy of our illustration in every experience of life from childhood to adulthood. Suppose one is afflicted with suffering. The more you talk about it, and the more you allow other anti-cheerfuls to "tootsie wootsie" you, the worse your pain will become. If you should be surrounded by such unpsychological humans, seek a quiet place and there strive to be peaceful, calm and at rest in Infinite Love. Assert, I feel well and happy; all of the organs of my body are functioning normally; I am strong, harmonious and well. Do this without ceasing, and you will swing yourself into a peaceful mental attitude which will soon have its effect upon your nervous system and physical being.

Should things go wrong, and your sky-line of experience become cloudy and life irksome and monotonous, the more you talk about monotone and tiredness and awful experiences of life, the more keenly will you feel what you are passing through and the more you allow others to talk about it, the worse you will become. Get away from them unless they can talk in terms of positive, comforting, and encouraging philosophy. Get away from them. Find a quiet place to repose. Lie down--flat on your back without a pillow. Stretch the arms out horizontally from the body. Take a few deep breaths and then talk to yourself something like this:

The riches of the Spirit now fill my mind and affairs, and I am prosperous always. I think only of prosperity; I talk only of prosperity; any I know that success is mine.

Infinite Supply meets all my needs. Abundance, prosperity, plenty, and opulence are mine now, to have and to enjoy.

There is abundance in the world for me, given by the bountiful hand of Omnipotence I gratefully claim and accept the supply for all my needs.

God is supplying all my needs from his illimitable riches

I am one with the infinite Source of all the wealth in the universe, and that wealth is flowing through me now and meeting my every need fully and completely

I am the all-wise, all-loving, all-conquering son of God.

I rule supreme in all the affairs of mind and body. Infinite Wisdom guides me. Divine Power prospers me; I am successful in all that I undertake.

I rise above my circumstances. I rise above all handicaps, all hindrances, all conditions. I rise above my environment, and I control my life. I am success, and I have success.

I WILL: there is nothing impossible to me.

I am the captain of my soul; I am the master of my fate.

The power within me surmounts all obstacles.

I am unconquerable. I am achieving my desires; I am the captain of my soul and master of my fate.

The Spirit of good goes before me, making easy, healthy, happy, prosperous and harmonious all my ways.

I meet all the conditions of my life, and I know that I am using them all to my good.

Spirit is spurring me to action and I am going swiftly forward. I have the strength and the courage of a real man, and I am not being kept down. I am strong, successful, and happy.

You have all noticed that a hypnotist, returning every year to your town, to give the public a huge laugh at the pranks his "subjects" play, always makes use of certain old "subjects." The reason of this is that they are trained, not to sham, but their subjective minds are trained to respond with promptness to almost any suggestions the operator may make. It is usually easier to produce a physiological effect upon a trained hypnotic subject than upon another person; not because the trained subject has greater powers, for he has not, but because his subjective mind has been trained to obey and put into operation the suggestions and instructions given to it.

I should rather consider, from all evidence that I can find, that the hypnotized subject has no greater power over his own organism than another, but that his mind obeys suggestions--either from another or from himself --with greater promptness and attention to the work to be performed. That which can be done through hypnotism can likewise be done without hypnotism. It is subjective training that counts in these matters, not special states.

Train the subjective mind, through auto-suggestion, to become an obedient servant--one that will give its attention to work and duties committed to it. It has powers beyond our most sanguine belief. It has knowledge concerning the mysteries of the cells and organs of which we know objectively so little. Trust it, then. Give it large tasks to perform, and give it inspiration and encouragement through auto-suggestion. Guard the mind against adverse thoughts, which, remember, become adverse suggestions.

One suffering from a chronic ailment and habitually thinking of the hopelessness of his ill, saying to self and others, "I fear I will never get well," is like a man searching for a lost article in the night, and continually turning his back to the shining moon, and thus casting a shadow upon the part of the ground he is searching. He not only denies himself the light of the moon, but darkens the place of search. The sufferer not only denies himself the aid of his subjective mind, but turns it against himself in all its awful power to deplete and destroy.

But someone says to me, "I can't help but be discouraged and apprehensive, my mind will dwell upon my ailment. My ailment is present with me to remind me of it." Such a person has allowed the bodily condition to train the mind into thought habits concerning the bodily conditions. The mind thus trained reacts upon the ailing part with harm.

Contrast this condition with the chances of an organ where the habit of the mind has become one of cheer and hope, and the auto-suggestion, "I can get well,--I will get well,--I am growing better and better. I have the power to surmount this difficulty. I will, I will," have become a part of one. Added to these auto-suggestions should be the principles of love, which I will speak of in a chapter later in this work.

If your habit of mind is gloom, fear, worry, apprehension, remember that you have fallen into a bad habit, and must reverse the condition by making a new habit.

It is your privilege, on the whole, to govern the general course of your thoughts. It is true that the mind is influenced by conditions, but we must not acknowledge ourselves automatons, without power to arise above conditions or steer our course to miss the reefs ahead.

No Royal Road

There is no royal road to success in autosuggestion. All that any practical psychologist can do is to send out a warning to all those who are about to travel this wonderful, marvelous pathway of life. Many fall by the wayside because they fail to struggle on. They give up just too soon. Many become foot-sore and soul-weary, in traversing this straight and narrow path of life because they fail to pay the price in thorough vigilance and persistency. In autosuggestion beware of slothfulness.

And, just as there comes a time in the experience of everyone, when the line between success and failure is so thin you cannot tell where one leaves off or the other begins, so in autosuggestion and suggestion a very faint line divides success from failure.

Everyone should fortify himself against early surrender. He should know what to expect. The critical hour may arrive any moment when one thinks that there is nothing to autosuggestion, when he argues that although he has been talking to himself for some time no results are apparent. When he becomes discouraged and ready to quit, that is the very time to hang on. When you think you are going to give up--don't do it. Stick 'er out. Pass the crisis and success is yours.

The longer the subconscious mind is trained to serve the will and the oftener it is exercised, the more readily will it respond and the more effective the results. This is not unlike training the body for the performance of physical feats. The pianist must keep in training and practice to retain his skill and dexterity.

"Such subjective education inspires a feeling of confidence in one's own powers. Fear and apprehension find less room for growth. One will pass through an epidemic in greater safety and with less harm to himself. You can't afford to live in fear or anxiety. Strengthen the inner man. Put it on its guard and about its business to maintain bodily health and moral purity."

Power Over Cells

In "Mind Power and Privileges" by Albert B. Olston, the reader will find much food for thought along the lines of autosuggestion.

When we remember that every thought in the objective mind is an auto-suggestion, and in some way affects the subjective mind, and recall the powers of the subjective mind over organs and over the very cells of our body, the question of what we shall and shall not think becomes one which deserves our highest consideration and greatest enthusiasm.

The greatest obstacle in the way of auto-suggestion to heal and cure lies in the objective and subjective ideas that it "can't be done," "I don't believe it." I must again insist upon the importance of the active reiteration of suggestion, and the withdrawal of any open criticism of progressive judgment on the matter. Give the auto-suggestion a chance to instruct and educate the subjective mind by withholding any adverse suggestions in the way of adverse or doubtful thoughts. Rather say to yourself, "It will be done."

One well-authenticated case is recorded by Mr. F. W. H. Myers of an experiment in which two patches of skin, alike in size and shape, were removed from the arm of a subject in the hypnotic sleep. The suggestion was made that the one wound would heal rapidly, and give no pain or sore-ness; while the other would become sore and painful, and cause, on the whole, a bad sore. The one healed more rapidly than usual, while the other place did as was suggested. To one wound was given the assistance of the subjective mind with its mysterious powers, and the metabolism of the cells was increased by its influence. A healthy tone was imparted to that region. To the other part was given the morbid effect of the subjective mind. Instead of it building a healthy tis-sue it destroyed and made sick the part. That, no doubt, could have been carried to the point of great harm to the arm.

Who can measure the effects and destructions of morbid thoughts habitually carried on? To the subjective mind of the person upon whom the two patches of skin were removed, a destroying suggestion was given concerning the one part, while concerning the other, suggestions of growth and health were made.

How different the processes of the two wounds! But someone will say, "That was done under hypnotism." So it was, and we will also grant that the person was especially susceptible to sug-gestion. It must, however, be borne in mind that the suggestions were made to him on one occa-sion, merely repeating them a few times so as to fix them upon the mind. In the case of a chronic disease the destroying and doubting auto-suggestion is made hundreds and thousands of times. It is repeated and repeated. The morbid, discouraging thought is often almost continuous. This often is carried to the extent that the person somehow seems to take a delight in recounting his suffering to every other person he sees.

He is the worse off for each such conversation. It all amounts to the education of the subjective mind, which comes to believe that the suffering must be; and under such premises it usually takes place. At least the body in its tendency to mend has a formidable barrier to crowd out and fight against. It is this thing that so often baffles the skill of physician and nurse. The effects of discouragement, fear, and morbid thoughts upon the organs and functions of the body differ quite widely in different people. Some suffer harm directly and do not seem to be able to escape the ravages; while others seem to have a more natural independence of the body, and less sensi-tive to the moods of the mind.

Everyone has noticed that people suffer differently from the same degree of harm. This is due to several things. Chiefly among others is the degree of attention given, and the matter of determi-nation not to suffer. Determination, exercised habitually by the objective mind, finally develops its character in the subjective mind, which produces its effect in any crisis, even though the ob-jective mind be otherwise employed. If one wishes to exercise the sense of touch upon something which requires a delicate touch, he will give it an undivided attention. Some people hold the same attitude toward their bodily ills. Instead of diverting the mind from the diseased part, they fix upon it such an attention as to increase the suffering, and, as we have come to know, to do harm by the thoughts of apprehension.

Stage Fright

As an instance of how autosuggestion can do most anything, we quote in full, as an example, Geraud Bonnet's prescription for the cure of stage fright:

Let us suppose that, on some approaching day, you have to sing at a private party or on a public platform.

You have a good voice, and you are quite familiar with what you have to sing; you know that the audience will be friendly, and that success awaits you.

But you are panic-stricken; you feel certain that when the time comes you will be seized with stage fright.

You are sure that you will be terrified by all the eyes that will be concentrated on you when you appear on the platform; you will become uneasy, will sing wrong notes, and will finally break down.

This is an involuntary autosuggestion, which has taken possession of your mind.

You can combat it by a voluntary autosuggestion.

Isolate yourself in a room where no one will come to disturb you. To make assurance doubly sure, lock the door. Settle yourself comfortably in an armchair; or lie down, if you prefer it, on a sofa or on your bed. Close the eyes; and if you are afraid of being disturbed by some noise from outside the room, plug the ears with cotton-wool.

Relax your body to the utmost, for this physical inertia favors mental passivity, and renders the mind more accessible to suggestion. When your nervous energy is no longer dissipated in making movements or in other work, it will be concentrated in the brain, and you will be better able to devote it to the idea you wish to realize.

At the outset, endeavor to stop thinking altogether. Try to think of nothing at all for a time. Then direct your thoughts towards the idea which is worrying you, and counteract it by its converse, saying to yourself "I don't suffer from stage fright; I sing well; I am perfectly easy in my mind."

Take a deep breath. Wait for a moment, and then say once more: "I don't suffer from stage fright; I sing well; I am perfectly easy in my mind."

Repeat the process several times; repeat it five times, ten times, or more, according to the amount of leisure at your disposal.

Have a number of such "sittings" every day--in bed, at night, just before you go to sleep; during the night, if you happen to be awake; in the morning before you get up, immediately after waking.

If you carry out this plan with assurance and conviction, success is certain.

Dr. Schofield says:

I think from such cases as these, and the fact that the hypnotic state is generally produced through the eyes, that there is a closer connection of the mind with sight than with the other senses--or in other words, what has been considered the worst affliction to man, and the most difficult to heal, is so intimately allied with the power of mind that blindness becomes one of the easiest afflictions to heal.

Deafness Easy to Heal

I might add that in my own classes I have found about the easiest of anything to heal is deafness --deafness of long standing--deafness of twenty to forty years--deafness where the ears have pronounced punctured ear drums--no ear drums-- ear drums destroyed, people who never did have ear drums--according to specialists' diagnosis.

In nearly every psychological campaign which the author conducts and in all classes following these campaigns, people have sight restored. In a recent campaign three people, blind, received their sight. One woman who was totally blind in her right eye had instantaneous healing. Another man, twenty-five years of age, who had been born blind in one eye, who had seen many specialists, a number of whom had recommended that the eye having no life at all, should be removed, during one of our "silences" felt vibrations in the eye with such a force that when he opened his eyes, he was surprised to see not only an effulgence of light, but he was able to see me on the platform some forty feet away--the first time he had ever seen any object of any kind out of that eye since birth.

Another, a brick mason by trade, had met with an accident. In breaking a brick to fit in construction, a piece struck him in the right eye, causing instant blindness. Two and a half years following this he had sun stroke, which caused the other eye to go dead. He went to five specialists, they said, they had done the most they could do, and the best they could do and to no avail. A number had pronounced him absolutely blind forever-- hopeless. When I opened my campaign he was being led about the streets of his native city by the hands of a boy--his son. In less than two weeks he was able to get around the city without any help, his eyesight gradually becoming better and better.

It's a most interesting commentary upon the mistakes which even celebrated specialists can make when it is related that this man, after having had his sight restored, went back to visit one of the old specialists who was so obsessed evidently with something else than healing, examined the man's eyes and said they were no better and yet he was seeing. There is one red signal sign of danger which I should like to imprint on every page of this book namely, don't believe everything you read in the "item," only about one-half you see and very little that you hear if it's negative or destructive.

More Evidence

A famous medical authority gives the following illustrations:

At the siege of Breda, in 1625, the whole garrison was down with scurvy. The Prince of Orange smuggled into the town three small phials of essence of camphor, and his physician put three or four drops into a gallon of water, and the men recovered and saved the town.

As to this, we may remark that it is a matter for curious conjecture as to how far generally the cure we now attribute to drugs will soon be considered to be due to psychism.

Sir Humphrey Davy, wishing to experiment with some new preparation on a paralyzed 'patient, put first a thermometer under his tongue. The man, believing that this was the new comedy, soon felt so much better that Sir Humphrey told him to come the next day, and in a few days, with the thermometer applied for a few minutes each day, he was well.

Dr. Eanierie Gerbe, of Pisa, cured 401 out of 629 cases of toothache, by making the sufferers crush a small insect between their fingers, that he represented was an unfailing specific.

An amusing case is that of a paralyzed girl, who, on learning that she had secured the affections of the curate, who used to visit her, got out of bed and walked--cured: and afterwards made an excellent pastor's wife.

And, on the other hand, we give an illustration as to the curative effect.

Pertaining to the curative effect of the patient's own conscious suggestion to the unconscious mind, and through it on the body, in "The Life of Father Chiniquy" we read:

In 1837, Pastor Chiniquy got severe typhoid fever in Canada, and four physicians told his bishop there was no hope of his recovery. On the thirteenth day they said he had only a few minutes to live, and his pulse could not be felt. He then in a vision saw his favorite saint, St. Anne, to whom he cried for cure with every power of his soul, and he heard her say, "You will be cured." He recovered, and Quebec rang with the miracle. He was examined by two Catholic and two Protestant doctors.

Dr. Douglas, a Protestant, showed Chiniquy his recovery was due to his being a man of remarkably strong will, and determination to resist death; that the will had a real power over the body, and his strong will had conquered. Chiniquy listened but preferred his saint, and had a votive picture painted of her for fifty pounds. A priest who saw it then told Chiniquy the cure was no miracle, and that most of the crutches hanging round the church were left by imposters; and the rest by those cured by the power of the mind over the body.

Till 1858 that picture, representing the saint telling Chiniquy he would be cured, was in the church. In that year he again got typhoid fever in Chicago, and once more was given up as dying. But this time he did not cry to the saint, but made a determination to get better and soon felt life returning. He then saw the saints had no part in his previous cure and took his picture down and burnt it.

What Is It Heals?

It is evident, therefore, if some believe in signs, wonders, miracles, saints, charms, touching the King's garments, horseshoes, rabbit's foot, horse chestnuts, medicine or various negative thoughts and are healed--" according to your faith so be it unto you"--but the unprejudiced, open-minded, thinking person will have his faith strengthened by understanding that all things are in divine order, in harmony, logical and scientific. Knowing that this infinite power is all-wise, with certain laws that always act and react the same, whether for sickness, or health, abundance or poverty, failure or success, gives an added impetus to the thinking person so that he understands that it is not signs, wonders, miracles, that heal but the superstitious and ignorant person may have the faith in these things aroused which effects the healing, but none of these things in themselves have any healing virtue. It is the life-giving God-presence, health-restoring power within each person to do the will of the Father so that the healings are effected.

In "Psychic Healing," Swami Ramacharaka gives another illustration of the power of mind to heal:

It is that the person may give himself just the suggestions that he would give a patient. The "I" part of you may give suggestion to that part of the mind that runs the physical organism and manages the body from cell to organ. These suggestions will be taken and acted upon if given with sufficient earnestness. Just as people may make themselves sick by improper self-suggestions, so may they restore themselves to health by the proper suggestions given in the same manner.

There is no mystery about this--it is in accordance with a well-established psychological law.

Make the treatments vigorous--just as earnest as if you were treating somebody else instead of yourself. And you will get wonderful results.

There is no special mystery about this self-suggestion.

It is merely your "I" telling your instinctive mind to get to work and attend to its affairs properly. And by right living you give the instinctive mind the material with which to work and the conditions conducive to success

Just speak up to the instinctive mind just as if it were another person who had charge of your body and tell it what you expect it to do. Do not hesitate about being in earnest about it--put some life into your commands. Talk to it in earnest. Say to it, "Here, you instinctive mind, I want you to get down to work and manage things better for me. I am tired of this old trouble and I intend to get rid of it I am eating nourishing food, and my stomach is strong enough to digest it properly, and I insist upon your attending to it--right away, now.

I am drinking sufficient water to carry off the waste matter from the system and I insist upon your seeing that my bowels move regularly every day. I insist upon your seeing that my circulation is equalized and made normal I am breathing properly and burning up the waste matter and properly oxygenating the blood and you must do the rest. Get to work--get to work." Add to this any instructions that you think well and then see how the instinctive mind will "get down to business."' Then maintain the proper mental attitude, bracing yourself with strong affirmations until you get things going right. Say to yourself, "I am getting strong and well--I am manifesting health," etc., etc. Now we have told you how to do it--then GET TO WORK AND DO IT'

Method of Healing No. 13

"William Walker Atkinson, famous American writer on mental healing, has a most interesting addition, he thinks, to auto-suggestion. Instead of using, "I am well, etc.," he says the second person, "you," even when an individual is taking an affirmation for himself.

It is always a stronger suggestion for the healer to use a certain person, "you"--for instance, "You, John Doe, are well, whole and complete," but now Atkinson adduces a workable hypothesis which he says is better than this, when an individual is healing himself, John Doe is the patient ; John Doe desires to heal himself. Following Atkinson's suggestion, John Doe auto-suggests to himself in this fashion: "John Doe, you are well, whole and complete" (instead of "I am well, whole and complete").

In this respect, Atkinson says, "On the planes of the Subconscious are performed many of those processes of classification, analysis, synthesis, adjustment, relation, combination, etc., which are usually regarded as being performed exclusively by the conscious mentality."

Three Reasons "Why"

Self-help,--auto-suggestion, does not always heal. In the first place, the person may not be able to make the suggestion of the conscious mind strong enough to the subconscious to open the little trapdoor to get the counter suggestion into the miracle-working, inner mind.

Second, auto-suggestion will not always avail, for the effort of the individual to try to concentrate or to bring about a healing makes him more conscious than ever in the matter, so that he is afraid that he is not going to have his demonstration or he holds the thought, "Will I have it! It doesn't seem as though I am any better." He keeps his mind on the trouble, whereas the best way to have a demonstration is to hold the thought, take your formula, either by yourself or others, and then forget it. Trying suggestion without assistance from someone falls short of the mark to some good, well-meaning, trustful, delicate, sensitive people who rely upon others. They must have their faith inspired by the presence and help of other people.

Third. Self healing does not always take place because one's imagination is not under control. He is either not able to stimulate his imagination to perfect health or his imagination pictures sickness, catastrophe and ill health, instead of the opposite--perfection.

Method of Healing No. 14

Another method of treatment by suggestion and auto-suggestion is given by Wm. Brown, M.D., in "Suggestion and Mental Analysis."

The best method of employing suggestion and auto-suggestion would be one that avoided artificial dissociation altogether. This may be carried out by asking the patient to lie on a couch with eyes closed and all voluntary muscles, as far as possible, relaxed and to think passively of sleep. The patient must avoid all effort, and if thoughts thrust themselves on his notice he should quietly turn his attention away from them and let them, one by one, pass by. He is to allow his mind to dwell upon the idea of sleep throughout the whole time that he lies on the couch, and to pay no attention to the words that the doctor will address to him later on. Although he will no doubt hear these words he is not to listen (actively) to them. For the first few moments the doctor suggests relaxation, passivity, and sleep in calm tones, and then proceeds to give his suggestions in a low voice, speaking with calm certainty.

The suggestions are both special suggestions in reference to the actual symptoms and to their causes, so far as they may have become known through previous mental analysis, and also general suggestions of sound mental and physical health. The further suggestion is also given that the patient will be able to help himself by auto-suggestion, which he will practice the last thing at night and the first thing in the morning until recovery is complete. The patient is allowed to lie on the couch, thinking of sleep, for an hour at a time, and the suggestions are given him every five or ten minutes. It has been previously explained to him that, although he is not listening to the suggestions with his conscious mind, yet his subconscious mind will receive them and act upon them. It is also explained to him that, should he actually fall asleep during the hour, it will be normal sleep, not hypnotic sleep, and that the suggestions will be received all the same. Almost all patients are able to be passive for an hour at a time in this way, and experience no restlessness whatever while doing so.

They often express surprise at this, and state that they could never do this by themselves at home. The rest itself appears to have a specially recuperative effect--like a concentrated rest-cure, as one of my patients remarked to me. After a few hours of treatment most patients find themselves able to carry out auto-suggestion satisfactorily. My advice as regards auto-suggestion is that the passive state should not be pro-longed for more than about a minute at any one time, for reasons already stated.

Permanent improvement may be obtained in this way, especially if the suggestion treatment is preceded by an adequate mental analysis. Almost all patients need help by suggestion from another person before they can obtain much success through auto-suggestion. This is not surprising, since suggestibility is an essentially social characteristic. It is only secondarily that one becomes suggestible to oneself as to an alter ego.

Remember that one of the biggest words in auto-suggestion as well as suggestion and mental healing is REPETITION. If you do not succeed in your healing or in maintaining your health, be sure that you repeat and Repeat and REPEAT to your subconscious mind.

It may take some people only a few minutes-- with others a day--some may have to repeat to the subconscious mind and take the affirmation several times a day for a week--others will find it necessary to do this for two or three or four weeks--with some it may even linger into a month, or months, but whatever you do, remember that repetition is the biggest thing in mental healing. If at first you don't succeed, try, try again is as necessary in the practice of mental healing as in anything else. Repetition. Repetition. Repetition!

This great creative principle that is scientific and logical, love, peace, joy, happiness, fellowship and brotherhood and fatherhood, is with us, will help us, guide us, lead us, make us well and prosperous and happy. That spirit is now with you and is a part of you. Accept it, believe it, and the peace that passeth all understanding shall be with you forever and forever.

SEMI NEGATIVE

Four Kinds of Affirmations

Generally speaking there are four kinds of affirmations, namely:
1st.--Positive,
2nd.--Negative,
3rd.--Semi-negative, or Semi-positive,
4th.--Post-positive and Post-negative.

Method of Healing No. 15

Inasmuch as we have offered in this series different methods and ideas of healing, this policy will be followed in the affirmations.

The old way of negation, denying things as they are, including sickness, poverty and diseases, has healed thousands, but a quicker, surer, more reasonable and a purely scientific way is to acknowledge that the sickness is in the body but to assert the real spirit is not and never could be sick, for this spirit is God. We, however, are

'For the way in which this healing takes place see Practical Psychology and Sex Life. Vol. Ill of this series presenting in this work various methods of healing and are not emphasizing absolute denial. Inasmuch as that belongs to the first stage of mental healing, dating back to the last half of the nineteenth century, such a bold assertion as the following, taken from "Divine Healing" is emphatic if not elegant, but it also is unreasonable and represents an archaic method. I quote verbatim: "Here is one, for example, who is troubled with the belief of a severe headache. What is that so-called headache! Nothing but a lie! It is not true." The author of this, teaches emphatically that you must deny everything that you do not want. Such teaching for people who have come into a higher consciousness of mixing reason with our thought needs no comment.

Why We Have Colds

As a rule, the most effective way to achieve a healing is to take an antidote--a counter suggestion, affirmation--to that which has produced our sickness, leaving out the denial or negative part of the affirmation. In most cases I say this is more effective. Yet there are certain types of people and certain ailments which may be more readily eliminated and corrected if we take an affirmation semi-negative. For instance, for a cold, which is recognized to be one of the hardest things over which the ordinary newcomer into mental science faith has to demonstrate.

A person may so charge the subconscious mind with this affirmation "I am well, whole and complete" that the cold will never come but there may be other types, and I have known them in my classes, who have taken the following semi- negative affirmation and with it healed themselves from colds. " My subconscious mind I desire and command you to rid my system of colds forever and forever" or, "my subconscious mind I desire and command you to eliminate from the organs of my body the thought of colds. I am perfect."

While the most effective is the positive antidote--the constructive opposite thought or counter suggestion--yet the wise patient or practitioner will be willing and ready to apply any method which will bring about a result. So, if a person is of the opinion that he or she needs a semi-negative affirmation, as per the illustration of cold above, do not hesitate to try this formula given.

Perfect Memory

Or take as another illustration memory. Suppose a person has poor memory. The positive suggestion would be, "You have perfect memory. You are life. You are vitality; you are strength. You are a part of universal intelligence and all mind is memory. You are a part of universal mind and memory and are therefore all mind and have perfect memory."

But with other individuals, it will be found helpful to give such a thought as, "He is freed from forgetting or free from whatever malady he may have." Then there are teachers who believe that all treatment should be specific in designating the symptom which should disappear and the harmony that should come in its place. For instance, one has heart trouble. He talks to his subconscious mind in this fashion, "My subconscious mind, I desire and command you to relieve the strain on my heart and make my heart function normally day and night."

This is a semi-negative suggestion. It brings up into the consciousness of the individual the fact that he has trouble with his heart, yet this method is used with many, many people very successfully. You see this book is trying to point the reader to the idea that there are many angles to truth and many ways to operate the laws of health, success and happiness.

The more positive thought probably is such an antidote as this, which does not mention to the consciousness anything about the heart's irregularity, to-wit: "My subconscious mind, I desire and command you to make all of the organs of my chest well, perfect, harmonious and whole."

Eating

Suppose we are having trouble with digestion or assimilation. This will serve as an example of one way to make semi-positive affirmations. It is one used by Dr. A. A. Lindsay.

Hare no fear or thought about food and you will find that every meal will be digested properly and you will want three good meals daily and regularly. Your stomach will perform its offices in secreting the right fluids to treat the food--its muscular and nervous activities will be normal. The liver will perform its appointments naturally, and the intestinal functions will be carried on successfully. The assimilation of your food will be perfect; every cell shall take from your food the elements needed. The irritation of the skin, showing a lack of elimination, will disappear. Improvement in every direction shall continue from this moment until you are perfectly well in all respects.

This same kind of a treatment can be used to break bad habits.

Every healer must use the power of the spirit at his own level of consciousness. That is why this series is of such great service to man. It offers the many and different ways of healing so that each healer and each one to be healed may attract to him and use every means best needed in his present state of consciousness.

Christ's Method

So, we say that the semi-negative will demonstrate its value as illustrated in the affirmation taken for a cold or heart trouble. On the other hand there are those who will be healed by making a direct denial as has been practiced by some in denying sickness, denying matter, denying mistakes or failures, denying sin, in fact, denying most everything except the universal spirit.

Christ, however never used denials. He used the positive, "I am," and "I will," "Be thou clean," "Thy faith hath made thee whole," "Rise, take up thy bed and walk," "Go and sin no more," "Take heed," etc., etc.

According to the measure of our own positiveness do we open the channel for the cosmic forces to flow through us, and according to the faith of the patient does he open the channel for the healing forces to flow into and through him it matters not what method is used so long as this faith is aroused.

While we suggest that the individual healer and patient use the semi-negative denial, the actual denial, or the positive, according to his or her plane of consciousness, we believe that most people will be more successful with the positive.

If you can get results by negative methods or semi-negative methods, use those methods. Some people do.

Oliver C. Sabin uses them successfully. While we do not agree with him entirely, yet his explanation of his procedure as given below may help those who elect to use his method.

Examples of Negative Healing

We have had two cases where the fever had run two or three weeks, and with all the work that we could do we could not heal before four or five weeks. The universal thought around the patients was that the fevers had to run their course. We could keep them out of delirium, we could keep them comfortable, but to get them out of the hospital was impossible because of this universal thought. But if you can apply the Truth absolutely and perfectly against any kind of error you absolutely and perfectly destroy the error; you annihilate it.

For instance, here is a dark room, very dark. You think that darkness is real. I turn one of these electric buttons. What is the result? The light comes out, the darkness is annihilated. It did not go anywhere; it was nothing; it was simply the absence of light. So with error of any kind or character. It is the absence of Truth. Let the Truth be demonstrated that the perfect child of God cannot be sick and is not sick, that it is impossible for it to be sick--let that Truth be demonstrated and all the so-called errors in the world are gone. That is the thought that heals the sick.

Let me illustrate further: Here comes a messenger boy with a telegram for someone in this audience. It says that some friend has been injured and the person is asked to go immediately. We will suppose further that the telegram is false, came here through a misapprehension. What is the effect of that telegram upon this person before me? It strikes what we call the mind first, and instantaneously goes down through the body, and the body becomes distracted because of that story.

Suppose, before the person has time to leave the room, here comes another telegram stating that the first telegram was based upon misinformation, and that it was somebody else who was hurt. What is the effect of that second telegram? It annihilates the first one. Do you not see that it annihilates the first? The first statement was a lie; it never had an existence. Why? Because the person alleged to have been hurt never was touched; it could not be the Truth. Then the last one simply annihilates the first one, because the last one was the truth. Whenever the truth comes in contact with any kind of error it destroys that error.

Elizabeth Towne says:

I used to quickly heal myself of the blues, which often possessed me as I waked in the morning--if I forgot to go to sleep with a cheerful mind. When I waked "blue" I gave myself a few vigorous denials and affirmations--"I am not blue--I am full of soul-shine!'" I would say; and then put on a smile and go quietly about my work. Next time I thought about it I found myself vibrating with the shine-statement.

Such worked for her, it may work for you. Use the method best suited to your belief and temperament.

How Others Do It

Other schools of metaphysical or religious healers treat the patient by impressing upon his mind the fact that God being perfect, good and loving could not be guilty of creating evil, pain or disease, and that such things are non- existent in the "Divine Mind," and are merely illusions, errors or false claims of the "mortal mind," or "carnal mind," of the patient; therefore, if the patient will deny their reality, and will admit as existent only such things as are held in the Divine Mind, i. e., the GOOD things, then the evil things, being merely illusions and untruths, must of necessity fade away and disappear and perfect health will result.

Others treat their patients by impressing upon their minds the idea that sickness and disease is either the world or "the devil," or of the "principle of evil," the latter being described as "the negation of truth," and similar terms; and that therefore fixing the mind and faith upon the "principle of Good," or God, must result in driving away the evil conditions. Others hold that disembodied spirits are aiding in the cure. There are thousands of variations rung on the chimes of metaphysical or religious suggestions in the cults. And they all make some cures, remember--in spite of their theories rather than because of them.

Method of Healing No. 16

If wisely used the Semi-Denial is, in some instances, a powerful method for healing but a dangerous one if wrongly used. For some people to deny sickness is the best way of quickly loosening the hold of the inharmonious claim, but this denial must be followed by a strong positive affirmation.

In my classes I teach this semi-denial method, as one method of healing but I am always careful to insist that my students and patients follow the denial with the strongest positive affirmation possible.

Jesus gives us a good example of the denial method. When he was accused of doing the works of Beelzebub and of possessing a devil he said, "I have not a devil but I honor my Father, and ye do dishonor Me." When St. Paul was accused before the king of being mad he said: "I am not mad, most noble Festus; (notice the strong affirmation following) but speak forth the words of truth and soberness."

The following affirmations for health will give the reader an idea of what we mean by denial being followed by the positive: For instance, HEADACHE--"My head is aching less and less, it is going, going, going." (Notice the positive which follows.) "I am perfect, whole and harmonious."

ASTHMA--"My subconscious mind I desire and command you to drive my asthma away so that it shall never return (note the positive which follows.) I am harmonious in body, mind and spirit."

COLD--"My subconscious mind I desire and command you to make it impossible for a cold ever to enter my system (note the positive which follows). Every organ of my body is functioning normally. I am healthful, strong, and harmonious."

HEART TROUBLE--" My subconscious mind I desire and command you to make my heart function naturally, normally and rightly, beating in natural rhythmic pulsation's, sending the blood to every atom of my being, cleansing, purifying and bringing it back into the lungs with ease, with power, and poise." (Note the positive which follows :) "My subconscious mind I desire and command you to make all of the organs in my chest to the reason we prefix "my subconscious mind" to the state-and torso function in their normal capacity and with perfect action in every particular."

Indeed, any negative statement carries a wrong suggestion. Therefore, denial is a harmful form of suggestion unless it is immediately followed by a strong, positive and constructive affirmation.

How Boyd Does It

So if you do use negative suggestion, I think Thomas Parker Boyd's method is best, namely: to follow the negative by positive suggestion, as he explains in "The Finger of God."

Be perfectly still, physically, then mentally. Next, use a process of denial. Say to yourself, "In heaven there is no pain; there is no sickness; there is no lack; there is no fear; there is no weakness." Now follow it with the positive affirmation, "In harmony or Heaven there is perfect being; in Heaven there is perfect health; in Heaven there is perfect life; in Heaven there is perfect power; in Heaven there is perfect harmony." Then let your mind rest upon the fact that Heaven is the Inner Kingdom.

Scientific understanding unlocks for us the secrets of the Kingdom, for here, especially, is the great law of action and reaction operative. Every thought we hold, be it good or bad, reacts upon us of its kind. The law is universal. The thought of health steadily held reacts upon its holder. The thought of lack and want reacts as a state of poverty.

How Leavitt Does It

C. Franklin Leavitt, commenting upon this same side of affirmations in "Are You YOU?" says:

Many ask when denials should be used. Now remember, it is never the words which influence the subconscious. It is the IDEA conveyed. Some denials are, in effect, affirmations. The so-called denial, "I am NOT sick! I am NOT all in.' I am NOT unhappy!" given with a certain defiance and spirit, certainly suggests anything but weakness--rather, it suggests determination, energy, fighting spirit. On the other hand, an affirmation (in words) of strength, can carry a suggestion of weakness. Suppose you have suffered from insomnia for a long time. It is highly probable that each time you affirm, "Tonight and ever after I shall sleep soundly and well," that through the force of association of ideas, you will THINK of not sleep, but sleeping! What is to be done?

Why, this-- simply affirm once or twice in the morning and in the evening, quietly, almost with indifference, "I shall, of course, always sleep well, from now on, because there is no good reason why I should not do so. I expect to sleep." Then forget it! A healthy person doesn't think about whether he will sleep or not. Act like a healthy person and the suggestion of health will be given to the sub-conscious, and acted upon. Besides such specialized forms of thinking as affirmations and visualization, you should reorganize your general thinking--in your consideration of any matter adopting a mental attitude of serenity, courage and optimism.

But generally speaking, a positive, a constructive statement is the best vehicle of suggestion, because it goes directly to the point. It is like an arrow aimed at a target, it shoots in the direction it is sent. A negative suggestion carries a wrong idea.

The subconscious mind must overcome the negative before it can become positive.

Most Important Method

Elizabeth Severn says:

The more important mode, however, is one of Direct Suggestion. This is really the distinguishing feature and crux of the whole system. It is indispensable as a means of reaching the subconsciousness, and through it is supplied that force of will and initial impulse which all sick people lack in regard to themselves.

Some healers use suggestions made with reference to the disappearance of disease symptoms by confidently asserting that the disease will disappear as we have shown in the illustration of cold and heart trouble above.

Negative Method of Healing No. 17

When we deny a pain, either by "persuasion," declaration, or affirmation, it takes a much longer time for the demonstration because the very denial is a contradiction. Coue has met this situation by using the method "It is going, it is going, it is going." He has his patients say this so fast and so often that they haven't time to think of anything else. This is hopeful, it inspires the subject with confidence and is not contradicted by actual feelings and common sense.

This method would be, for instance, if you are suffering from headache, to affirm, either to yourself or to your patient that it will disappear. If it is self-healing, isolate yourself as much as possible, close your eyes, and without any effort whatever, repeat the phrase in an audible tone, moving your lips, "It is going, it is going, it is going," over as long as it may be necessary. The pain will subside, and as its passing becomes evident, conclude your phrase,

"It is going, it is going, it is going," with an emphatic, "It is gone, it is gone, it is gone."

Partial Negative Method for Headache

After the patient has been seated and made comfortable in a semi-reclining position, relaxed in mind and body, the healer may or may not make passes about the head or body of the patient while he speaks in a monotone to the effect that the headache, for instance, is about to cease, that it is already ceasing, that it is gone. During this time the patient will use his own phrases in the reiteration of the declaration that the head is better, that there is complete harmony among all of the organs of the body, that the glands, pores, secretions and functioning of all bodily organs are normal, restful, quiet and natural.

How The Healer Talks

The healer talks directly to the subconscious as though it were a separate and distinct entity. The early practitioners, pursued a method which is still used by many healers employing negative or partially negative suggestions. They would for instance, treat headache in some such way as this: A strong suggestion that the headache is about to cease is made and repeated in various ways a number of times. Then a strong suggestion that it is already ceasing follows, the suggestion being repeated in various ways for some time and then finally the word given that it has ceased. The suggestion should be made in the form of spoken words, in something of a monotone, yet very decisively and positively until the desired effect is produced. When the pain has left, a strong declaration should be boldly made that the pain has entirely ceased. "If any remnants of the pain are felt, the fact should be ignored and the suggestion proceeded in, that it has ceased. This should be followed by the declaration that there will be no return of the symptoms and this should be made with an air, tone and feeling of perfect confidence."

In other words, it has been found that any positive suggestion made when the mind is in a receptive state is likely to be carried into execution more readily.

The negative or semi-positive affirmation also gets there but it is a longer, more roundabout way.

And remember, the denial method should always be followed by the positive.

H. W. Dresser is right when he says:

"Rational mind cure thrives, not by denial but by understanding; it urges both the sick and the therapeutist to make sure that all the facts are taken into account."

We present the following as an illustration of the positive method, and contrast it with the negative:

Timidity

Suppose one says: "I am not timid," and repeats over and over, "I am not timid." At the beginning the more frequently he says "I am not timid," the more he brings timidity up to the threshold of consciousness so that eventually he may feel more timid than before. On the other hand, if he were to take the affirmation "I am strong, courageous, powerful and harmonious," he will feel wholesome vibrations immediately.

Of course, if he continues to deny his timidity long enough, with persistence enough and will not give up, he is bound to change the current of his thinking.

The timidity, however, is more quickly overcome by taking the antidote for timidity which is an affirmation just the opposite to such as mentioned above, viz., "courage, strength, power, harmony."

So, if one wants to overcome the habit of poverty he will come into the fruitful field of abundance much more quickly by asserting such a thought as this "The spirit of good goes before me, making easy and prosperous all my way," than by denying poverty in words such as "I am not poor, I am not poverty stricken, I have no lack."

The positive thought of prosperity and plenty displaces the poverty thought of lack and limitation more quickly than by denying poverty and limitation, just as failure gives way more quickly to the persistent thought of success than by asserting "I am not a failure."

We believe more in the positive affirmation than in the negative or semi-negative. Nevertheless, use that which helps you the most.

Post-Positive, Post-Negative

A post-positive or a post-negative affirmation demonstration may be well illustrated in the experience of the hypnotic subject who is told that at a certain time tomorrow, or in the future, he is going to perform a certain act and does perform it at the time stated--post suggestion.

"Post" means the action takes place after the prediction and in the future. So if one holds a thought for healing diseases, poverty or unhappiness, the healing may not take place immediately but will at some time in the future.

For instance, hay fever. You may treat a person for hay fever weeks or months before the periodicity is due, or after the seizure has taken place and suggestions again may be given so that it will not return at the next cycle of recurrence.

In fact, most of our demonstrations are post, or effected in the future. This must be borne in mind or your demonstration may never be accomplished. Remember that most things take time, any kind of a demonstration must have time, and if you do not become a new creature overnight, a millionaire in a week, or happy as a lark in a fortnight, it is the way of life. It takes time to break old habits and make new ones, but if you have suggested well and rightly to yourself, as we have outlined in this volume and will allow the element of time to effect a healing, you may expect to have it. Your healing or whatever you are endeavoring to demonstrate will come. Maybe not at once, but remember that whatever method you may use to affect your demonstration, that demonstration will be accomplished if not at once then in the future--post-healing.

HETERO SUGGESTION

Different Methods

Hereto-suggestion is that which is given by one or more persons to another; it may be given verbally or mentally.

This is simply another way of saying that" two heads are better than one" or "let us put our heads together."

The world is so filled with fear, and our heritage thereof through the centuries is so heavy that our conscious mind very often unconsciously and almost automatically plants seeds of doubt in our subconscious when we try to demonstrate for ourselves. Hence, it is necessary for a second person to give the suggestions to others. This helps to produce the passivity of mind and create the subjective expectancy which is necessary before a demonstration may be completed.

When any doubt exists about the results, make a strong auto-suggestion without becoming impatient or allowing yourself to examine the progress you have made, such as "I do believe and know that I can do it. It will be done!"

There is a power, far beyond the usual reader's expectations, is such an oft repeated statement.

Some people again are like a sensitive hothouse plant or flower. It is of little avail for them to make the usual affirmations or formulae for success, health or happiness. They have relied so much upon other people and others have ministered so much to their wants that they feel unequal to the task of holding thoughts to help themselves. Such patients will secure beneficial results from having others demonstrate with or for them. This is called Hetero- Suggestion.

The great Master said, "Where two or three are gathered together in my name there am I in the midst of them." Psychologically speaking, Jesus understood and tried to impress upon his followers that man is a social being, that while we are dependent upon God, the Infinite, yet we are "members one of another" and are so constituted that we feel better when in company with others. We feel stronger when groups gather, when clansmen and tribes federate, when states are made one. Our dependence is not only upon God but we rely one upon the other. There are few hermits, few recluses and mighty few Robinson Crusoes--and then, even Robinson had his man Friday.

Man a Social Being

So we feel stronger and better when we have human support. It helps us have a greater confidence and a greater faith in God. In learning, therefore, how to take our counter suggestions for health, success or happiness, if two people sit down together, the one desiring help and the other longing to give it, the result is sure to be beneficial.

Then, if the suggestion for health, success or happiness is not strong enough, when given by one to help the other, if we add two or three or four or five or six or seven more people in hetero-suggestions, usually a more speedy demonstration takes place.

So, in taking our opposite or counter suggestion, many people find they are not able to heal themselves. They try the various methods we have already outlined here and elsewhere. They find their mental kink; they put their finger on the cause. They know the reason. They have tried to suggest to themselves by using one formula or another, one affirmation or more, and yet find they are not much better than before they attempted treatment.

At this point the patient needs the help of some one else or of many. Therefore, that person should have two, three or more persons suggest to his subconscious mind thoughts counter to those which he himself is holding.

To induce some individual or a number of people to help get these truths anchored into the subconscious mind is of utmost importance when one cannot do it himself by auto-suggestion.

If a person is not getting the results from auto-suggestion he thinks he should have let him secure the help of some other person or persons.

This of course he gets, when treatment is given by a practitioner, but results would perhaps be better if more than the practitioner were to help give the suggestion. Four minds are stronger than one mind, three minds are stronger than two. Let three or four or even more suggest to the patient giving the same affirmations and results may accrue that have not been noticed before.

Anyone may be invited or commandeered to help in hereto-suggestion, the only requirement being that whoever makes a suggestion in the presence of another will enter into co-operation and sympathetic relation with the subject to whom the suggestion is made.

When auto-suggestion does not bring about results try a healer.

When results from the healer seem to be slow, try hereto-suggestion--having several persons suggest to you.

Subjects may become electromagnetic, which is the greatest power that one can possess. Let a circle represent a great ocean of mind, holding in itself all power, wisdom, etc., and if a dot in the center of that circle represents a living person all that belongs to that ocean may be poured into that person to his fullest capacity because he lives in that ocean. Being also a center of force all the energy about him can be used. This will make him electromagnetic and very powerful in his life. It will be surprising to the operator how the subject will be able to help him- self and others if he gets these truths anchored in his mind and graphically sees these things.

In all cases of normality it is necessary for whoever makes a suggestion to another to enter into co-operative and sympathetic relations with the subject to whom the suggestion is made.

Scripture tells us in effect that if two or three are agreed upon a certain thing it shall be given unto them.

This is another way of saying that where two or more people center their minds upon a given object, the result which they desire may be expected.

As an example: If two or three are agreed together that pain shall leave a stricken body and perfect physical harmony be restored, or if two or three are agreed that success, prosperity and new channels for vocational success shall come to one, the result will be effected, much more quickly as a rule, than when a person works alone.

This is what we call hereto-suggestion. That is the reason why we recommend and indeed strongly urge that patients call upon practitioners to help them and why, immediate personal treatment not being available, we recommend absent treatment.

LARVATED – PLACEBOS – (MASKED) SUGGESTION

Bread Pills and Colored Water

Mental healing should embrace the use of every form of suggestion that leads to health of mind and body.

Any reputable physician, if he were to draw back the curtain of light to show you the truth of healings in many cases where he didn't know what to prescribe, would tell you that in such cases it is very common for physicians to administer "placebos"--(larvated suggestion) make- believe medicine, colored water, bread pills, sugar- coated pills, etc. This is very often given when physicians do not know the cause of the trouble and is administered because people are so educated that they want a physician to prescribe some kind of medicine. The administration of placebos is originally intended to quiet the patient and satisfy his expectation of medicine, but in addition to this, most any physician will tell you that people are completely healed by these make-believe medicines.

The power of the mind over the body is so universally accepted now that it does not seem necessary to even give illustrations. One or two might be given in passing. Dr. Hack Tuke, the famous English physician, in making his investigations on imagination effecting sickness and healings, tells of an army officer who was subject to severe cramps of the stomach which powerful remedies had failed to cure. The doctor finally gave him "powder containing four grains of ground biscuit." This was to be taken every seven minutes with a caution by the doctor that it should be taken exactly on time, owing to its great power. The man was cured in a short time, the "powerful drug" acting upon the imagination of the patient to make him well.

Another unique experiment Dr. Tuke relates is a case in which the house surgeon in a French Hospital experimented with one hundred persons, prescribing sugared water for them. Then with a great show of anxiety and concern announced that they had given them a powerful emetic instead of the intended remedy. No fewer than eighty -- four-fifths of the entire number--were unmistakably sick.

Do Not Always Diagnose Correctly

In the hands of the prudent physician, who is distrustful of his own diagnosis, the placebo is of the very essence of conservatism. It conceals the ignorance of the doctor--which is in itself a measure of great therapeutic value--and it supplies the patient's strenuous demand for medicine. It gives the physician time to study the case, and "nature" an opportunity to do his work for him. Best of all, it does no harm; and when accompanied by an intelligent therapeutic suggestion, it often does much good.

Masked Suggestion

"Masked suggestion"--placebo, brings about an effect because the subject is told positively that the drug or treatment which is being administered, will bring about certain results and this suggestion having been repeated in different forms until the mind of the patient confidently expects the stated results, and then the "thought takes form in action."

Commenting upon Larvated Suggestion, Chas. F. Winbrigler says :

The sick man who goes to see the doctor is examined and wisely informed that he has a serious illness, but that he can be readily cured by taking the medicine prescribed. He swallows the drastic drug and soon begins to feel much better. He believes the medicine (larvated suggestion) has done the work, whereas the examination and the assurance of the doctor were the secret of cure through the vital functions of the organic life. Bread pills or other things in the Materia Medica could have been just as efficiently used as the medicine which was prescribed and taken. We are coming to a time when this wonderful law of suggestion will be as generally used as medicines have been, and perhaps more effectively and less deterioush.

And Thomson Jay Hudson in "Mental Medicine" also states:

Indeed, I know some physicians of high standing in the profession who never administer anything in the form of medicine except the placebo, accompanied by a vigorous suggestion as to the expected results, firmly believing that the therapeutic value of all medicines is due wholly to suggestion.

It may be noted, in passing, that one of the most hopeful indications of advancement in medical science consists in the fact that the profession now very generally recognize the placebo when diagnosis fails. Manufacturing pharmacists consequently derive a large income from the sale of the ready-made placebo. That many fatal mistakes have been avoided by its employment, and many cures effected, goes without saying.

So They All Work

So, you see, from every side suggestion of various kinds are being used more and more.

There are many recognized international authorities, both in medicine and laymen with whom I agree--that ultimately suggestion will take the place of medicine entirely. The heyday for medicine is passed. The new age for nature to help itself is dawning. The kingdom of man is approaching, and the kingdom of God is not far distant. It is within each individual.

Quite Ethical

In fact, Placebos, is considered quite ethical these days as a substitute for "Mental Healing."

Hugo Muensterberg, himself a physician and one of the world's acknowledged authorities on psychology gives added emphasis to the wise use of Larvated Suggestion when he says:

This belief in the future entrance of a change frequently demands an artificial reinforcement. There belongs first the application of external factors which awaken in the background of the mind the supporting idea that something has been changed in the whole situation or that some helpful influence has made the improvement possible. Medicines of colored and flavored water, applications of electric instruments without currents, in extreme cases even the claptrap of a sham operation with a slight cut in the skin, may touch those brain cells which words alone cannot reach with sufficient energy and may thus secure the desired psychophysical effect. The patient who by merely mental inhibition has lost his voice for weeks may larynx with a mirror and has held an electrode without battery connection on the throat.

Repetition

Repetition. One of the axioms of Suggestive Therapeutics is that "Suggestions gain increased force by repetition." A constant repetition of the suggestions fastens it firmly upon the mind of the patient, therefore the healer should repeat the key-word of the suggestion again and again--

not so as to become monotonous--but in a different arrangement of words, remembering to bring the key-word, or principal suggestion into each new arrangement. Remember that planting a suggestion is like attacking a fort. It must be attacked from all sides, and so a repetition of the suggestion in different forms is important. In repeating the suggestion, let the key-word ring out strong and vibrant.

Henry Wood in Ideal Suggestions Through Mental Photography, says.

This deeper or transconscious mind can only be gradually changed in most cases, and that by means of a stream of changed conscious thinking, which must be poured in for a considerable time. It may be compared to a cistern into which a small stream of turbid water has been flowing for a long period, until the process has rendered the whole contents turbid. Now begin to turn in a stream of pure sparkling water, and gradually the character of the whole aggregation will be changed. Just so by a controlled thinking power we can now begin to rectify the reservoir of mind by turning in a stream of pure wholesome thought, until the quality of the whole is purified.

When this has been thoroughly accomplished the deeper ego will not accept or fear disease and contagion, but will go among them unscathed. Realizing the importance of a rectification, we should each lose no time in turning such a sparkling rill of positive thought into the submerged mentality, as will make it grow clearer and stronger, so that when disorder or inharmony knocks at its door, it will respond: "Depart; I never knew you!" The recognition of man's two differing minds, and a reasonable discrimination between their provinces and operations, explains a great mass of phenomena otherwise unintelligible.

Making the Brain Over

As Swami A. P. Mukerji in "Spiritual Consciousness" has also said:

At first when you start forming a new habit, there is resistance from your brain and many heroic efforts are necessary. Then gradually the task shall become easy and really pleasant. Another important fact to remember is that if at some hour today you go into your room and send forth an intense thought, next day the same thought shall start up in your mind at the same point of time.

This is known as Periodicity. Therefore, supposing you want to perform some difficult task with which your mind is not accustomed to cope, sit up a few hours previous to that time and suggest to yourself, "I wish you, subjective mind, to prepare yourself for the performance of such and such a task tomorrow at 4 o'clock. Be sure you do it. Now prepare yourself."

Next day you will find yourself quite prepared to accomplish the task. Suppose you wanted to get up at 4 o'clock in the morning. Before retiring to bed say to yourself on your subjective mind:

"Look here--I wish you to get up (or wake me up) at 4 o'clock. Be sure you do it.".

You will wake at that hour.

Always concentrate your attention upon such autosuggestions and repeat them till you feel sure your commands will be obeyed and they will be, if you insist upon their fulfillment positively and persistently with confidence. Believe in your power to succeed and everything in nature shall rush to your aid.

There is always a way to be healed by mind. One should not only keep repeating formulae, but should also continue to seek help.

The author of the book of Silent Prayer, printed by "Unity" expresses the idea, which all seeking health should commit to memory.

Pray Without Ceasing

By experimentation, modern metaphysical healers have discovered a great number of laws that rule in the realms of mind, and they all agree that no two cases for healing are exactly alike.

Therefore, one who prays for health should understand that it is not the fault of the healing principle that his patient is not instantly restored. The fault may be in his own lack of persistency or understanding; or it may be due to the patient's dogged clinging to discordant thoughts. In any case he must persist in his prayers until the walls of resistance are broken down and the healing currents are turned in.

In everything give thanks

It was long thought and steadily maintained that the stigmatists did wonders. As we have explained earlier in this volume, it will be by repeated thought, as the stigmatists steadily maintained, not by intermittent, spasmodic endeavor, that those seeking health, success and happiness, will finally have that which they desire. Results are obtained not by half-hearted visioning, but by steadily holding in the chamber of imagery "seeing," the picture and desire that one wishes to materialize.

Impatience a Handicap

Those who seek health, success and happiness through the inflexible laws of life, namely, by conforming to hygienic, spiritual and natural conditions, aided by the power of mind, often become like the novitiate studying the piano--impatient.

Many of us act almost childlike in our inability to maintain a continued state of mind for that which we desire, we are impatient for quick results.

A child too young to understand, when given music lessons and kept playing the scales or exercises, wonders, when tunes would be so much easier, so much more pleasant, what it is all about. But the music master knows what he is doing. Practice makes all technique a habit, accordingly, later on, the player will unconsciously have everything at his fingertips, and his execution will be as nearly perfect as possible.

It is similarly true of mind healing. We must have the repetition of thought, the repeated exercises, the steady concentration, the drill and relaxation, the continued holding of the thought until our mental technique becomes a habit and we accomplish what we desire.

We must hold certain thoughts in the conscious mind day after day, month after month and in some cases, year after year, until those thoughts become an essential part of our being, until they reach the subconscious mind and there become a fixed habit.

If a person desires to have abundance, prosperity and success, he must hold thoughts reflecting those conditions in his mind until they bring results. No fleeting thought of success, no passing thought of prosperity, no flitting thought of abundance, can bring the ideal state which one aspires to. The thought must be held day by day until the desire has been accomplished.

The subjective mind will be found to respond more faithfully with each succeeding success. After much training it will act with power and celerity. It will perform with fidelity the labor entrusted to it. Give it instructions with objective confidence, and it will be found a useful and faithful servant. This confidence is to be stimulated by autosuggestion and faithful endeavor.

"I Will Succeed"

Should you not succeed the first time, even though you had labored an hour, do not stop to question future attempts, but repeat and repeat the same every day or oftener if you can. In the meantime say to yourself many times a day: "I will succeed. My subjective mind has the power, and it is going to obey." In time the subjective mind will become an obedient servant. It has the power. All it wants is the training. Persistent auto-suggestion will accomplish its obedient assistance, even starting from the objective mind's disbelief. Remember the premise of its amenability to control by suggestion.

Cease, then, all adverse autosuggestions and employ all favorable suggestions. In this way a man may persuade himself even against his first premise.

It is well known from every one's personal experience that a physical act becomes more natural and more easily performed the oftener it is repeated. "Practice makes perfect" is the common adage. Do physical acts, after being often repeated, become purely automatic; an act without the direction of the mind? Is it the muscle and nerve that has been trained, or is it an intelligence, the mind?

Do It Now

Elizabeth Towne's experience in "Self Healing by Herself," presents a wonderful history of her own physical cure, after which she says:

"Then I set to work with good will to understand the law of wealth and live it. I meant to make of myself a magnet which should draw gold and silver and greenbacks, instead of steel filings. I meant to let the spirit of me (God), lead me into the ways of wealth--out of the ways of poverty into the ways of plenty and peace and pleasantness.

"I had been years making a healthy woman of myself, now I meant to charge myself with real dynamic power for attracting money. I meant to be so right with the kingdom of Good that good money would not only follow me but catch up with me.

"I went to filling myself up on I-shall-be-wealthy statements. I could see no results but I kept at it. For hours a day, whilst busy at all sorts of work, I poured in those future tense statements. I kept it up for months in spite of the fact that I could see little results if any. I could have kept my soul and body together on the money I took in, but there were other souls and bodies to be kept, and still those old ends that would not quite meet, even yet.

"Then suddenly it came to me one day that I was putting off my wealth to some future time. I must claim wealth NOW.

"Then I began to say, I AM wealth--I AM. I said it actually millions of times. And I tried to imagine it true, and to live up to it. When I had not money enough to buy a thing needed I consoled myself by calling it mine anyhow--as we used to do when we were children. When we needed something and I did have the dollar for it I imagined that dollar as one of a boundless store, and I spent it willingly, smilingly. I blessed it and bade it Godspeed. I took infinite pains to get into the wealthy attitude of mind over the spending of every five-cent piece that went through my purse. You see, I used to squeeze every nickel and hate to part with it, because I saw 100 places where it "ought" to go. Now I was taking great pains to spend as the truly wealthy spend, with that sense of plenty always in reserve.

"By little fits and starts more money came to me. My success grew by fits and starts. There would be quite a swell in the tide, then apparently a dead level; then another swell. But always there would come a little higher swell.

I was healing and teaching along like this (doing lots of "charity work'" too, as every healer, even a doctor, must), and my finances taking little rises in the right direction, when I found that somehow we were holding our own--no new debts were being added. Still the old ones stood and there was no prospect of liquidating them. But deep down in my heart I found for the first time a sort of steady faith that I was really getting ahead, and that in due time I would be able to pay all those old debts. There were not so many of them, nor so great, but there were enough to be a millstone about the neck of my spirits whenever I remembered them.

"To my mind this is the greatest self-healing I have ever done. So I have told it to you in the hope that you will understand and be inspired to the persistence necessary to the working out of your own problems of finance."

It Gets There in Time

No idea held in the conscious mind, if it be persistently maintained fails to receive attention in the subconscious. Everything we read or hear, think or feel or in any way consciously experience, is entered as a factor in the subconscious processes.

An idea may be so strongly held in conscious action, that its effects in subconscious will be indelibly fixed. Or the milder idea may be repeated often enough to produce the same ineradicable impression. Because of its one way of reasoning, it is the side of consciousness given up to habit. Having started to do a thing in a certain way, only profound impression of an opposite idea can change its action. This element combined with the fact that the memory of the subconscious is perfect, explains its marvelous tenacity in reproducing things in body, mind and disposition for which we no longer have any need. This is seen in the more than forty vestigial remains of an animal ancestry in the body, of more than thirty animal impulses as seen in the emotions and disposition, and in its reproduction of hereditary marks of all sorts in body, mind and character.

So, in this process repetition is also most valuable. Repeat over and over again, at stated intervals, day after day. Thus we give depth to the impression. Eternal vigilance is the price of liberty and demonstration.

Affirmations and suggestions are useful in arriving at a knowledge of a given truth, but when it becomes one's habit of mind to think in a certain way, it has become a matter of his permanent conscious state. He has only to turn his attention to the fact in consciousness and act at once upon it. It ceases to be a series of affirmations and becomes a state of realization.

Final Admonition

Someone has well put it in this fashion: Permit me to emphasize the training of the subjective character. Make it a strong, useful servant, one that will defend you when a crisis comes, and it will repay you in a rich fruitage every day of your life.

HEALING CHILDREN

Children are particularly open to suggestion because they have not had the experiences which develop reason to make them skeptical and cautious.

The secret power within the child is that this spirit of healing meets with little or no resistance. If medicine is kept away and no disturbing influence or fear be allowed to interfere with the natural process and the mother has the faith and the confidence she can better fill the office of health restorer than anyone else.

We can successfully treat children, youths or adults by oral suggestion if we can get their attention long enough. The difficulty with children is that they are so active we find it difficult to get their attention for any length of time. The older children may offer objections because of their being at that particular age when they "know everything." They may not agree with mental treatment, especially if they are being treated for perversion, correction of bad habits or undeveloped character. They may not only demur mentally but outright which opposition would make a strong counter suggestion.

Big Handicap in Treating Children

In healing children we are not constrained by the same limitations of doubt and questioning as with the adult.

Children are much more sensitive to the thought forces of those about them than are grown-ups.

The chief difficulty in dealing with children lies too often in the faulty attitude of the parent, for a highly organized child is easily affected by the false beliefs and nerves of his elders, so the healer must always endeavor to get the co-operation of the father and mother or other near relative. If this co-operation can be secured, healing a child is easy, otherwise it is hard, unless the child throws himself upon the "mercy" of God and you, which is rarely the case if there is a strong opposition manifested by the parents. Fortunate the practitioner who has to deal only with parents not skeptical about mental healing.

In any event, do not argue, merely present your case giving the same reasons for healing as you give your patient, then draw attention to the greater sensitiveness of the child. If the doctors have failed most parents will yield at least a negative co-operation in healing their children by mind.

Sometimes the parent by scolding, nagging, lack of self-control, worrying, etc., not only makes the child sick, but continues the vibration which prevents the child from being healed.

The only thing to do in a case like this is to tell the parent to play on his own cellar door and keep away from the child as much as possible--to dig up the weeds in his own soul's garden.

It is either the case of a parent staying on his own side of the fence, and giving the practitioner and the child a chance to help nature, or surrendering to the negative forces that be.

After you have taken the foregoing precautions it will not be difficult to get the attention and interest of the child, for the child has great faith in God. It is an inborn instinct.

Explain to the child that God has given him a perfect body, that God is always close to him, ready and willing to keep him strong and well, that

right now he hears and understands, and in spite of the clouds that seem to be drifting along his skyline of health God hears and will make him well.

Faith is an inborn attribute of childhood.

Narrate stories of Christ's healings. They always have a strong appeal to children. Then give a treatment in your own way, as your good judgment dictates, and go upon your way rejoicing.

For just as the child is more sensitive to the influences or inharmonies about home, so is he more sensitive to the influences for good and for health. Remember, "it is never God's will for any of these little ones to be sick."

Treating a Baby

In treating a baby it is easy to treat through the Mother, or some other person who has charge of the child, because the baby will be more responsive to the suggestion and helpfulness of the mother or someone particularly close to it than to others. Instruct the mother in your presence how, when you are gone, the child should be treated.

Use the same method as you would for an adult, but put it in a child's language.

The child is most susceptible to telepathic impressions from its mother.

In Applied Psychology and Scientific Living we point out the experiences of women who, nursing their babies in highly emotional and temperamental states, have poisoned them until convulsions have taken place and even death--the babe actually poisoned to death by the mother.

But the child is, by way of the breast not only physically receptive to the mother's mental condition but is influenced by telepathic suggestion from her. If the mother is in a highly emotional state, such as envy, fear, dread, worry, anger; if she receives a shock, is frightened or is the recipient of bad news (whether the child nurses or not) this chemical state is communicated and as the child's physical resistance is less than an adult's it is made even more ill than the mother.

"Most Sensitive"

Just one instance of a hysterical woman and her child will show receptiveness and susceptibility to healing which characterize childhood.

The mother constantly parades her symptoms before the child, in whom, through the paramount juvenile instinct of imitation, similar manifestations are quickly aroused. Furthermore, when such a child is delicate as is frequently the case, it often complains of petty ailments and succeeds in evoking expressions of maternal sympathy or alarm which only fan the flames. With a tendency to self-consciousness and hypersensitiveness already existing in the child, the manifestations of sympathy produce undue exaggerations and pave the way for the outbreak of nervous symptoms. Such a child, and this is of course true of other children also, should be taught to bear trifling ailments patiently.

A mother may hear a doctor, nurse or neighbor discuss the symptoms of spasms. Telepathically the child catches these vibrations. That night the mother may be startled to see her child shudder, shiver and go into convulsions purely from suggestions reaching it.

Many a child while unable to talk or, apparently, to understand its mother's tongue, hears negative talk about sickness of various kinds and takes on the symptoms which he hears discussed. These symptoms, unless uprooted will stay by the child all through life.

If you have been unable to find the cause of your sickness, probably your mother or those who attended you in infancy will be able to recall the unfavorable suggestions which were given in your hearing while very young.

In such an event the healing takes place by counter-suggestion the same as suggestion for other wrong thoughts which have caused one's sickness.

HOW TO GIVE TREATMENTS

Surroundings

All the treatments should as far as possible be given amidst surroundings that do not distract the patient's attention. All sights and sounds which may disturb the patient should be removed. Close the windows and pull down the blinds of the room so that neither sight nor hearing will be disturbed.

It is a known fact that few people can concentrate in the open where even a delicate breeze is blowing. In order to reach the inner consciousness of the patient and help the suggestion to have its best effect, the milieu should be as near ideal as possible.

All surroundings should conduce to impress upon the patient that something is about to happen. Thus, will his mind become the more receptive and the more completely will suggestion take effect.

Passivity being sought, relaxation of the body should be urged and neutral environment be provided. The patient must be comfortable and forget his body if possible.

The Healer should either sit or stand beside the patient or else behind him. Since there is no hard and fast rule, let your little monitor (the hunch) act for you in these matters.

There is a force more subtle than that of the spoken word or affirmation, especially if the Healer is able to throw himself into the subjective state of deep concentration. Whatever the healer thinks or formulates in his mind for the good of the patient will invariably be transferred to the patient telepathically. Many successful Healers never speak out loud, but quietly hold the thought which performs wonders.

The influence of the spoken work is of course very great. And merely by the vibrations of sound and carefully chosen words the healing is often effected. In nearly every campaign I conduct, I ask those, who have been healed by the tones of my voice to hold up their hands. There is always a response that represents a large percentage of the audience.

In a positive, convincing manner backed up by your own faith and belief, tell the patient that his pains will cease, his strength return, and all of his inharmonies and difficulties be smoothed away. This gives an added faith and confidence to the patient.

One may alternate his treatments by audible instructions and exhortations of comfort with silently holding the thought. There is something deeper and more far-reaching in thought than in the spoken word. Very often there is an interchange of vibrations between the healer's mind (which is in a state of poise) and that of the patient so that thoughts of disease, failure, lack, unhappiness are eliminated and new hope transferred, by some invisible psychic process, into the very heart and soul of the patient.

You cannot help the patient until he is in a passive state and will follow your specific directions. To accomplish this the patient should be taught to relax his muscles; to allow his hands to be limp, to fall at the side and then to be raised high above the head. Repeat this a few times.

The practitioner may set a good example by seating himself in a chair and telling the patient to let go in his own way. This may be helped by using such an affirmation as this: "Now, make yourself perfectly comfortable, easy, restful, quiet. Easy, comfortable, restful, quiet; easy, comfortable, restful, quiet." This suggestion will pro- mote physical as well as mental ease and relaxation, and will draw attention from the nerves.

Study your patient and converse with him according to his particular requirements, speaking only things which will produce quietness and calmness of mind. Be careful to avoid subjects that will bring about argument or arouse antagonism. The main object of the wise practitioner will be not to convert his patient to any particular belief or faith but to cure him.

Other Things to Do

The practitioner must firmly impress upon the patient the necessity of proper nutrition and proper elimination. This instruction must be given not only before healing may be expected, but must be pursued if the healing is to "stay put." An instantaneous healing by the strongest psychic force is no guaranty of a permanent cure if the primary, physical laws of life are neglected.

Theron Q. Dumont, in "Mental Therapeutics" expresses this at great length. We quote briefly:

By proper treatment it may be encouraged to resume normal and natural functioning; but the patient should be told to treat it properly in return. In treating the stomach, address yourself not only to it in itself, but also to the glands manufacturing the gastric juice--it is astonishing how these glands will respond to an earnest appeal, and will manufacture a sufficient amount of gastric juice with a sufficient amount of pepsin in it to do the work properly. Treatment of this kind just before a meal will often give the patient a keen appetite, and will result in perfect digestion of that meal. The experiment is most interesting and instructive.

After the food-mass has been treated by and in the stomach as I have just described, it is passed on and out of the stomach on the right-hand side, and enters into what is known as the Small Intestine. The Small Intestine is a long tube, entrail or gut, which is from twenty to thirty feet in length, but which is so ingeniously coiled upon itself as to occupy but a comparatively small space in the body --this intestine must not be confused with the Colon or large intestine which carries away the refuse or garbage of the system to be discharged from the body. The Small Intestine is an important part of the main organs of nutrition. Its surface is lined with a velvety substance which brushes against the food-mass which passes along it, and acts to absorb the fluid food-substance when properly digested.

When the food-mass enters the Small Intestine it is met with a strong, peculiar fluid called Bile, which becomes thoroughly mixed up with it and worked into it. The Bile is manufactured by the Liver to the extent of about two quarts a day, and is stored up for future use in what is called the Gall-Bladder. There is also poured into the food in this stage another strong fluid, called the Pancreatic Juice, which is manufactured to the extent of about one and one-half pints daily by the Pancreas, or '"sweetbread," an organ situated just behind the stomach. The work of the Bile and the Pancreatic Juice is to act upon the fatty portions of the food-mass so as to render it capable of being absorbed into the blood; the Bile also acts to prevent decomposition and putrefaction of the food as it passes through the intestine, and also to neutralize the gastric juice which has already performed its work and is no longer needed by the system.

In cases of digestive trouble, the practitioner should always treat the Small Intestine, the Pancreas, and the Liver. The first two organs are, like the stomach, quite receptive and responsive to mental treatment--in fact, they are rather more gentle than even that organ, and rather resemble the intelligent well-bred hunting-dog in their mental character. The Liver, on the contrary, as I have said before, is stubborn, rather stupid, and "heavy" in its mentality--it is like the pig or the mule, and must be treated vigorously, firmly, and positively, and emphatically told that it must get to work properly and efficiently.

The food-mass in the Small Intestine is a soft, semi- liquid substance produced by the process of digestion of the food originally taken into the mouth. It reaches the Small Intestine from the stomach in the form of a pasty substance called Chyme. This Chyme is transformed by the intestinal juices and Bile into three derivative substances, namely: (1) Peptone, derived from the digestion of albuminous substances; (2) Chyle, derived from the emulsion of the fatty substances; and (3) Glucose, derived from the transformation of the starchy substances. It should be noted, however, that the fluids taken into the stomach as drink, as well as the fluids liberated from the solids in the process of digestion in the stomach, do not reach the Small Intestine at all--instead, they are rapidly taken up by the absorbent apparatus of the stomach and carried into the blood, and thence to the kidneys and bladder, and finally voided from the system in the urine. Some of the fluids, of course, are retained in the body to perform necessary work therein.

It is always well to be supplied with plenty of mental ammunition relative to the power of the mind over the body to heal. This can be obtained by reading books, attending lectures, by meditation and prayer.

It is always best to begin treatment of the patient by pointing out to him what you aspire to accomplish; explaining to him how the mind heals; assuring him that countless others have been healed; and forecasting the probability of his own healing, etc.

Do not let yourself be drawn into an argument with the patient. Stick to the effects to be produced and do not dwell too much upon theory. There are plenty of facts and actual demonstrations for you to dwell upon. In giving treatment you do not have to repeat our exact words or our formulae unless you so desire. No doubt you have memorized a number of affirmations which you will string together like a necklace of pearls while you talk to your patient about the power of the mind to heal or to bring about success, prosperity and happiness.

Getting Down to Treatment

You have already spoken to him about the power of the mind to heal and the necessity of nutrition, elimination, fresh air, and water, so the following suggestive treatments may now be considered.

Sample Treatment No. 18

After establishing the patient in proper surroundings as recommended above, relaxed, in a reclining position or prone; exhort him in some such way as this:

"Mr. Doe, you are resting; you are quiet and peaceful. Your body is relaxed and your mind at ease. Your nervous system is calm. Your heart beats normally and all the organs of your body perform aright their natural functions.

"While I speak, you feel more restful and quiet. As you listen to my voice your muscles become more relaxed, your nerves less tense and you are more at peace in your mind.

"You are feeling more quiet, comfortable, easy, and serene. You are at rest in Infinite Love. You now feel a spirit of peace and poise creep into your being that gives you strength and courage, hope and health.

"We will now proceed to give strength and harmony to various organs of your body. First, your stomach and organs of nutrition are all restful, harmonious and strong. My suggestion will cause your stomach to digest your food easily; will cause your body to derive nourishment there- from; and the process of elimination to be performed normally. This nutrition is giving strength and power to your body, courage and power to your will. It is carrying to all the cells of your body, strength and harmony for natural functioning. You need perfect nourishment and I am now going to cause your organs of nutrition to give it to you.

"Your stomach is strong, strong, well, well, whole and complete, whole and complete. Your stomach is able and willing to perform its natural functioning with ease and strength. It can digest the food necessary for your nourishment, and begins right now to manifest strength, power, so that it will digest your food properly and naturally.

"In order to be well you must have proper nourishment, therefore we begin with the stomach and the organs of nutrition. They are strong, strong, strong. They are willing to perform their task with ease, ease, ease. As I slowly speak, you perceive a feeling of rest, quiet, calm, and poise permeate your being, and you are strong, strong, strong.

"You are going to help nature perform its natural functioning, by maintaining a cheerful mind, an optimistic outlook, and the spirit of faith. Bright, cheerful thoughts are going to help your organs of nutrition. Right now, you are at peace and rest in Infinite Love. Right now you are bright, cheerful, and happy. While I silently think these words, repeat a number of times to yourself, I am bright, cheerful, and happy. I am optimistic, courageous and faithful.

"We are now going to equalize, energize, and stimulate your circulation. There is no organ of the body that works with more cheer than the heart. It delights in healthful pulsation, in sending the blood received clean and pure from the lungs back to all parts of the body in life-giving fluid, re-energize and re-vitalize. The heart responds wonderfully well to a little thought from the patient.

"The blood will course freely and cheerfully through your body, vitalizing, energizing, yielding health and power.

"Your lungs are co-operating with the heart, inhaling fresh air, supplying oxygen and strength to the blood received from the heart. The heart sends out fresh blood and pumps the impure to the lungs which burn up the waste-matter of the cells and other organs of the body, and replace worn out poisonous tissue with fresh and good material in the blood.

More

"Now, breath deeply a few times and while doing so feel the live-giving energizing power as you inhale it from the circumambient. You are breathing in health, you are breathing out impurities. You are inhaling strength, you are exhaling waste matter. You are breathing in health and strength. The sub-conscious mind is taking up my suggestion that you are breathing in health and strength. You are feeling stronger and stronger. You are feeling better and better.

"Remember, Mr. Doe, you are going to help nature in the process of nutrition and elimination by being careful what you eat and by drinking plenty of pure water. You must increase your supply of fluids. You must drink water often during the day, and as you drink, take a thought such as this: 'I quaff this water to cleanse my system from impurities and to bring about new, normal, and healthy conditions.' Every living thing depends upon water, needs water, must have water. Indeed, much of our illness is due to the fact that we have formed the habit of drinking too little water. So help nature and God by partaking of more of the necessary fluids.

"This increased fluid supply will cause your bowels to move regularly every day, thus carrying off the waste matter of the system. Your bowels will begin tomorrow morning to move naturally and normally and will soon form a regular habit. You must hold this thought yourself several times during the rest of the day, and as you drop off to sleep at night, you must repeat to yourself, 'My bowels are functioning normally, easily, and will function naturally in the morning.'

"Now, Mr. Doe, rest a few moments. Be quiet and reposed as possible. (Here the practitioner pauses and holds a silent thought). Mr. Doe, you are feeling stronger than you did. Your nerves have relaxed and the tension of your body has 'let go.' Your mind is at peace, and you feel much stronger and better than you did when you came. You are going to continue to feel this way. You will be better tomorrow than you are now. You will feel stronger and better day by day. You feel stronger now. You feel better now. You ARE stronger and better now. You are at rest in Infinite Love. The Spirit of Good goes before you, making easy and prosperous all your ways. You may rise and go your way in peace, filled with the Infinite Spirit of health, success and happiness."

The foregoing is a general treatment which may be modified or lengthened by the Healer. The same kind of treatment may be given for success, and prosperity. In the place, however, of speaking directly to the organs of the body, speak directly to the man's mind and soul assuring him that he is prosperous and successful; that he is feeling stronger and more courageous; that he believes in himself now as he never did before; that his old time strength is coming back; that the ambition of yesterday is again aroused. The desire to achieve, stimulates him into action. He feels certain that nothing but courage, and faith, and power, and achievement, will be entertained in his consciousness; that things he dreams about will be realized; that the desires of his heart will become actualities; that his castles in Spain will be built of material things; that he will come into his own.

The reader may add to the treatment for success and prosperity suggested above, according to the dictates of sound judgment, but the way to give this treatment, the position, the surroundings, the conditions, the tone of the voice, etc., are identical whether in giving the treatments for prosperity, for success, for happiness, or for physical healing.

All of the other organs of the body can be treated in the self same way--headaches, reproductive complaints, nervous troubles, in fact any physical or nervous trouble. Self treatment, likewise, can be carried out in the same way.

HOW TO TREAT AND GIVE TREATMENTS – CONTINUED

How Healers Work

There is one thing that an operator must always observe; that is, he must give his suggestion in a plain, precise, and direct way to the patient. If this is not done, there will be hesitancy on the part of the subject, and the results will be unsatisfactory. Suggestion ought to be direct in order to be quickly and effectively realized.

To be able to do this the practitioner should cultivate a good "Suggestive Voice."

"The use of the voice may be in words spoken, either loudly, moderately loud, softly or in a whisper." But whatever may be the pitch of the voice, it should be vibrant with sympathy, love, helpfulness, courage, faith and power.

Learn From the Actor

A good way to cultivate this manner is exactly as an actor practices his lines before a mirror.

It is said that Nat Goodwin would take a line or a scene whose rendering hitherto did not satisfy his artistic sense and go over and over and over the words until he had the inflection, tone and gesture that wholly suited him. Surely, the profession of a mental healer is fraught with as much importance and demands as much earnestness and practice as that of the actor.

Imagine yourself, therefore, treating a patient by suggestion. Imagine him in a chair in front of you or reclining leisurely on a couch by your side. Give to the imaginary patient the affirmation or the thought which you would give to an actual seeker for health. Carefully pick out the words that seem to you to be the strongest and repeat these words, or whole sentences containing the words, in a tone of conviction, with a spirit of helpfulness and the expression of power. Perchance you will have to repeat a certain word over and over until you can get that downward inflection of sublime faith which strikes home into the very soul and being of the patient.

Take the words strong, powerful, harmonious, and whole, and repeat these words over and over again in some affirmation which you compose to give the imaginary patient. Give your affirmation until you feel vibrations of strength, power harmony and conviction.

Practice your affirmations before the imaginary patient often, until you feel the vibrant, highly suggestive tone of a man who believes in the profession he follows. Then, watch the eye. See that it does not shift. Look directly at your imaginary patient with intensity of purpose until you have cultivated a firm earnest gaze of the eye. Now assume a compelling glance. A person always gazes earnestly and strongly at the thing which holds his attention. You never saw a person in love but whose eye flashes diamonds of affection. The eye of the Healer must flash the diamonds of faith, courage, helpfulness, love and health and flash them until the very walls of the room will react with ocular vibrations.

This in no wise has necessarily anything to do with hypnotism. It is calculated to develop the expression of the eye until it can be projected into the very recesses of the patient's soul and be felt.

Of course, such exercises must be backed up by confident, faithful, honest belief by the patient that he can be healed.

Speech and Voice

The sympathetic vibration of the voice and skillful words and suggestive movements may be all that is needed, but without some power of awakening this feeling of personal relation, almost of intimacy, the wisest psychotherapeutic treatment may remain ineffective, especially in cases where the patient's psychical sufferings are misunderstood or ridiculed as mere fancies or misjudged as merely imaginary evils.

From sympathy it is only one step to encouragement, which indeed is effective only where sympathy or at least belief in sympathy exists. He who builds up a new confidence in a happy future most easily brings to the patient also that self-control and energy which is the greatest of helping agencies.

We do not mean that the practitioner should cultivate a stilted, affected, elocutionary manner of expression. But we do mean that he should have earnestness, feeling, and strength in his tones. He should endeavor to have his thought and desire so permeate his voice, that the vibrations may be felt by the patient.

He should be so filled with the desire to heal with a knowledge of his profession, and with enthusiasm for health, that the very tones of his voice will vibrate health, strength, courage, power, love.

Firmness

It may seem almost paradoxical that a healer must be both extremely sympathetic and firm at the same time, yet this is of the utmost importance. The healer must have all of the patient kindness in the world and yet must have enough firmness to insist that his patients follow the regimen of a well-rounded way of living, to include exercise, breathing, eating, sleeping formulae, etc. When giving personal treatments he must know how to be firm and see that the patient carries out to the best of his ability, the instructions which the teacher is giving.

Never speak to a patient in a doubtful or hesitating manner about his case. In the first place, you should not take a case unless you believe you can help and heal. This settled in your mind, and you are confident that the patient can be cured, speak up with the courage of your convictions and the vibrations of your faith and assert bravely in a positive manner, "I can cure you, sir."

Do not talk to patients as many doctors do, in such a tone as this," Well, you are in a pretty bad condition. Don't know whether I can cure you or not, but I will try. We can tell better what can be done as we go along," or "There is no hope for you," or "Your days are numbered," or "Better put your affairs in shipshape condition, because you have not long to live." You may just as well tell a patient to go home and stay there. Such talk has killed thousands.

When people are sick they want a physician that can heal, not one who doubts his methods or himself, or who has a timid manner. No matter what the school or what the method used, the successful healer will squarely face his patient and say, "I can help you, sir."

Up To the Patient

With certain individuals and temperaments the practitioner may get better results by throwing the patient upon his own resources and telling him that today he should take his affirmations at stated times every half hour or every hour and that if he will do this perseveringly for one day or two days and then come back you will give him help.

You will have to know your patient in this kind of treatment for most people feel they must have the assistance of someone else. They lack confidence regarding the value of their own efforts and this acts as an adverse auto-suggestion. On the other hand, a person who is independent and resourceful will feel the responsibility that you put upon him by telling him to work by himself for a few days.

Often it is wise to give the suggestion, not from without but to prescribe it in the form of auto-suggestions For instance, advise the patient not only to have the good will and intention of suppressing a certain fixed idea or by producing a certain inhibited impulse but to speak to himself in an audible voice, every morning and every evening, saying that he will overcome it now. Here, too, the autosuggestion may become effective by the frequency of the repetition or by the urgency of the expression or by the accompanying motor reactions.

As a rule no matter how many ailments the patient has, all of his needs should be treated at each sitting.

HOT TO GIVE TREATMENTS - Continued

The Chronic Invalid

The chronic invalid is not only treated for immediate relief from pain or mental disturbance but for complete restoration to health and such a patient may require as you would naturally expect, systematic and educational treating to break the old sick habits so that the health habits may be firmly established and grounded. One of the most successful healers I know, says: As a rule, I do not treat patients for any special thing, but rather treat them for perfect health and harmony, because it is difficult, many times, to diagnose a person's disease and locate exactly the physical organ that is out of harmony with the rest of the body. Less than ten per cent of the practicing physicians are always right in their diagnosis of a patient's trouble and that is one reason why so many of them fail to "make good" in their profession.

Another Method of Healing No. 19

Another mode of healing used by some practitioners is first to have the patient tell the healer what are the symptoms or what seems to be the matter. Then to have the patient sit in a reclining position in a Morris chair or rocker tilted back, relax, close the eyes, remain quiet and let the mind drift indifferently.

You will notice this differs from some other methods. While some require the patient to think with the operator and others want the patient to be relaxed and think of nothing, there are those who suggest to the patient that he let the mind go as it pleases and then again to become absolutely indifferent to what the mind does.

Then in a few minutes, say three or five minutes, the operator gives audibly in a low tone of voice suggestions pertaining to the cure of the particular disease or symptom saying that the symptoms are disappearing and they will disappear, that they are becoming less and less noticeable or gradually leaving, leaving, leaving.

My own opinion is that, before the patient is dismissed, such an affirmation should be followed by strong positive suggestions for a decided improvement. I believe the very best way is to make suggestions that the body is well, whole and complete, harmonious, strong and normal in all functionings.

Then again it is well after the suggestions for healing have been given, to sit silently by the patient, thus telepathically continuing the treatment free from audible vibrations. Some healers have great power this way and many sensitive people receive healing treatment with more force given in this manner.

If this kind of a treatment is given, the audible suggestions should probably be repeated three or four times during the half hour's treatment, each one followed by a silent treatment. If not each one, then at least the last.

The same method with suitable affirmation may be used to demonstrate success, prosperity or anything one desires.

Personal Magnetism

It has long been recognized that there is an out-going, subtle force from each individual, and this out-going force will be, of course, strong in any one who has developed the power of healing.

Jesus and his disciples recognized this. Christ said, "I perceive that virtue is gone out of me."

At another time he said, "Come ye yourselves, depart into a desert place and rest awhile." This indicates that in the impact of one individuality upon another through the agency of physical touch, some force or power leaves the healer, which has a tendency to deplete his vitality.

Healer Taking On Conditions of the Patient

We all know the dragging effect of certain personalities and if the fluidic radiations of the body could always be seen it would not be so difficult to understand why this occurs. There are, unfortunately, human vampires, unconscious though they be, and very little is to be gained in permitting an absorption of one's energies by such sponges. It is all very well to claim an inexhaustible supply of strength, but we have not yet arrived at the point where this can be wholly demonstrated, and it is therefore necessary, especially in giving magnetic treatment, to observe some precautions and use it with care.

Or as Thomson Jay Hudson says:

Some healers fancy that "they take on the conditions of the patient," as they phrase it. That is, they feel the symptoms which afflict the patient. There is no question but that those who enter upon the treatment of a case with that idea firmly fixed in mind will experience the anticipated sensations, often to a marked degree. But late scientific experiments disclose the fact that such phenomena are always the effect of suggestion. The physical exhaustion which some healers feel after the treatment of a case is also largely due to suggestion. These effects may always be counteracted by a vigorous autosuggestion; and, moreover, the same means may be effectively employed to produce exactly the opposite effects upon the operator. That is to say, the mental healer, by whatever method he does his work, may always cause his treatment of a patient to redound to his own benefit, as well as to that of the patient, by the exercise of the power of autosuggestion.

You may be so happy in your healing as to want to go out and tell others about the joy you have and so do your bit in healing others. You may follow any one of the methods which we have outlined in this series. You may be of great service to some other sufferer, perhaps heal him, and then feel a strange sensation yourself. In fact, you may take, for the time being, the very conditions and pains of the person you have helped. Sensitive and sympathetic practitioners sometimes temporarily suffer thus, but remember there is no danger that you will take on the condition of another, UNLESS YOU THINK SO.

You may have the identical pain, you may act as a human magnet and draw from the patient the precise pain into the same organ, in which the patients' distress is located, but remember this is only temporary, unless you become frightened and allow your fears to take possession of the sub- conscious. Then you may get sick, but let me repeat, there is no danger if, when you take on the condition of the patient, you instantly take a health affirmation.

Healer, a Human Magnet

The healer very often feels the identical pain in the same region or organ of his own body as that of the one whom he is treating. The more sensitive and the more intuitive the healer the more is he prone to take on the conditions of the patient he is treating. He acts as a human magnet, he actually extracts and draws from the patient the pains his subject is experiencing.

Not only is the healer a magnet drawing the actual pains from the patient, but the patient who is throwing off the thing he does not want is, in turn, drawing strength, energy, vital force and power from the healer.

Nevertheless, a positive affirmation, a positive healer and positive formulae prevent much of this taking-on-the-condition-of-the-patient.

Therefore, if the healer is positive in all of his statements, formulae, thinking and practice, he will save himself many an unpleasant experience.

Suppose the practitioner does feel the same pains as the patient, there is nothing to fear if the healer dismisses the thought at once. If the healer allows his subconscious mind to cling to the thought pains which he has extracted from the patient, he may, indeed bring those conditions into his life, but by taking instantly such a thought as this, "I cleanse myself from all negative thoughts. I am and I know I am and nothing is greater than I am" he is using a positive antidote so that the sick conditions of the patient will not remain in his consciousness.

This affirmation, "I cleanse myself from all negative thoughts. I am and I know I am and nothing is greater than I am" should also be accompanied by a physical suggestion such as placing the right hand on the left breast and making a gesture with the extended arm as though throwing away from the body something that may cling to it. This gesture may be taken two or three times as the affirmation is repeated. Then place the left hand upon the right breast and with the same full arm gesture as though throwing or expelling something from the body, take again the same affirmation with the same gesture. This having been done, there is no danger of the healer's taking on the permanent pains of the patient.

This personal fluid, or human electricity, or vital force, whatever we may call it, is put to excellent use by some successful healers, as "Magnetic Treatment."

Method of Healing No. 21

If one has a vivid imagination, or is a good visualizer, he may use the method which has equipped some healers with additional force. This is effected by adding to their verbal or silent treatment, a mental picture or image of the thought currents actually leaving their minds, traveling toward the patient, and then enveloping and surrounding him.

In giving a mental treatment, remember that no two patients are of equal receptivity. One patient will be able to take a simple statement from you that his pain will cease from this hour, and it actually will. Another will be required to sit down, or lie down in a reclining position, have his forehead stroked, work out his vasomotor nerves and explain that you are doing this to help his nervous vibrations and treat his heart and liver and stomach, and this will quiet him and he will take the suggestion. In other words, you have to rub the suggestion in.

A most helpful method of healing, both for healer and patient, is for the healer, just before he goes to sleep, to take up his patients, one by one, or collectively, get a mental image of each or all, and send them such messages of health, comfort and good cheer as they need.

Many healers will find, unless they have set their mind not to drop to sleep before finishing the list, that they will go to sleep while sending messages to others. But the Subconscious Mind, which is all wise and has perfect memory, will, as you drop to sleep, continue sending the messages. Such a habit will react in inestimable good to the percipient--sender--as well as to the recipients.

Keep It Up

KEEP-AT-IT-IVENESS, persistence in suggestion and auto-suggestion, is the one big thing to bear in mind. Many will succeed where others fail, because some will keep at it while others give up. Stick to your healing treatments!

In the second place mental conditions differ. Some will find that their subconscious minds respond more readily than others, who will have to exercise more patience and be more persistent in their efforts.

Third, some types are more highly sensitive than others. Mental telepathy, or spiritual communication, can be exercised by some people without any previous training. Some get the impressions more readily than others, all however, can reach a high degree of efficiency in helping others, curing themselves, etc., if they will yield obedience to the laws of physical and mental hygiene and keep forever at it.

There is still a fourth thing to bear in mind, and that is, not to be discouraged or disheartened if you fail to get immediate results from your treatments. As intimated, above, results are not infrequently long delayed but if you are faithful and persistent they come at last. A great philosopher has said: "God does not always refuse when he delays. He loves persistence and grants everything."

Remember the parable of the woman who repeated her request until finally it was granted because of her importunity. She got what she wanted by hanging on. The successful healer must do likewise and the wise patient ditto.

If You Relapse

If you have relapses and set-backs in your progress toward health, do not let them discourage you or dishearten you. There is a rhythmic swing in growth everywhere. This has been discovered by Professor Bose of the University of Calcutta in studying the laws of growth in plants. He invented an instrument by which he could measure this growth which was wholly imperceptible to the eye. He discovered that plants grow upward for five seconds, shrink downward for five seconds, remain stationary for ten seconds, then start upward again and repeat the same round. But notice this great law: in shrinking downward the motion is slower than in pushing upward. The five seconds of slipping backward or downward do not take the plant back as far as its starting point, so that on the whole it gains in growth and stature. Then note, that the five seconds of shrinkage and the ten seconds of remaining stationary, are as three to one to the upward push. Practically this amounts to three steps backward as compared with one step forward. But in terms of growth the forward step outranks the three backward steps. So, in seeking health, if your progress seems to be one of going forward, slipping backward, remaining stationary and then starting all over again; going forward, and slipping backward and again remaining stationary, do not complain. You are getting ahead, you are gaining ground.

All Growth Forward and Backward

It is therefore very important for everyone who is trying to apply these principles to understand that all progress and all growth is forward a little, backward a little, then marking time; forward a little, backward a little, marking time. All progress is vibratory and uneven.

The heights are reached only through a long series of "ups and downs."

To the careless observer, and to one who has not been trained to note that he is going forward a little, slipping back a little, and staying where he is a little, it may appear that he is retrograding in conscious, physical growth instead of gaining ground. He may think he is back at the starting point. Back in so far as outward signs indicate, but in reality he has gained.

I know of nothing the practitioner should so seriously impress upon the patient and the patient should bear in mind so sedulously as this: that the law of growth is up a little, down a little, forward a little, back a little, then stationary.

And this will be true in development of higher consciousness as it is in the physical growth. You will feel Oh, so much better today in mind and spirits and then, ah, me, how bad you feel tomorrow. Up in the mountain tops of ecstasy today, down in the valley of the dumps tomorrow. But, decide not to stay dumped, and, if you continue to hold your thought or your affirmation, you won't.

By continuing to hold your thought or affirmation, you are remaking yourself as surely as the plant grows to maturity, even though in the process, it slips down in its upward climb. The better side of man is bound to triumph. The lower and false self will fight like "all get out," with the desperation of demons, but will finally yield if the better self insists upon claiming health, success and happiness.

Remember then, our mental and spiritual growth also is up a little, down a little, ahead a little, back a little, stationary, but meantime, very surely climbing upward. The better part of man prevails in the end. The better part of you is bound to triumph.

In a tug of war, there often comes a time when both sides are about "licked." It is sometimes only a matter of a little twitch of muscle that swings the winning side into victory. That is the way with a man's mental, spiritual and physical development. There is that conflict within the individual the conflict of the lower self with the better self. The tug of war Of the two personalities within the individual is on. Especially is this felt and seen when the better self-determines to assert for health, for spiritual or mental development; when we are determined that we shall climb to the mountain tops of ecstasy and remain there. At this time, one feels the tug of war more than ever before. The fight is on. The lower and false element in man makes its last struggle to maintain the upper hand. It does not give way without a desperate struggle and this is felt very appreciably by the person who is going upward.

So, when you feel that you are slipping back a little you are being given the best evidence in the world that you are making progress. The Dunce does not know that he is a Dunce--sometimes. The cabbage-head does not know that it is a cabbage-head. But when the better part of man begins to pull he soon catches the vibration that he is not what he ought to be; that he is not where he should be; that he is not making the progress that he ought to make. May I repeat with all of the emphasis at my command that when you feel you are not getting ahead the way you ought, the great struggle is on. The tug of war has reached its climax. You are at the critical point of your experience. You are making progress because you feel that you are not. That's the best evidence ever. Hang onto your thought a little longer, and the better side will surely win. The count is on your side. Victory is yours.

When you feel that you're not going forward, that is the time you are actually making the greatest progress.

The purifying fire seems to burn us, but in reality it destroys only "the wood, hay, and stubble" which claim our selfhood. With all its threatenings it only cleanses, polishes, and brings out in high relief, the beauty of the divine humanity. All so-called evils and disorders are existent as conditions, but have no reality as entities. Conditions and educational experiences serve their purpose and come to an end, but all true verities are eternal, because they are divine.

Whether it be a new experience for the subject or not, the organism within resents, at times, innovations or changes of habit. Consequently the patient, although he has been healed of other troubles may experience a reaction from the first few treatments, or he may get a reaction at the very start. But do not be discouraged, these symptoms are indicative of good. In fact, you may now be better and then a little worse, again better and then a little worse, for a considerable time, but will gradually improve until at last, if you are faithful, you will arrive. Be strong and of good courage, for the crown is to the victor. Let your motto be "I can and I will."

The rise and fall of the effects of the treatments is with some types natural. It can be explained by the state of mind of some people who are sick. It indicates merely a rebound from low mental and physical states. Protracted sickness, for instance, is inclined to make some people depressed. Even when they get better gloominess may creep over them and the physical condition being weak, one reaction may play upon the other. The patient should remember, however, that each little slump is going to be followed by a higher rebound for health than before. In fact each ascent after each slump will actually be a little higher and better than the one previous. If the patient understands this, there is no occasion for discouragement. Knowing this to be the natural tendency, he can fortify himself against despair and raise his courage to the mount of transfiguration of health, success, prosperity and achievement.

After Healing

Sometimes former patients will ask leave to come occasionally to sit in the chair or be in the room where they have received treatment. There seems to be holy associations in the room near the healer or around the healers, association which gives added confidence to the one-time patient, for offering expressions of thanksgiving and gratitude and to go forward with a positive assurance that everything is well for them in the future. That tomorrow holds nothing but success, health and happiness for them.

AFTER THE HEALING – WHAT?

All Is Mind

I believe that all advanced thinkers, practitioners and teachers in this great movement of mental science are beginning to realize that there are certain fundamental laws, physical as well as mental, which must be observed and followed.

True, "All is Mind" but mind has a better chance to operate if it is given ideal conditions. The ideal condition, therefore, for mind to demonstrate to the best of its wonderful power is for man to try to keep his body physically fit. If the mind has to spend too much time, energy and strength in repairing the waste tissues of the body and restoring run down cells, or depleted vitality, it must of necessity, since the mind is working through the physical, have a certain amount of limitation. If it has to spend time overcoming foolish inharmonious weaknesses and sicknesses caused by irregular living, wrong eating, overwork, negative and inharmonious thinking, lack of proper exercise, sunshine and fresh air; too great a burden is laid upon it.

We, therefore, believe that after the healing, one of the most important things is to see that a right regimen of dietetics, exercise, breathing, recreation, accompanies right thinking.

All Is Mind – But...

While "All is Mind" this mind is now encased or tabernacled in the physical body. The physical has limitations. The physical may overtax the mind so that the mind in turn will not be able to produce the maximum amount of efficiency for success, prosperity, abundance, love, joy, peace and happiness as it would, if the mind had a perfect human channel through which to operate. It is absurd for anyone to think that while this spirit is in the physical that our bodies can live with- out nourishment. "All is Mind" but while we are in the body, we must eat to live. God gives us life, but we have to conform with his laws to have life at all. Mind is the basis of this life; in fact, mind is the God life, but our minds will not remain long in our bodies if we do not help the God laws to help the mind to keep us alive. For example, God gives us life, but we have to breathe to maintain that life. A man who plugs up his nostrils and shuts his mouth and tries to "think" that he can live forever without breathing is next door to a lunatic--or a half-brother to a jackass. So there are other fundamental laws—physical laws which man must conform with to have the maximum amount of success, health and happiness. You would not expect a man to live forever if he does not sleep. Nature requires a certain amount of sleep while we are in the physical, if our minds, our spirits are to remain in our bodies. Therefore, after healing, we must be sure that we have rest, that we have our necessary sleep, that we have recreation, as well as right eating, exercising and fresh air.

Help Nature to Adjust Itself

A man cannot continue to break the physical laws and still expect his mind to keep him whole and harmonious and well. The late Professor James no doubt was right in saying that most of us only do about 10 percent of the work we can do. No doubt there is a great deal in the assertion that some people sleep more than they ought to sleep, but I believe if a person is living a normal life, that nature adjusts the hours of sleep to suit the individual. Some people may get along with less sleep than others. If you are eating properly, having plenty of fresh air, exercising and thinking rightly, nature will see that you desire only the necessary hours of repose and sleep for the daily rebuilding and rehabilitating of the body.

Be sure, therefore, that you play fair with nature by adhering to the rules of the health game in right eating, thinking, exercising and breathing.

To Help Certain Laws

But there are certain health laws which if rigidly kept will help the mind to help the individual to help God to help him to keep well. To say that because mind is all we can eat anything is almost as absurd as the conduct of a faith healer I know who limps in his walk, who has fits of indigestion and who has to remain away from his office and his practice for weeks at a time because of his irregular living or something inside him put out of whack and yet his great slogan is "Mind is All, man can do anything he wants to do if he has the right mind."

These mental healers have but one angle of truth. Many of them are so warped and prejudiced that they are not able to apprehend any aspect at all of God given truth. Otherwise they would not say "you can eat anything you want to eat, it doesn't matter what--." Absurd, absolutely absurd. More sickness in America is due to overeating, fear, selfishness and worry than to any other one cause. Much of our sickness, however, can be corrected by dieting, sunshine, fresh air, drinking plenty of water, and exercising.

The next step, therefore, in the development of mental science is to get away from our lopsided, warped idea that everything is mind and that we can abuse all of the physical laws of nature. We must return to the common sense basis that, although all is mind, we must be in complete harmony with all physical and mental laws. Only thus can the efficacy of mind and its superiority over matter be demonstrated.

If I get a splinter in my flesh, nature in time creates a fester, pushes up the skin and makes a slight enlargement through which the festering enlargement bursts the skin. Then the impurity around the splinter is released and the splinter expelled. Nature in time gets rid of the splinter.

But isn't it an easy thing to do, won't it save time and trouble and help nature, if I myself take the splinter out?

Nature is the most wonderful workshop. A needle may be broken off in the palm of a person's hand and in time will force its way up through the surface of the skin an inch or more from where it entered. But who wants a needle forcing its painful way through the tissues of the hand, if by one little twitch the broken steel may be removed ?

We therefore believe that all practitioners of every stripe and color, of every school and cult, will in time subscribe to complete and scientific conformity with the material laws of nature.

Recognition of the power of the mind to heal combined with respect for all natural laws is a program we recommend as a perfect whole to every healer.

The Master Knew This

Even Jesus could not have made his healing invariably permanent if the patient himself were not solicitous for his own recovery. In fact, all that Jesus did, or any other healer ever does, is to help the patient to help himself to get in harmony with the laws of nature. After the patient is helped into harmony with the laws of God, it is then the obligation of the patient himself to keep in harmony with these God-given laws. If the laws of nature are disregarded or treated with contempt, it is not reasonable to expect that mind will be efficient in its healing processes. There's a parable of a maniac who suffered a relapse because he didn't fill his mind and heart with right thoughts and his hands with useful service and the second condition of that house was worse than the first. It is one thing to be healed. It is another thing to remain healed.

"Mental inefficiency may result from functional derangement occasioned by the continued effort of the brain to do its work under diseased conditions. Nerve impulses may be obstructed or diverted by the physical condition of the nerves through which they pass. Since the brain is, first of all, a physical mechanism, and as such cannot be exempt from physical limitations, mental efficiency rests primarily upon a vigorous nervous system healthily environs. We should know the part that reflex neuroses play in mental hygiene, and in their preparatory training they should learn to recognize the indications of these affections in order that the nervous irritation may be relieved before it becomes a serious menace to brain growth and mental development.--Chas. E. Swift, "Mind in the Making."

The proper use of air, water, food, and exercise will produce physical perfection if the mind activity is ever constructive and creative.--Terry Walter, M. D.

No system of healing, no healer, regardless of the doctrine held or the method pursued, can guarantee health without the intelligent cooperation of the patient.

Tit for Tat

It is important fully to understand that when the brain is restored to health by good nerve tissue and healthy blood, it can be made by suggestion to exercise as healthy influence over the body as it previously exercised a harmful one. If ideal centers can produce ideal diseases, surely the rational cure is first to bring these ideal centres into a healthy condition, and then make them the means of curing the ideal disease. Mental disease requires, and can ultimately only be cured by, mental medicine. When will this be understood? And when will nauseous drugs cease to be ministered to a mind diseased ?

Of the usual remedies given, Dr. Russell Reynolds says: "The whole list of anti-hysteric remedies--musk, castor, valerian, and the like appear to have this one property in common: that they do no good, and delay the real treatment of the case, which is not one to be cured by nauseous 'gums,' but largely by mental, moral and social management."

Verily, H. W. Dresser, is right:

In the long run it is right living that secures health, and every man who has failed to adapt his conduct to nature's requirements must learn the art of health with regard to the matters in question. He who would truly possess permanent health in contrast with the supposable health of the anxious and the nervous people who consult a physician every time they feel a slight pain--should be able to take the matter into his own hands so that he will be able to avoid the life that breeds disease.

No one who has followed the writer thus far, who has noted the emphasis he puts upon the power of mind to heal the sick, to inspire the discouraged, to uplift the downcast and to strengthen the weak, can possibly misunderstand him when he says that to do something is much more important than merely to assert something. If we are using our forces in the wrong way we must, whatever our affirmation, begin to employ them in the right way.

Aye, affirmations cover a multitude of sins for those who want an excuse for irregular living.

A suggestion--affirmation--will not plant corn, harvest wheat or bake bread. Affirmations must be used with as much intelligence and good common sense as are called for in any human situation. We cannot by taking an affirmation live without eating or sleeping. All the affirmations in this world or kingdom come won't supply oxygen for the body unless we do our part in breathing.

There is no formula that will enable a man by substituting affirmation for accomplishment to make headway in life. Of course, everyone must believe in himself to succeed but he must back up that belief by effort and work.

There is no "prosperity treatment" that can change a man's condition from non-prosperity to prosperity other than that which inspires him to go out and bring prosperity home by preparation, work, effort, love and expenditure of time.

Complete cures can better be made if a regulation of life habits, a correction of wrong mental attitudes, and an establishment of a different way of thinking and living are demanded of the patient. Reeducation and persuasion play heavy roles in the transforming process.

If our sickness has been caused by irregular living, environmental conditions, inharmonious vibrations or wrong thinking, it then is most essential if we are to have our healing and maintain health that we change these elements.

How to Help Yourself

Mind can accomplish most anything, but the mind that is hampered by over-eating, poor air, cramped conditions, etc., is a mind that has to spend much of its energy in overcoming those conditions, when it should be devoting itself to keeping health, success and happiness.

Therefore, besides keeping your minds clean and open it is most essential that you give attention to your bathing, to your eating, to your exercising and to your breathing.

A mind that is unhampered in a healthy body, of course, will not have as much work to do as the mind which has to overcome physical limitations. By keeping your body fit, therefore, you help your mind, to bring and keep success, health and happiness.

It is a sad reflection upon human nature that the comfort, ease of mind and pleasure obtained under treatment by the suggestion method often tend to make the patient indifferent to health observation.

After the healing has been effected, the patient should under no circumstances allow himself to become indifferent to health rules and regulations. He should be more desirous, more eager, than ever to yield whole-hearted compliance with the laws governing health of mind and body.

Effect of Body on the Mind

We have put great emphasis upon the power exercised by the mind over the body. Now, we should like to direct the attention of the careful student and the sincere aspirant after truth to the fact of the vast influence exerted by the body over the mind. In the mental science movement this has been one of the neglected truths. The observant and unprejudiced will unquestionably agree that there is an influence exerted by disease or by a disordered physical body upon the mental state and the moral tendencies.

The careful student is compelled to recognize that in many instances it is the physical disorder which is to blame for the depressed mental state. Destructive states of either mind or body react, the one upon the other, each tending to make the other worse, until such a time as the body regains its equilibrium of health, or the mind recovers its lost mastery of feelings and emotions.

Dr. Wm. S. Sadler has well said,

All thoughts which are evolved in the brain and which finally find expression in various ways, are actually constructed out of literal, physical impressions, transmitted over the nervous system from the organs of special sense to the brain.

It is true, physical disturbances of the circulation or of the digestion are often contributory to hypochondria; in fact, most hypochondriacs are sick both in mind and body, but the mental state is usually the determining factor. Most hypochondriacs would speedily recover if they would but become confirmed optimists. Faith is the important remedy and the essential element is the cure of hypochondria. In this unfortunate and imaginary disease--none the less real and painful in its effects because it is imaginary--the entire brain seems disordered.

No one will seriously question the fact that pain invariably exerts a deleterious influence upon the mind. Intellectual activity and mental usefulness are restricted or well-nigh destroyed by severe or long continued pain in any part of the body, resulting from any cause whatsoever.

Many people are sick because they violate the laws of their physical nature.

Health Is Natural

Health is both a natural and a contagious thing--more so than sickness, else we should have been swept into oblivion long ere this. With obedience to the laws of breathing, exercise, diet, sleep and right thinking presupposed, we need never get sick.

We Must Do Our Part

After our healing, how can we go on breaking the laws of nature and expect that nature will continue to keep us well? There are certain things which Mother Nature demands and if these requirements are not met, our good old mother has to spank us again. Overwork is one of the prevalent causes of nervous disorders as well as of many physical disturbances.

When you believe that you can do more work than you have been doing, there is no doubt but that you will. It is the preying of the mind upon work to be performed that is vastly worse than the work itself. Therefore, if it is necessary for you to play the work horse, go about your tasks cheerfully; do not allow your work to drive you, but you drive the work. In any event observe moderation. There is a limit even to work.

The late Professor James tells us that we can do nine times as much work as we now are doing and still have the spirit and strength for more work. But, even at that, there is a limit. Know your limit. Be wise.

After healing, what! Conform to all the hygienic laws of life.

The most lasting, satisfactory and helpful element in mental therapeutics springs from teaching patients how to help themselves and how to help others, and not from what the healer can do unaided.

After a patient has been healed, it is advisable for him to make occasional visits to a practitioner to attend lectures, to join classes and associate with people of like mind. Further than this he should himself "carry on" for at least three months after the healing. "Whatever method or methods have been employed in effecting his cure, whatever the methods which particularly appeal to him, he should at all events practice the Silence once or twice a day. He should, moreover, continue to take healing thoughts, to charge the subconscious mind just before retiring at night and upon awaking in the morning, and to comply faithfully and religiously with nature's requirements as to diet, sunshine, exercise, breathing, work and rendering service unto others.

Keep Normal Laws

Wise care of one's self means simply steering into the currents of law and order- mentally, morally and physically. The physical, mental and moral man are all three actually interdependent but all the care in the world for each and all of them can lead only to weakness instead of strength unless they are all three united in zeal for a useful life for the benefit of others.

In other words, we can be only at our maximum efficiency by taking good care of the mind and of the body which tabernacles the soul. Therefore after we have been healed, to maintain our healing and our maximum amount of mental and bodily efficiency we should be sure that we keep strictly the laws of life.

We have made a careful study in these pages of the crux of the whole disease matter and if we have succeeded in making anything at all clear it is this: that when we live in harmony with nature's laws, mentally and physically, it is im- possible to be sick. Sickness and disease are breaches of natural law so it is apparent that each person should subscribe to partnership with the Infinite. The wise seeker after health will do everything to be a good partner with nature by observing her health rules and regulations.

We Violate Natural Laws

Health is but life under normal conditions; hence, disease is life under abnormal conditions. We are living in a civilization which has forced us into a more or less unnatural mode of living. We do not eat naturally, sleep naturally, drink naturally, breathe naturally, or dress naturally.

"We have done those things which we ought not to have done, and we have left undone those things which we ought to have done, and there is no health in us"--truly we can add, at least, there is but little health in us.

Ignorance Is the Fault

It takes a big mind, to perceive that the root of disease is ignorance, that somewhere along the path of life law was violated, and to face himself like a man and say: Of my own ignorance I created this. This diseased condition is the result of destructive mental forces generated in wrong thinking, I am responsible for this, I will arise and go to my Father in whom is all resource for my healing. --Helen Rhodes Wallace.

Mind and Body Inter Correlate

"One can no longer understand life unless one admits that mind and body are one."

Andre Tridon has put some authority in his statement when he thus expresses himself on this subject:

It is only the profoundly ignorant who at the present day pretend to know the limits of the physical and of the mental and attempt to attribute certain phenomena to the mind and others to the body.

The truth meanwhile occupies, as ever, the medium position between the two, there being times when the body sways the mind, and other times when the mind sways the body, the two being, as has been forcibly expressed by Miss Cobbe, something like a pair of coupled dogs; sometimes one and sometimes the other obtaining the victory, and sometimes both pulling together in harmony.

"If mental strain, and depression can produce constipation, then constipation arising from other causes may and does produce mental depression and nervousness. In fact in most nervous disorders there is some such vicious circle as this."--Thomas Parker Boyd.

The chief objection to most of these therapeutic sciences is that they put forward a theoretical, one-sided mental scheme, thereby ignoring half of life. A theory of health to be of real value must be founded on established evidence and natural laws. However noble the spiritual structure reared upon it may be, Man, whatever else be true of him, will be a natural being as long as he lives in this physical world.

There are partisans of various therapeutists who insist that any workable knowledge of the organism of man is unnecessary; that even to mention physiological science is to compromise with materialism. They see no virtue in physical exercise, in the regulation of diet, correct breathing or proper mastication of food. For all of these they would substitute the affirmation of thought, and the spiritual realization of ideals, and then dogmatically proclaim that the art of health preservation is known only to them!

Such people should remember that their claims like the dogmatic implications of "revealed" religion must, of necessity, undergo the critical scrutiny of unbiased, thinking people. We are in an age where we accept nothing which runs counter to nature. We must have a reason for our faith, something more than mere creed or dogma. "We must have an educational philosophy of health which any reasoning man might accept whatever his metaphysics or religion.

Cause of "The Blues"

Most cases of the "blues" for instance are due to imperfect elimination caused in its turn by overeating or underdrinking, improper breathing or by all three.

Atkinson says, in "Mind and Body":

This action and re-action works along the lines of building-up as well as tearing-down. For instance, if a person's Mental States are positive, optimistic, cheerful and uplifting the body will respond and the Physical

Conditions will improve. The Physical Conditions, thus improving, will react upon the Mental States giving them a clearness and strength greater than previously manifested. This improved Mental State again acts upon the Physical Conditions, improving the latter still further. And so on, an endless chain of cause and effect, each effect becoming a cause for a subsequent effect and each cause arising from a preceding effect.

Likewise, a depressed, harmful Mental State will act upon the Physical Conditions, which in turn will react upon the Mental States, and so on, in an endless chain of destructive cause and effect. It is a striking illustration of the old Biblical statement: "To him who hath shall be given; to him who hath not shall be taken away even that which he hath."' In improving either the Mental State or the Physical Condition, one gives an up- lift to the whole process of action and reaction; while, whatever adversely affects either Mental State or Physical Condition, starts into operation a depressing and destructive process of action and reaction. The ideal to be aimed at is, of course, "A healthy Mind in a healthy Body"-- and the two are so closely related that what affects one, favorable or unfavorable, is sure to react upon the other.

Man Compared to Trees

Herbert A. Parkyn, M. D., well states the action and reaction of Mind and Body, as follows:

A tree is much like a human being. Give it plenty of fresh air, water and a rich soil, and it will flourish. In the same degree in which it is deprived of these does it wilt, and the first part of the tree to wilt when the nutrition becomes imperfect is the top. This is owing to the force of gravity; the blood of the tree, the sap, having to overcome this force of nature when nourishing the highest leaves. The blood of man is also affected by this same force, and the moment a man's circulation begins to run down, owing to stinted nutrition, we find that the first symptoms of trouble appear in the head--The brain failing to receive its accustomed amount of blood, such troubles as impaired memory, inability to concentrate the attention, sleeplessness, nervousness, irritableness, the blues and slight headaches develop; and the impulses sent all over the body becoming feebler, the various organs do not perform their functions as satisfactorily as usual. The impulses to the stomach and bowels becoming weaker and weaker, dyspepsia or constipation, or both, soon follow.

As soon as these, the main organs of nutrition, are out of order, nutrition fails rapidly and more "head symptoms" develop. Every impulse of the muscular system leaves the brain, and the strength of these impulses depends upon the nutrition to the brain centers controlling the various groups. As the nutrition to these centers declines, the whole muscular system, including the muscles of the bowels becomes weaker and the patient complains that he exhausts easily. The impulses for elimination becoming weaker, waste products remain in the circulation, and any of the evils, which naturally follow this state of affairs, such as rheumatism, sick-headache, biliousness, etc., are likely to develop. The centers of the special senses feeling the lessening of the vital fluid, such troubles as impaired vision, impaired hearing, loss of appetite (sense of taste) and inability to detect odors quickly soon follow. The sense of touch becomes more acute, and it is for this reason that one in poor health becomes hypersensitive. Lowered circulation in the mucous membrane of the throat and nose is often the cause of nasal catarrh appearing on the scene as an early symptom.

Why Conform to Nature

No organ of the body can perform its functions properly when the amount of blood supplied to it is insufficient and we find, when the blood supply to the brain is not up to the normal standard, that brain functions are interferred with to a degree corresponding to the reduction in the circulation. Since the amount of blood normally supplied to the brain is lessened in nervous prostration, we find that the memory fails and the ability to concentrate the attention disappears. The reasoning power becomes weakened and the steadiest mind commences to vacillate. Fears and hallucinations of every description may fill the mind of a patient at this stage, and every impression he receives is likely to be greatly distorted or misconstrued. Melancholia with a constant fear of impending danger is often present. In fact, the brain seems to lose even the power to control its functions, and the mind becomes active day and night--The reduction of the nutrition to the brain lessens the activity of all the cerebral centers also, and digestion becomes markedly impaired, thereby weakening the organ itself upon which the supply of vital force depends.

Animals Observe Nature's Laws

When it comes to the satisfaction of his bodily wants the animal has more sense than man. It does not violate the laws of nutrition as man does. It lives nearer to nature and eats things in the way nature intended they should be taken into the we can fire food. The diseases of man are the penalty he pays for violating nature's laws.

The average length of life among the Mohammedans is one hundred and he often remains a youngster at that. Dr. Miller's studies and surveys in the Balkans have shown that many men are now living there one hundred twenty and one hundred fifty years of age who do not look over forty or fifty. These people live in the fresh air, next to nature, eat cheese, fruit and sour milk.

All forms of animal life known to man except man himself live eight times their maturity. Man matures at twenty-one. Measured by the scale of other animals he should, therefore, live to be at least one hundred and sixty-eight years of age as body. Man, on the contrary, has invented a dozen and one ways of cooking so that we are beset on every side with some newfangled idea of how we compute time. The average age is forty. Man has got away from nature. He's paying the penalty.

He eats wrongly; he coops himself up in an ill-ventilated office; he lives in a cubbyhole of an apartment he calls a residence; he puts on outlandish clothing, which interferes with respiration and shuts out the sunlight, nature's chief source for health. In other directions he has got even further away from nature. The complexity of our present-day civilization and the keen competition to get ahead results in man's being filled with fear, hatred, envy--to say nothing of prejudice and the other negative thoughts--most of which, if not all, paralyze the assimilation, clog up and poison the system so that the natural sequence is sickness and chronic diseases. Emotional states registered in the flesh as anger, fear, prejudice, hatred, envy, revenge, also produce acute disease. Thus a natural way of living has been perverted by man into a way of living, eating, dressing and yielding to mental strain wholly at variance with the laws of nature and the laws of God.

Intelligent functioning of thought with action and the application of psychology to everyday problems is not to "demonstrate over" the laws of nature but to understand these laws and work in accordance with them.

Health is our normal condition. It is our birth-right. "It is as natural to be well as it is to be born." All diseases are the result of a transgression of natural law. Man's ignorance about the natural laws of health has produced the thousand and one ills that flesh is heir to.

Terry Walter in "The Hand Book of Life," expresses it this way:

We say that the body affects the mind and the mind affects the body--that the two do not function independently one of the other. We walk with our head or our heels, which? If our head did not say walk, should we do it? The mind is the control and if this control is not in good working condition it does not guide us in the right direction. On the other hand if the body is not cared for with regard to proper physical requirements, the blood stream, the quality of which determines the quality and activity of thought, does not produce a healthy brain, and so we first show the necessity of lung development, body sanitation, within and without, proper diet, and systematic and intelligent exercise; in other words, to get well or to keep well, you must properly use the four physical essentials of all life--air, water, food, and exercise.

Health Is Supreme

Nature has everything called for in the process of making or remaking itself. Health is the supreme work of the normal body. A. A. Lindsay, physician of over twenty-five years practice says "that the soul has a preference for, a trend toward Construction, and a power deficit for Healing"; that a constructive suggestion is in accord with its innate ideals and, therefore, the impulse to reorganize for harmony is ever present. This explains why one who has an acute disorder will recover if he has proper nursing, hygienic and dietetic attention and is free from artificial things as obstacles to his recovery. Purely medical authorities declare that with the sort of attention above mentioned ninety to ninety-five percent of the people with acute disorders recover, and many times, they also say, "they recover in spite of the medicine."

The words that John writes in his third epistle are suggestive: "Brethren, I desire above all things that thou shalt prosper, and be in health, even as thy soul prospereth." To do this one must conform to the laws of life.

Gentle Lady and Bunions

As told by Villette H. White:

One of the gentlest of ladies happened to mention to a friend--an enthusiastic adherent of a healing cult—that she had a bunion; to which her friend replied, "Oh, you must hate somebody !" A little common sense would have suggested that an ill-fitting shoe, and not a state of mind, was responsible for the trouble. So there may be many immediate causes for disease aside from mental states.

F. W. Sears, M. P., shoots straight at the mark, when he says:

Many persons will say, "Why, could thinking make me well, I would have been well long ago." Let us see how much they have thought of health ? How much they have recognized their oneness with it? They have recognized it in this way: They say, "I wish I could be well; I want so much to be well." They would make these statements a half a dozen times perhaps and then they would spend a couple of hours in telling about how much sickness they had in their lives. Some persons will spend hours each day in talking about their ailments, when they can find someone to listen. Is that living in the consciousness of health ? No! It is living in a continued consciousness of disease, of lack of health, and it is impossible for us to have health while we continue to build a consciousness of disease. On the other hand, it is impossible for us to have disease, when we have lived in and acquired a consciousness of health and harmony.

Healthy people, those who have established a "health consciousness" so that it is natural for them to be well, never think of being sick, never fear sickness, and never are sick unless through anger, hatred, envy, jealousy, impatience, intolerance, worry, anxiety, resentment, resistance, condemnation, criticism, fear, etc., they generate the negative energy which later on creates so much interior-soul-inharmony that it registers in the body as disease. This is the only way such persons ever can become sick.

Nervous Energy

It seems to be a law of the nervous system to find its equilibrium by a series of "ups and downs." Progress in anything in life is seldom steady, but if the general trend is toward recovery, there is no reason for discouragement but rather for getting a little stronger grip on one's self. Improvement may be rapid at first, but slower later. The reason may be found in this statement from Hoffman: "Nervous energy for any kind of response is limited. If the stimulation is continuous the response must become gradually less energetic." This would indicate that in the use of the will the nervous reserve is first drawn upon, and afterwards the improvement is to be made by building up impaired tissue, which is a much slower process.

However, we must continue to use the stimulus of the will, as "long continued stimuli tend to make new reflex paths in the nervous matter."

We are told that a certain amount of stimulus is expended in rousing nervous matter.

If no more is added, the inertia will not be overcome. Does not this show the need of perseverance in sending, not weak suggestions, but imperative commands over the nerve paths?

So the necessity of reading, studying, and continuing charging the subconscious mind for health, harmony, power and poise is so important that all of the mental healers combined cannot overemphasize the necessity of people who want to maintain health by doing something to help themselves.

"We have mentioned elsewhere that the hardest part of our healing is to reach that frame of mind where we are willing to dig up the roots of wrong thinking and throw them into the ash can of forgetfulness.

Very often a person will not play fair with himself after he has effected a cure. He thinks it's all over, that health is restored and that he need feel no sense of obligation to himself, his neighbor, or his God. He is well and again begins to travel the treadmill of wrong living and wrong thinking the same as before.

If our sickness is due to wrong thinking and wrong living and we are healed, no one in the world can guarantee that we are going to remain healed if we go back to the old way of living and thinking which originally produced our sickness. We can no more begin a new life living wrongly and thinking wrongly and be well than we could live the old life in that manner successfully. After our healing it must be right about face, forward march. We must toe the line of right thinking and right living without hewing to the right or without wobbling to the left.

Perhaps more sickness comes from selfishness than from any one thing. While not all deafness comes from selfishness, yet most deaf people can trace their affliction directly to their own selfishness. If a person, deaf because of selfishness, is healed and then continues to live a selfish life, of course he's going to revert.

I healed a woman in one of my campaigns who had been deaf for twenty-two years. She said her deafness was a great impediment to her business success. When she was healed, I told her that her ailment came directly from selfishness and that to maintain her hearing she would have to change her way of living. (The woman confessed that before coming to me she had spent thousands of dollars to be healed.)

In the face of my statement and her costly experience she strenuously attempted during the public lectures of my campaign to return a thumb-worn and badly soiled copy of Applied Psychology and get a fresh copy in exchange. On top of all this, be it remarked, she has not yet paid for her class!

Think of it! A complete healing after twenty-two years of deafness, and after thousands of dollars spent upon other methods to regain her hearing! Then, after I warned this woman she must if she were to keep her healing change from her selfishness into a life of charity, giving an abundance, she indulges in the contemptible nickel-pinching piece of selfishness above stated.

And they wonder why they are sick!

Hence, after our healing it is absolutely essential (it cannot, in fact, be made emphatic enough) that we change our way of thinking and our way of living.

What the Others Say

In my search to ascertain how other authorities and healers work, I ran across the following illuminating paragraph:

A thoughtful young physician said not long ago to a Christian minister: "I am sometimes disgusted with my work. I am expected to cure a man of disorders and diseases which may be largely the result of his evil appetites and passions, and then, without touching his soul, leave him to return again to wallow in his evil. All that I am doing, as I see it, is to set at naught the stern lessons whereby a man is taught, through suffering in the body, that he has sinned in the soul. I wish I could deliver him from the sin in his soul while I am delivering him from the suffering in his body."

The foregoing suggests a similar experience of mine. One of my patients from a distant land wrote somewhat to this effect: "I took your class and was healed in mind and body. For three months I did not have an ache or pain. Life was one sweet song. For the last few weeks I have felt the old trouble returning. Can you tell me what is the matter?"

Of course I could. If anger, grief, sorrow, reverses, misfortune or any emotional state (in other words inharmonious thinking) has caused the sickness, and the person is healed, he is healed because he changes his mind--right about face.

This correspondent, like many another good person after having been healed for three months, and thinking that the trouble was gone forever, reverted, went back to the old way of living, the old way of thinking. It is obvious that if hatred and jealousy or grief or sorrow brought about our first sickness that the condition will be duplicated if after the healing has taken place you go back to the same way of thinking and living as formerly, and this woman after her healing no doubt not only went back to her old way of thinking but neglected her reading.

This we must emphasize. The very first condition for most people, if they would maintain, restore or keep their health, is to live in a healthful mental atmosphere. This is one of the most important things we have to learn. Our thinking, our daily thinking, must be done along lines which are wholesome, aspiring and uplifting. And it must, just as far as possible, ignore and inhibit thought of disease and diseased conditions.

We must always recognize every department of that all important factor which both effects healing and maintains our health after we are healed. Not only must we change our way of thinking, by surrounding ourselves with a better "atmosphere" for healing, but we must also observe the laws of nature which are the laws of God.

One Weakness

Paul Ellsworth speaks with much authority when he says:

There seems to be an inherent tendency in carnal mind to throw over its allegiance to God or natural law as soon as it finds itself in possession of even a measure of direct power over physical things. This is the danger in direct healing--that it will stimulate the carnal consciousness to say in effect, "All right, God, now I can look after myself; you won't need to bother about me any longer." Remember that in healing, as in all other things, only the consciousness of unity with spirit can quicken within the personal will that serene mastery which says, "Let there be health," and it is so. Never allow yourself to drift into the belief, no matter how successful you may be in mastering your body, that you are now independent of Infinite Love and Wisdom and Power. For it is only as these work in and through you, only as you become one with these spiritual elements, that your word can continue to go forth with power.

Keep yourself in the thought-currents of Infinite love, wisdom, and power. Keep yourself in the frame of mind which assures you that you are master of your body, environment and conditions.

Someone has well said:

In like manner a man may say, "I am health," and go on sleeping in an unventilated room, neglect to take proper exercise, or feed his body on an unbalanced diet, and in general fail to observe dietetic, hygienic, or other laws of health, and wonder why his "thought" doesn't create a perfectly healthy body. "Faith without works is dead," said St. James, a noted healer of the early church. Health without observing its laws is impossible.

Thomas Parker Boyd, the eminent authority on mental science, knows whereof he preaches when he says in "The Voice Eternal":

No scheme of the spiritual philosophy of health can be complete which leaves out a due consideration of the material means that make for the welfare of the physical body which is the temple for the life of God that for a time dwells here. The body is a fact on hand and no amount of mental jugglery can alter that fact. Its welfare is tremendously influenced by the materials that we take into it. It is the life of God expressed in material form just as the soul is the life of God expressed in immaterial form. The life of God is governed by certain laws of expression which vary according to the form of life. If the

Infinite life is expressed in spiritual form, then it flows into that form by direct spiritual contact of the individual life with the spirit of all life. If life is expressed in material form then it is constantly maintained by life imparted through material forms, as the living soil imparts its life to vegetation, and vegetation to the animal, and likewise both of these to man's body. In other words the human body receives living energy- from various material forms such as food, water, air, etc., while his spiritual body receives its energy direct from God, and even here the process is greatly helped by certain symbols and material forms. No sane man expects his body to be fed by purely spiritual means without the agency of material forms. And there are certain laws by which these material agencies are made to minister their energy to the body most efficiently. To know these laws is the first duty of man. No reference is made here to materia medica because its use is assumed, and the physician is regarded as God's man dealing in divine forces which many people need at times to use. The author is not a physician and is writing for the people who do not need material remedies, and whose attention needs to be turned rather to the menial and spiritual forces in and about them.

Do You Want to Stay Healed?

I have emphasized with all the power at my command, both in writing and in my public lectures and classes that to be healed the patient must urgently want to be healed and will try to assist the healer, or try to help himself. Do you really want to stay healed? That's the question right now. Do you want to be well or not to be well, that's the big problem for your subconscious mind to answer. If you want to be well, rest assured that the subconscious mind will make you well and keep you well. You are healed now, you can hear people speak, your pains are gone, the aches are no longer there, life is different from what it has been. Now, play fair with yourself, take account of your mental stock, be honest in making an inventory of your mental states. Do you want to remain healed?

No one can answer this but yourself. No one can keep you well but yourself.

To keep your healing, therefore, remember that these few simple things must be adhered to.

First. Positively desire to remain well.

Second. Forever keep away from negative and inharmonious thinking.

Third. Continue charging the subconscious mind with affirmations when you go to sleep at night, awake in the morning and during the day.

Fourth. Practice the Silence.

Fifth. If discord, inharmony or association with individuals or groups of negative people have come into your life, cleanse the aura.

Sixth. Do not give a thought to past afflictions until you become so grounded in your health that by referring to your old troubles you are strong enough to prevent them from returning.

Seventh. Associate with people who have like minds, who believe in mental healing and the power of mind over all conditions, both bodily and environmental. Do not allow yourself to associate with people who are skeptical and who scoff and speak lightly of mental science. Remember you are now but a babe in the new life. Negative thinking from skeptics may flash into the subconscious mind and stick there. You may begin to doubt that you are healed, that you will remain healed, that you have been healed by the right means. It is most necessary, therefore, that you have proper association.

Until you become strong and very positive that nothing can shake your faith, enter into no arguments with people who tell you that there are methods of healing other than those which you have become acquainted with. Bear in mind that there are all kinds of envious or self-seeking teachers in this wonderful new age who are un-psychological to such an extent that they may deliberately or unconsciously poison your mind by leading you to believe that yon have not the truth.

All Healers Have Truth

I have known many and many a person who has had a complete healing by one healer, then some other, either ignorant or jealous practitioner, has told the former sufferer that he was not healed by God or that his healing could not be permanent because it was not right, or that there is only one way to be healed and this practitioner has it, so that those who have been healed have lost their anchorage. They begin to question whether they are really healed or not and of course, they revert.

Remember this is a new movement we are in--mental science--less than three-quarters of a century old, as we moderns understand it, and that we may expect all kinds of angles of truth to be added to that which we have.

Mental Science and the Church

The differences and the contentions and the jealousies and the backbitings of the modern teachers of mental science are analogous to the growth of the Christian church. One branch of the Christian church claimed that they had all of the truth, then up sprang another branch and said, "You are wrong, I have it." One branch said, "There's only one royal way to heaven and that's mine." Another said, "No, you are wrong, God has given into my keeping the only way to get into heaven. You must tread my narrow path or be lost." One branch of the Christian church said, "You must be baptized by immersion." Another said, "No, you must be sprinkled," etc., ad lib infinitum. This made all kinds of strife and contention. Then comes along another branch and said "you don't have to have any kind of baptism except spiritual." Each church claimed that it had the only truth. That has been going on now for some 600 years or more, I suppose we could say, 2000 and be nearer right.

This modern movement of mental science though still in its infancy is splitting up the same way. One man says, "I have all the truth." A woman says, "I have all there is," the next teacher declares, "There can be no truth unless you get it from me." Up springs another leader who contends that God has put the pass key of success, health and happiness into his keeping and the lock cannot be opened unless he lends you his magical pass-key opener.

This is all wrong. It should not be. It must not be. If you are to keep your healing, you will not listen to any narrow-minded bigoted doctrinal mental science practitioner who tries to undermine your faith and ruin your health by saying you have not the truth, that you need his teaching and his healing, and that of nobody else.

Remember the truth can come from any place. Truth is truth no matter where it is and what livery it wears. How do you know that you have pure law, pure science, pure psychology, pure mental science, pure healing? How do you know when you have the truth?

How to Know When You Have Truth

That's easy. If you have been healed, whether of physical afflictions or mental disturbance or domestic inharmony or business perplexities, or worry, doubt, fear or anything, all is well. Your healing is evidence that a Simon pure law or method was used--you have the truth for you.

One person gets his healing from a Christian Scientist. Another gets his healing from a Psychologist and someone else gets his healing from another mental practitioner, but if you are healed, there can be nothing but truth in that particular mental science which you have taken hold of--for you!

To be healed is to have received the truth, no matter from whom you got it, who administered it, where it came from, whereof it is born.

If you are healed, you are healed and it must of necessity be a true healing; it must be the law of truth which has healed you. God doesn't deal in falsities or trickery or sham, and everyone who has been healed has been healed by some natural law, whether that law has been well understood or not. That law is God given law, hence it is the God power. Why should you care who has healed you, how you have been healed, where you have been healed, what system was used, what method was manipulated, so long as you have been healed?

To be healed is to know the truth. To be healed is to have been helped by natural law. I grant you that some people only have an inkling of this law, some get nine-tenths of the law wrong and one-tenth of it right, but when you are healed, you have had the one-tenth of a law that is true. That is power, that is Godly.

So, let no one disturb your mind, perturb your soul, or upset your physical condition by telling you that you have not the truth. God is God and God is Truth and all healing is the operation of a God given law and where God is, there can be nothing but Truth. Flee as from a plague from that bigoted individual who would tell you you have not the truth--that he has all there is.

Eighth. Do you associate not only with people of vigorous minds, but attend meetings where you will hear various angles of mental science expounded. If you have firmly grasped what has been stated in the foregoing paragraphs, about Truth, you can hear a lecture or discussion on mental science anywhere without uprooting your faith.

Ninth. Exercise.

Tenth. Breathing.

Eleventh. Eating.

Twelfth. Fresh air.

Thirteenth. Rest.

Fourteenth. Work--hobby.

Fifteenth. Bathing and cleanliness.

We cannot, of course, pretend to include everything relative to sickness and health, anatomy, physiology and hygiene in a book of this size. In fact that is not necessary. The thing of chief importance is to admonish our readers to keep the main channels of health open.

The fundamental demand of nature in the physical, mental, psychic and spiritual planes is for cleanliness. In the physical plane this law is as rigidly enforced by nature's police as anywhere. She permits no latitude here. She is inexorable!

Bathing

Regular, thorough and easy cleansing of the system can easily be incorporated in one's habit complexes, although the practical details of method can be taken up more advantageously in the classrooms of sane and progressive teachers.

Be as scrupulously attentive to the matter of cleanliness, internally and externally, as you are in following the injunctions of your prayer book.

Psychological good sense speaks thus:

Surround yourself with cleanliness and helpfulness; they are suggestions. Fill yourself, and be filled with cleanliness and helpfulness. It will provide a powerful suggestion for the subconscious mind and will prepare a good channel through which may flow a realizing of your aspirations toward further knowledge, wisdom and power. It will form for you a glowing internal constellation which, with its stellar or cosmic correspondences, will bend to beneficent and fruitful purposes your growing knowledge of all that is helpful.

In the matter of bathing one should avoid extreme temperatures. The water should be neither too hot nor too cold.

Use the temperature of the water which you most enjoy. Do not take a daily cold plunge just because someone tells you to take it. How do you know but that it is too much of a shock for your body? Moreover, do not devitalize your strength by staying in hot water too long or entering it too often.

Sixteenth. Elimination

Elimination means "to drive out, to dispel, to discharge." The body eliminates its waste matter in four ways.

First, through the breath; second through the skin in perspiration; third through the kidneys in urine; fourth through the bowels in the feces.

Mental practitioners are coming to see that the wise "first aid" to all sickness is the method of the sensible doctor, namely to see that the kidneys and bowels act freely. The mind will have a whole lot better chance to heal the body if the four avenues of elimination are well taken care of.

When the cause of constipation is removed, the original cause of a great majority of ills that flesh is heir to is removed, and the symptoms of many diseases will disappear. Do not overlook this all important request of nature--that you are scrupulously attentive to the elimination of bodily waste.

Reading

And finally, be sure that you read, read, read, along these lines. Inoculate your mind with a taste for mental science study. Saturate your consciousness with constructive mental science reading. Concentrate while you read.

The maxim of the ancient Greek philosopher, communicated to the pupil who would become a great orator, was action, action, action. Modern psychologists will tell you that one of the surest ways to become well and to remain well is by reading, reading, reading.

We cannot afford to remain ignorant of these laws or to neglect to put ourselves in alignment with them as the first measure in maintaining health or in regaining it when we have slipped through temporary carelessness. If we neglect these basic laws--as one might put it, the Master Suggestions of the Eternal Mind--then the successful working out of our subsequent suggestions can hardly be expected.

As Doctor Sidney Murphy says:

Certainly all experience declares and all physicians will admit that where vital power is abundant in a man he will get well from almost any injuries short of complete destruction of vital organs, but where vitality is low, recovery is much more difficult, if not impossible, which can only be explained on the principle that vitality always works upward toward life and health to the extent of its ability under the circumstances, because, if it worked downward, the less vitality, the more surely and speedily would death result.

Disease, in its essential nature, has a deeper significance than simply abnormal manifestations. It is really a remedial effort, not necessarily successful, but an attempt to change, or have changed existing conditions. And for this reason any improper relation of the living organism to external agents necessarily results in an injury to that organism, which by virtue of its being self-preservative, immediately sets up defensive action, and begins as soon as possible to repair the damages that have accrued. This defensive or reparative action, of course, corresponds to the conditions to be corrected, and hence is abnormal and diseased; and its severity and persistence will depend upon the damages to be repaired, and the intensity and persistence of the causes that produced it. Serious injury present or impending will demand serious vital action; desperate conditions, desperate action. But in all cases the action is vital, an attempt at restoration, and the energy displayed will exactly correspond to the interests involved and the vitality that is available.

Pain Our Best Friend

Whenever a pain is felt, this is the red light danger signal which God is flashing in front of the on-rushing man doomed to sickness. Pain is a "stop, look, and listen" signal. "Wise is the individual who, immediately upon recognition of any kind of pain, stops, takes account of stock studies the situation, his condition, and right about faces. There has been a breach of natural law somewhere.

We have given in this series of the Fundamentals of Practical Psychology, enough so that any rational human being can be his own physician, his own prescription writer, his own medical compounder, and his own healer.

After you have been healed, the slightest pain should inspire you to immediately look into the inner chambers of your being and see what is the cause of these pains. I reiterate, by again consulting the first volumes of this series, you will become your own doctor, save untold suffering, much money and loss of time.

Pain is your best friend. When he makes a call, get busy.

After Healing What? Conform to Nature's Laws

Listen to the admonition of Thomas Parker Boyd in "The Voice Eternal":

For as surely as obedience to the law of heat banishes cold, and obedience to the laws of knowledge eliminates ignorance, and to the law of prosperity ends poverty, and to the law of Christ ends sin, so also obedience to the laws of health emancipates from sickness, and we shall lay aside our crutches and walk forth as the sons of God, without spot or stain or any such thing.

After healing what? Adhere strictly to the laws of God.

I have met many upright, honest, conscientious and religious people who wonder why they are sick. Sometimes they compare themselves with people who are living far from moral lives. The reason is obvious. It is a matter of moral perception of moral standard.

The man who lies without compunction or conscience, who thinks there is no wrong in stealing, who approves of betting on a horse race, has a different standard of morals from the godly person. He may, therefore, without psychological or physical harm, do many things which according to Christian convention are reprehensible. Because he does not believe he is doing wrong, his acts have no ill effects on his mind and body.

On the other hand one who has a higher standard of morals, who pursues an honest, upright life, who does unto others as he would have others do unto him, is so conscientious that he is affected by even an approximate violation on his part of any of the moral laws by which he orders his life.

What is not wrong to one is distinctly wrong to another, and the significance to its perpetrator of a doubtful act depends mostly on how far he has gone toward violating his own accepted principles of right living. The "roughneck" may lie and think he does no wrong. But with you, just one falsehood may affect your consciousness sufficiently to lower greatly your sense of physical wellbeing. Do not regret the high standards you have set for yourself. Thank God for them. It is you, not the evildoer, who will get the Best out of life in the end.

BREATHING

Another very important element in maintaining our health after we have been healed, or to keep health, is this apparently simple business of breathing. Too much emphasis cannot be put upon the importance of right breathing. The author has written extensively on this topic and has presented

a system of breathing in Volume 3 of this series. It must not, however, be assumed from what I say about the vital importance of breathing properly that I intend to gloss over other digressions from physical and mental laws. I merely wish to make my position entirely plain that to become and remain well we must breathe properly.

The importance of deep breathing is well given by Hereward Carrington, in "Higher Psychical Development," referring to deep breathing as taught by the Yogis:

Deep breathing and the regulation of breath are taught. (This is known as Pranayama.) The process of breathing is in three parts--inhalation, retention and exhalation. The time taken to perform each action is proportionate. The Yogis have discovered the proportion, and its apprentices are taught to breathe accordingly. Gradually the aim is retention, then suspension of breath. Anyone who will try the experiment will find that the brain works with dizzy celerity when the breath is held in the body. This, then, is the object. Another object it has--namely by suspending the breath, life--it is said --may be prolonged indefinitely.

How well Yogis have succeeded in this wonderful art may be gathered from various accounts which narrate the interment of Yogis in sealed, air-tight coffins for periods varying from seven to forty days. The experiment was tried on a Yogi, with his consent, by some well-known British officers, who testified to the incident on their word of honor, and also signed a paper giving an account of the whole experiment in all its details.

Nowadays it seems hardly necessary to tell of the effects of deep breathing. It is known to everybody that deep breathing makes the blood pure, the eyes so bright that they dazzle, the complexion clear and clean, the skin smooth, and that it fills the body with the exhilaration of health; but few know that it makes the body glow--actually glow. For many decades the occidental scientists laughed at the idea that the human body glowed and gave forth light; but lately, within the last few years, a series of experiments on chemicals and other substances sensitive to light, undertaken by French and also American scientists, have proved clearly that the human body does emit a form of light. Youth radiates more light than the aged, and the so-called '"beauty of youth" is said to be largely due to this glow.

Deep breathing produces more glow than most ordinary youths have--and brings new life, youth and beauty to age. It is a most noticeable and remarkable fact that Yogis, however old they may be-- and some of them are said to live three and four times the span of 70 years, an ordinary man's life--always look young, some positively handsome: all have brilliant eyes, and all are strong and healthy.

An advanced position taken by many investigators, which I have proved to my own satisfaction to be right, is that we do not get our nourishment so much from what we eat, as we do from what we breathe, and from sleep.

So, besides your regimen of wholesome living, of right thinking, eating, drinking, breathing and sleep, get an abundance of fresh air at night while you sleep, so that when you awaken in the morning, you will have a feeling of refreshment, vigor and optimism. Remember that the blues, mental depression and worry go with impure air and poor breathing.

Worry and bad breathing go together. All sick people are bad breathers.

Poor breathing leaves the blood filled with carbon-dioxide, which makes the brain sluggish, reduces its power and lowers the vitality of the whole system. Breathe deeply of plenty of fresh air. By all means have your bedroom windows open while you sleep. Do not permit your house to be overheated in winter. Get fresh air and plenty of it and breathe deeply.

After healing what? See that you add deep breathing to your program of health.

KEEPING FIT

Exercise

The day for all kinds of apparatus for physical exercise is like the proverbial phrase that "every dog has its day." The apparatuses have had their day.

In the good old days when we looked upon dumbbells and Indian clubs as a necessary adjunct and all of the weights and pulleys and other paraphernalia in gymnasiums, many a good soul thought he could not exercise unless he could afford such apparatus.

If you can afford apparatus and think that you must have these frills well and good but the main part of exercise is the use of your mind as yon exercise.

A famous authority on this has well said:

You do, however, need a large stock of desire, enthusiasm, and persistence. It is from the development of these that you will get the best development of muscles and health. It is the amount of mind you put into the matter that will give the best results. A great deal of mind---of desire and a little exercise will do wonders and give health and pleasure in living.

Exercise Is Mental

Eugene Sandow says :

It is all a matter of mind. Nothing will make a man strong save his own concentration of thought.

If you concentrate your mind upon a single muscle or set of muscles for three minutes each day, and say, "Do thus and so!" and make them respond by contraction, there will be immediate noticeable development.

It is mental first, physical afterwards. The whole secret of my system lies in the knowledge of human anatomy,-- in knowing just where one is weak and going straight to work bringing that particular part up to the standard of one's best feature,--for there is a best feature in every man as there is also a worst. And yet as a chain is as strong only as its weakest link, so is the body strong only as its weakest member. The secret is to "know thyself," as Pope says, and knowing one's weakness, to concentrate the mind and energies upon that weakness with a view to correcting it.

Why Blame God?

One of the important things for the human race to understand is that health and disease are not matters of chance, but are regulated by the universal laws of sowing and reaping; that health, when lost, is frequently regained by faithful cultivation of mind and close adherence to all mental and physical laws; that sickness is a consequence directly or indirectly (although we may be ignorant of just how we have erred) of a violation of natural laws. Hence disease is not due to the anger of the gods nor to the "Providence of God," and mental healing is not the result of a miraculous presto-change flip of a health coin flung by the fingers of a mysterious Deity to determine who shall be miraculously healed and who shall remain under the wrath of God. Law, not chance, rules the world.

We become sick and diseased by virtue of wrong living, as well as of wrong thinking. We are healed by the power of mind over the physical laws just in proportion as we conform to the divine operation of these mental and physical laws. To keep our healing, we must, therefore, continue to do our part, continue to keep in harmony with both the mental and physical realm.

Exercise properly and you stimulate good breathing, create thirst and arouse appetite. Of course, the appetite should be satisfied with the nutritious diet specified elsewhere. It is the idle person who is the shallow breather and whose appetite calls for stimulants and highly seasoned and concentrated foods.

The right kind of exercise, if carried out for six months or even less time will make you a changed person. Therefore, after your healing, be sure that you help God to help the laws to help yourself to keep well by exercising.

Walk

Besides exercising the muscles of arms, legs, abdomen, face, eyes and neck one should walk at least two to four miles a day, breathing deeply, the clothing loose, to allow free play to the muscles of the extremities, and of the vital organs.

While D. McDougal King, M. D., recommends:

Every normal person should walk at least four miles a day. Where it has not been a habit, it will be a little taxing at first, and should be extended by degrees.

Watch Lower Animals

Men can learn from the animals. Watch the cat, the dog, the tiger, as they stretch life into their limbs. Modern man sits and writes, humps up his back, doubles in his shoulders, contracts his muscles, without ever thinking that life and invigoration come from stretching his limbs, muscles and joints.

How It Is

A famous physico-mental therapeutist explains it as follows:

Between each spinal vertebra the nerves emerge, running to the various parts and organs of the body, and when the segments of the spine move easily and freely and are in proper relation to each other, the circulation is normal and the entire nervous system works efficiently. This condition can be brought about by the proper exercise of the muscles of the back as the determining factor is the proper functioning of these muscles which maintain spinal balance. To keep the spinal nerves unhindered in their function is one of the best ways to keep physically fit.

Nothing in the world, outside of the mind, has more healing power than the sun. Children can be cured of the rickets by keeping them in the sun.

Modern civilization has entombed man in clothes, sky scrapers and apartment houses so that the body does not get its much needed sun bathing.

Sun Cure

Every person should be at least one hour in the sun's rays a day, nude. Yes sir, nude. I suppose there is not one out of ten million who puts himself in that happy condition ten minutes every twenty-four hours.

Never mind what the other man does. Each must look after himself and if it is not customary in your house to go undressed with the sun beating through the panes, make it a habit. If you cannot get the full benefit of the sun's rays, get as much of the fresh air as possible on your body.

Arthur Brisbane, the distinguished journalist, also believes in fresh air and sun cure. He says:

A real sun cure means walking in the sunshine naked, except for protection on the skull. Exposing the whole body to the sunlight causes blood pressure to fall. The breathing becomes deeper and slower; the amount of air inhaled greater and the strain on the heart less.

Sunshine on the skin expands the little capillary veins, bringing blood to the surface, which is good for the surface and good for the blood, increasing both red and white blood corpuscles, the protective army of our blood system.

Let your body be exposed to the light, air and sun; help yourself to help your body maintain its healthy equilibrium.

Back to Nature

Another of the best methods of exercise in the world is to get down and crawl on the floor on your hands and knees. Better yet, crawl on the earth on your hands and knees. The body becomes magnetized when it comes in touch with mother nature. Take off your shoes and stockings and walk on the bare earth. If you live in the city and have only a patch of a back-yard, do it there in the summer, every day. On your vacation time, see that you go without shoes and stockings at least an hour a day. Of course, you are not to sit around on damp benches in the woods with your feet on the cold, damp ground, without exercising

The body also should be exposed to the sun at least an hour a day. Take your exercise with your windows open--nude.

If you live in the city, put up in vacation time some kind of a contraption without any roof, where you can sit in the sun stark naked. It will re-vitalize, re-energize the body in a marvelous manner. To keep perfect health, one must take pams to help nature.

After healing what? Plenty of exercise, fresh air and sunlight.

EATING AND MIND

The body requires certain life essentials--air, water and proper diet. All the affirmations and auto-suggestions in the world will not take the place of a glass of water or a few cubic feet of air. If physical troubles of any sort are due to the lack of these essentials no substitutes will suffice to keep the physical machinery oiled and steam generated within.

Diet is the fundamental factor in the cure of disease because it controls the action of living cells, and through metabolism or cell-changes it builds the body tissues and creates heat and energy.

Carl Bingesser,M. D.

One of the best books on Mind Healing right now, is "The Finger of God" by Thomas Parker Boyd. In this, Dr. Boyd says:

It is not an "accident" that an overuse of sweets over-load the body with heat energy and covers the face with pimples. It is not an "obsession of the devil" when one eats twenty or thirty per cent of his food allowance in proteins (meats, etc.) and finds his liver and kidneys diseased, and his body riled with rheumatic twinges. It is not a "mysterious dispensation of providence" that one who fills his body with pork and fats, finds his body cushioned with layers of useless and disfiguring blubber. It is not an "error of mortal mind" when one takes in fifteen hundred calories of food energy and uses up twenty-five hundred, that the body forces are depleted, its resistive powers weakened, and tuberculosis, cancer, and other destructive processes get foothold, and make headway. These are all legitimate results of a lack of intelligent thought application growing out of a state of consciousness which is out of harmony with the consciousness of the Absolute, and hence their building ideals and processes do not obey His laws of expression.

Catch Your Breath!

Paul Ellsworth does not deal in superlatives unless he actually means what he says. Harken to his punch:

I have known as many "Beefsteak drunks," and as many "bread and butter and potato fiends," as I have alcoholics or drug fiends; and I am stating that very moderately. Toleration and sympathy; the earnest, humble, kindly desire to help others out of the same bog of sensualism and ignorance in which we have wallowed--your patient will not get far until he learns this lesson.

A noted specialist has said that not one person in ten thousand fully understands the necessity of giving regular daily attention to the life essentials--air, water and food, or realizes that his health absolutely depends upon their being supplied to him in a pure state and in ample quantity.

Scientific Living and Thinking

Taking these facts into consideration it must be evident to every thoughtful person (and this is most important to the mind cure aspirant) that whether mental troubles precede or follow declining physical health, a patient should take steps to correct both his physical and his thinking habits if he would improve his general health. For with an improvement in the nutrition of the brain and body, there must necessarily follow an improvement in the operations of the cerebral and bodily functions. Being thereafter in better mental and physical condition the subject will experience an increase in the control exercised by the conscious mind over the subconscious thoughts and actions.

Thus by combining right thinking with right living in general; by giving seasonable attention to fresh air, at work and in sleeping quarters, to abdominal breathing, to regular physical exercise and proper eating, the patient will be able to reap one hundred per cent returns from his affirmations. In order to live harmoniously and rightly it is evident to one whose mind is unwrapped by prejudiced mental healing ideas that one must live simply and adjust oneself naturally to the requirements of one's whole being. When we live naturally, we live harmoniously. That is to say we've combine scientific living with scientific thinking.

Disregard of nature, over-taxation, or under development of our physical and mental powers, neglect of any of the laws of our mental or material being, may be evidenced in discord in mind or body.

We are living in a world where constant readjustment is required. For instance, our fore- fathers, whether on the New England farm or the rolling prairie, had no skyscrapers in which they imprisoned themselves all day, no stuffy apartment houses in which they slept a few hours at night without the necessary amount of good ozone. They did not have to adjust themselves to modern living so as to get fresh air. They had it--everywhere, all about them. Similarly with our and their eating habits. Before cook stoves were invented and cooking by gas and electricity was widely advertised, they ate a natural raw diet.

Thus they were as wise as nature herself, in adapting themselves to their environment, in adjusting themselves to the requirements of their situation. Should we not imitate them and in our day and generation be as wise as they!

"When this modern movement of mind cure was ushered in, it was such an innovation and such a change from the old methods of being healed by medical aid, that at first the mental science cults of various kinds, stripes and denominations rushed to great extremes. Their spokesmen averred that since everything was mind no concern need be given the physical body. It seems that even yet few understand that the simple natural living of one's life on the physical plane in its physical surroundings is necessary for a harmonious whole, and many continue to overlook the importance of having a scientific regimen for physical as well as for mental needs. It is not enough to think right, much as that is needed. To "think right," we must add "eat right, breathe right, sleep right, rest right, relax right, exercise right."

However, I am hopeful that in a short time all mental healers, practitioners and teachers will emphasize the necessity and beauty of the balanced life; combining a scientific mental and physical regimen, to produce a harmonious whole.

There is but one unerring test of a full-fledged psychologist. He is one whose maxim is right living, who preaches harmony on every plane. These, I believe, are the big desiderata; they are one and inseparable.

Strictly speaking, a raw, live diet without any meat is by far the best for most people. Some, however, have been so long accustomed to a mixed diet, including animal flesh that considerable time may have to elapse before it is possible for them to go without eating meat. The wise person who is desirous of obeying the call of nature, who wants to live in harmony with the digestive as well as spiritual laws, will be honest with himself in making up his daily diet.

There is considerable doubt in some quarters about the relative value attaching to foods but there is no escaping the fact that many good people are making themselves sick and others killing themselves from eating too much heat producing and energizing food, very often in bad combinations.

Surplus, or incompatible foods, generate in the stomach foul gases which are absorbed, enter the blood, poison the system and cause all kinds of diseases.

Apoplexy, burning fevers, splitting headaches, bilious vomiting, jaundice, diabetes, Bright's disease, painful diarrheas, sour belchings and profuse catarrhal discharges, are only a few examples of errors in diet.

These manifestations are like volcanic eruptions—they are explosive efforts of nature to spew out, cast off from the body, accumulated surplus and offending materials.

In some chronic, and in all acute or febrile diseases, all kinds of food should be stopped till they can be appropriated, nothing but water being allowed.

Use The Mind

Most cases of constipation can be cured by suggestion--in fact the hour when the bowels will move can even be stated--but right eating will never produce or be followed by constipation. To help suggestion for regularity and elimination; suppose you stop eating the regular cooked diet and, for two or three days, substitute the juices of fruits--such as oranges, grapes and grapefruit --and a goodly portion of water. Supplement this diet by taking hot baths nightly and constipation will soon be a thing of the past.

Some forms of chronic headache are due to the lack of acids in the body which fruits and other forms of unfired or uncooked diet contain. These headaches can be healed by abstinence from cooked food and the substitution therefor of a raw or live diet regimen containing a liberal proportion of juices from oranges, grapefruits and grapes, together with plenty of water. Pure cider is splendid.

If a protracted chronic condition exists let the subject abstain for three days from solid food of all kinds, the diet to be only the juice of fruits mentioned above and plenty of water. If this course be followed the headaches may disappear never to return provided the live diet becomes a regular habit. In any event, three days on liquid food only, consisting of the juices of fruits, then a week of ordinary eating and another three day period of fruit juices, instead of the regular diet, will effect a cure. It certainly will if during this time the suggestion or auto-suggestion is used.

Partial Fast

If one takes just a three-day lay off from heavy eating during which he will drink the juices of oranges, grapes, apples, grapefruit, or juices of any other fruits, twice a day, consuming as much of these juices and of fresh water as he possibly can, he will enjoy the three days immensely and when his partial fast is over, can adjust himself to almost any diet he desires.

"We most enthusiastically recommend this to anyone who, upon beginning the raw diet finds it difficult to keep wholly away from the mixed cooked foods. After this three-day partial fast he can then accommodate himself to the raw diet with ease and pleasure.

Drinking all of the juices of fruits one desires gives sufficient nourishment for the body. It is not an actual fast; it is merely giving the organs of nutrition a rest, while meantime supplying them with all the nourishment the body requires.

How to Reduce

For people who want to take off flesh, this is a splendid method. Many persons make the mistake of reducing too quickly. Three days of eliminating all heavy foods from the diet while drinking nothing but juices of fruits, and plenty of fresh water will reduce the average person to a sufficient extent. Should you try this once and find you have not reduced enough you may repeat the program within a week.

To keep in the pink of digestive efficiency, live on raw diet, as we have outlined in volume three of this series, and, for at least one day a month, eliminate all other nourishment, save the juices of fruits, and three or four quarts of water. Better still, especially if you are inclined to corpulence, live for two days out of every thirty on nothing but the juices of fruits and water.

Everybody should take a seven-day fast at least once a year, meantime remembering there is a difference between starving and fasting. Plenty of fruit juices and water is fasting; nothing to eat may be starving.

Probably the race would be better off if all of us took a forty-day fast each year.

Justice to All

The need of the hour in care for the health is prevention--prevention in medicine, prevention in metaphysics and prevention in psychology. There are several doctors who write daily articles on health which are circulated among millions of people. Here is one tinctured with real common sense, and which is worth thousands of dollars to the American public--aye, millions.

I should like to have the readers of this series be given an illustration of the scientific methods of the freedom of thought and the genuine simplicity of a really great member of the medical profession.

I give verbatim Dr. Copeland's write-up on drinking water:

"Foodstuffs would be of no more use to the human body than stones or dirt if they were incapable of solution. Until they're dissolved they are valueless. All the bodily acts having to do with the reception of nourishment are associated with the necessity of dissolving food.

Water

"First we chew the food thoroughly, thus mixing it with the saliva. Next we swallow it, so that the fluids of the stomach may act upon it. Then it passes into the intestines, where the bile and other juices attack it.

"As the food is thus prepared and dissolved, it is taken up by the body, furnishing the fuel and nourishment essential to life itself.

"The acids generated in the body require water for their making.

"About two-thirds of the weight of the human body is water. Like water outside the body, this will grow stale if not frequently changed. You cannot be healthy unless you supply yourself every day with an abundance of pure water. Make sure of the supply and then make free use of it for drinking and bathing purposes.

"There have been many arguments over the propriety of drinking water during meals. Forget all about these discussions and do not hesitate to drink at least one glassful at each meal. A second glass will do no harm.

"The best grounded objection to the free use of water at meal times is that many persons use water to soften the food instead of depending on the chewing and saliva.

"The starches require saliva in order to begin their digestion. The teeth are needed to give fineness to the food. Drink the water, but do not use it to rob the food of the necessary action of teeth and saliva.

"Every adult should take at least two quarts of water during every twenty-four hours."

Chew, Chewing, Chewed

The average diner at hotels and those who eat at railway stations in a hurry, consume three times as much as they need and yet feel "empty" a short time afterwards usually because they make use of some kind of liquid in washing down their food. A prolonged chewing of food is necessary to stimulate a flow of the digestive juices, and water is not a substitute for the juices. Drink plenty of water, preferably before meals, and not with meals, but be sure that you chew your food, and chew it, chew it, CHEW IT! Then chew it some more until it unconsciously and involuntary slips down the throat.

Masticate your food. Fletcherize!

Chew, chewing, and chewed will keep many a pale man from taking pink pills and will help many a "bucking" stomach to settle down and behave itself.

Teeth

Elsewhere in our works we have presented the scientific outline for right eating. In addition to thoroughly masticating the food--Fletcherizing-- the teeth and gums should be maintained in healthy condition for only when the teeth are good grinders is mastication thorough and the saliva able to do its best work. The importance of healthy gums and sound teeth cannot be too much emphasized.

Think Right While You Eat

Hold firmly in your mind the particular thought which you would embody in yourself, during the time you are nourishing your body and at least an hour afterwards. This will liberate certain finer forces from the food and nourish particular brain-centers that you are building up. Do the same when walking in fresh air and when having physical exercise. This will deepen the thought-channels in the brain. Remember, at first there will be resistance from the lower brain-centers, but as the higher centers develop they will take absolute control. Go on. Stop not; you must build up a new brain in which the higher centers will control the lower ones and this process of brain-transformation has to be done; now that you know these things, and see the absolute necessity of setting about the task, it is no use getting impatient.

Eating and Colors

We can scarcely over emphasize the importance of maintaining a cheerful attitude at the table. To this end you should, especially in your own home, be surrounded, at meal time, with light colors -- for these conduce to raising the rate of your vibration--together with every other sur-rounding condition which serves to add cheerfulness, joy and happiness to the hour of partaking of life's essentials.

It is very important that you sip your liquids slowly, eat slowly and masticate your food very, very well. Be sure to Fletcherize.

Eating and Demonstrating

If you make a habit of sipping your liquid, accustom yourself to carry meantime the mental at-titude and the thought you want to take for the demonstration you are working on. Thus you will couple up your scientific eating with the habit of using your mind for your life's demonstrations.

Even if you are in good health, with every sip comes a reminder that it is time to take your au-tosuggestion treatment--your formula for demonstrating.

Therefore, it is most essential that you begin your meal in a spirit of cheerfulness with the right surroundings. As you sip your liquids take this thought:

I realize that whatever I eat becomes a part of my brain and body and whatever I do I do for the good of myself and others. Therefore, these life essentials make me well, whole, harmonious and complete in mind and body. These life essentials are making of me a human, spiritual magnet to attract unto me and mine the maximum amount of success, health and happiness.

Then you may use any affirmation or formula you desire for health, success, prosperity or hap-piness, any affirmation or formula calculated to crowd out stray, unfriendly suggestions which may be trying to manifest themselves.

In order to keep the health you have regained and to prevent ill health in the future, be sure that you take time at each meal to affirm, "I realize that everything I eat becomes a part of my brain and body and whatever I do I do for the good of myself and others. Therefore, these life essentials make me well, whole, harmonious and complete in mind and body. These life essentials are making of me a human, spiritual magnet to attract unto me and mine the maximum amount of success, health and happiness." Then also remember that this is a splendid time to "hold the thought" for anything for which you wish to demonstrate.

Formulae to Use

The subconscious mind works continuously whether man directs it or not. Therefore, it is very important that we assign definite work to the subconscious mind. By so doing we strengthen our control over the subconscious and secure from it far better response. It's on the same principle as that of the blacksmith having more muscle in the arm which swings the hammer.

As you drink water or other liquid (which should amount to two quarts a day), sip instead of gulping it, and with each mouthful take such a thought as this:

This water will increase the secretions m my body and will help to carry off waste material. It will promote the secretion of saliva and I will masticate every mouthful of food thoroughly. It will increase the quantity of gastric juice and my stomach will perform its work of digestion properly. It is to increase the quantity of pancreatic juice and the quantity of bile, and my bowels will complete the digestion of my food and turn it into good, red, rich blood.

My appetite is normal. I am eating like a healthy man and am obtaining as much strength from my food as any healthy man.

My kidneys and skin are working perfectly. I am bright, happy and cheerful. I am obtaining perfect health from the life essentials.

Physical strength is the basis of success and courage. The life essentials are building up my body and I am becoming strong and robust. I have physical strength and I have determination. I feel my courage increasing. I am strong, courageous and fearless now. I am a man amongst men and I know my physical strength and courage will carry me through anything successfully. By thinking these strong thoughts I feel stronger; my actions are stronger and my confidence in myself is increasing.

The good, rich blood I am making now is carrying health to every cell in my body. Health is my birthright. There is health all around me. I am eating it, drinking it, breathing it. I am healthy NOW.

This mouthful of water is also a reminder that I must "eat some air" and I shall now proceed to educate my lungs to breathe deeply by taking half a dozen deep breaths.

I shall take a moderate amount of exercise commensurate with my store of energy, but am making certain that I am appropriating more strength each day, from the life essentials, than I am expending. Thus I am banking on my energy. I feel better and stronger this moment.

Herbert A. Parkyn, M. D., who uses the above formulae, says:

That these or similar auto-suggestions taken frequently every day, with a liberal supply of the life essentials, will benefit any physical sufferer--I care not what his complaint. Rheumatism, sick headache, neuralgia, constipation, feebleness, certain forms of nervousness, failing eyesight, nasal catarrh, etc., are all symptoms of faulty circulation, and by following the self-treatment I have outlined, the cause of the symptoms disappears, the symptoms themselves soon follow the cause; consequently in employing the auto-suggestions it is not necessary to think of the various complaints. Think the thoughts that will bring general physical improvement and the symptoms will be overwhelmed in the irresistible march of health that will surely follow the health thoughts all though the body. Thought is a positive, dynamic force that takes form in action.

And finally, follow the admonition of Joseph Perry Green, when he says:

Next try and realize the Omnipresence of God. The word "God" really means Good. When you drink water bear in mind that Good or God washes and cleanses your body as it goes through your blood and through your flesh and that you love the Good or God in the water. The same way with your food. Good in your food is God on the material plane to nourish your material body. Recognize it, praise it and appropriate it in a mental digestive act. So likewise in your breathing. For 5 or 10 minutes while you are breathing, make yourself conscious of inhaling the Good or God in the atmosphere and that this Good or God enlivens and quickens your Life and increases the abundance in your Life.

After healing what? See that you eat proper food, take periods of rest each month from eating and think right as you eat.

REST

Different People, Different Rest

I believe it is now recognized by all reputable neurologists that the chief causes of most diseases, functional and organic, are overstrain, wrong diet, lack of relaxation and insufficient rest. Therefore, the importance of regular, unbroken rest, is most apparent. We cannot disobey the laws of life and expect God to keep us well, any more than we can disobey the laws and God and expect him to heal us while these laws are not being lived up to.

It must therefore be plain that, no matter what your sickness has been, or what your condition may be, if you are tired, overworked, or overstrained, God cannot keep you well unless you have rest. You must not offer the excuse to yourself, "this has to be done," or, "I cannot get along without doing it," or, "it is impossible to do otherwise." Such excuses only travel in a circle, and presently you will find that you are headed again for the sick bench.

The foregoing injunction applies to the student who is overstraining his mental faculties, to the housewife, to the business man as well as to the athlete, who is overstraining nerves and muscle.

Another chief cause, the dietician will tell us, is overeating, or improper eating.

Backbone of Rest Cures

There is no doubt but that rest is a great factor in all systematic rest cures which for a long while were almost the fashion with neurologists. Many of their patients were, however, allowed to go to extremes with their stereotyped regimen and thus were often unsuccessful, because of overeating and lack of exercise.

It is necessary to have plenty of rest, but this should be combined with a well rounded out, organized routine of exercise, fresh air, right eating and right thinking.

To aid one's right thinking, he should spend at least twenty minutes a day (more would be better) in reading literature along the lines projected in this series. The reading will help induce relaxation, both in mind and body and stimulate brain cells to functional activity for mental energy and physical strength.

One should see to it that he has enough sleep for his physical requirements. No set rule can be laid down, the number of hours to be devoted to sleep cannot be stated for all individuals. Some people require more sleep than others. Let not foolish ignorance dictate whether you shall sleep five hours or ten hours. Take the number of hours your own particular constitution requires.

If your sickness has been caused by wrong environment, untoward conditions, overwork, or faulty vibrations, you must not return to the old surroundings, if these surroundings seem to "get on your nerves." Again, excuses to the effect that you cannot change, etc., are no excuses at all before the judgment bar of health.

Bernarr MacFadden, the widely known physical culturist, surely has had enough experience for his words to carry weight. He says:

Most Needed

Nothing will avail unless you get sufficient sleep to keep up your vitality and energy. Going to bed late is one of the greatest American vices. Thousands who would not think of drinking or dissipating in any other way will dissipate in this manner. Don't lose sleep even to read poetry, philosophy or religious books. It is dissipation. Get to bed. And sleep in the fresh air. If you can possibly arrange it, sleep outdoors. Fix up a couch on the roof, on the balcony, or anywhere you can, so long as it is out of the house. Try it. Do it not only for the benefit, but for the pleasure of it. You will enjoy it as you never enjoyed sleep before. And it will give you vitality.

After you have overworked, you must rest. If you don't get rest, the undertaker may get you.

Don't Blame Mind

And finally we have the indirect help towards the cure by the suggestive removal of pain. We have no right to say that it is a pure advantage for the treatment of the disease if the pain is centrally inhibited. Pain surely has its great biological significance and is in itself to a certain degree helpful towards the cure, inasmuch as it indicates clearly the seat and character of the trouble and warns against the misuse of the damaged organ which needs rest and protection.

To annihilate pain may mean to remove the warning signal and thus to increase the chance for an injury. If we had no pain, our body would be much more rapidly destroyed in the struggle for existence. But that does not contradict the other fact that pain is exhausting and that the fight against the pain decreases the resistance of the organism. As soon as the disease is well recognized through the medium of pain and the correct treatment is inaugurated, not only the subjective comfort of the patient but the objective interest of his cure makes a removal of pain most desirable.

A quotation from a book that has attracted the attention of two continents, "Power Through Repose," by Annie Payson Call, is well worth pondering by a person who really wants to help nature to help himself to be well.

"I do not understand why I have this peculiar sort of asthma every Sunday afternoon,"' a lady said to me. She was in the habit of hearing, Sunday morning, a preacher, exceedingly interesting, but with a very rapid utterance, and whose mind traveled so fast that the words embodying his thoughts often tumbled over one another. She listened with all her nerves, as well as with those needed, held her breath when he stumbled, to assist him in finding his verbal legs, reflected every action with twice the force the preacher himself gave,--and then wondered why, on Sunday afternoon, and at no other time, she had this nervous catching of the breath.

She saw as soon as her attention was drawn to the general principles of Nature, how she had disobeyed this one, and why she had trouble on Sunday afternoon. This case is very amusing, even laughable, but it is a fair example of many similar nervous attacks, greater or less; and how easy it is to see that a whole series of these, day after day, doing their work unconsciously to the victim, will sooner or later bring some form of nervous prostration.

The same attitudes and the same effects often attend listening to music. It is a common experience to be completely fagged after two hours of delightful music. There is no exaggeration in saying that we should be rested after a good concert, if it is not too long. And yet so upside-down are we in our ways of living, and, through the mistakes of our ancestors, so accustomed have we become to disobeying nature's laws, that the general impression seems to be that music cannot be fully enjoyed without a strained attitude of mind and body; whereas, in reality, it is much more exquisitely appreciated and enjoyed in Nature's way.

If the nerves are perfectly free, they will catch the rhythm of the music, and so be helped back to the true rhythm of Nature, they will respond to the harmony and melody with all the vibratory power that God gave them, and how can the result be anything else than rest and refreshment,-- unless having allowed them to vibrate in one direction too long, we have disobeyed a law in another way.

Our bodies cannot by any possibility be free, so long as they are strained by our personal effort. So long as our nervous force is misdirected in personal strain, we can no more give full and responsive attention to the music, than a piano can sound the harmonies of a sonata if someone is drawing his hands at the same time backwards and forwards over the strings. But, alas! a contracted personality is so much the order of the day that many of us carry the chronic contractions of years constantly with us, and can no more free ourselves for a concert at a day's or a week's notice, than we can gain freedom to receive all the grand universal truths that are so steadily helpful.

It is only by daily patience and thought and care that we can cease to be an obstruction to the best power for giving and receiving.

Child and Rest

Adequate and proper nourishment, scrupulous care for its sense organs, due attention to rest after fatigue, and especially long hours of undisturbed sleep are essential conditions in the intelligent and sympathetic rearing of children. The interferences with sufficient sleep are to a high degree responsible for the later disturbances of the mental life. It must not be forgotten that nothing but rest and sleep can make complete restitution for the decomposition of the brain molecules caused by active exertion. Physical exercise is certainly not such restitution. In the best case it brings a certain rest to some brain centers by engaging other brain parts.

However, the child needs sleep, fresh air and healthful food more than anything else, if his mind is active. Regular and careful examination of the sense organs and unhindered breathing through the nose are most important. Even a slight defect in hearing may become the cause of under-development of the faculty of attention.

"There is no other influence which builds up the injured central nervous system as safely as sound natural sleep."--Hugo Munsterberg.

Many people have become insane, have made physical wrecks of their God-given tabernacles, because of too much work and overstrain--if you are one of these, get rest.

Over-Work

With many people, sickness is due to overwork. When this is the case, it is obvious that the patient must have rest. But sickness very seldom comes from overwork per se. We are probably safe in saying, never from overwork, if the patient gets enough sleep. It is more likely to be a case of too much nerve or energy expended in performing the given work along with worry, anxiety or negative thinking, in connection with the tasks at hand. Or, again, dissipation might have caused the sickness. As a rule rest does not necessarily mean suspension from all work, but more rest mixed with the work one is doing. Illustrative of this theme Annie Payson Call presents an interesting case in point:

"I am so tired I must give up work," said a young woman with a very strained and tearful face; and it seemed to her a desperate state, for she was dependent upon work for her bread and butter. If she gave up work she gave up bread and butter, and that meant starvation. When she was asked why she did not keep at work and learn to do it without getting so tired, that seemed to her absurd, and she would have laughed if laughing had been possible.

"'I tell you the work has tired me so that I cannot stand it, and you ask me to go back and get rest out of it when I am ready to die of fatigue. Why don't you ask me to burn myself on a piece of ice, or freeze myself with a red-hot poker?'

"'But,' the answer was, 'it is not the work that tires you at all, it is the way you do it;'" and, after a little soothing talk which quieted the overexcited nerves, she began to feel a dawning intelligence, which showed her that, after all, there might be life in the work which she had come' to look upon as nothing but slow and painful death. She came to understand that she might do her work as if she were working very lazily, going from one thing to another with a feeling as near to entire indifference as she could cultivate, and, at the same time, do it well.

She was shown by illustrations how she might walk across the room and take a book off the table as if her life depended upon it, racing and pushing over the floor, grabbing the book and clutching it until she got back to her seat, or, how she might move with exaggerated laziness, take the book up loosely, and drag herself back again. This illustration represents two extremes, and one, in itself, is as bad as the other; but, when the habit has been one of unnecessary strain and effort, the lazy way, practiced for a time, will not only be very restful, but will eventually lead to movement which is quick as well.

For the young woman who felt she had come to the end of her powers, it was work or die; therefore, when she had become rested enough to see and understand at all, she welcomed the idea that it was not her work that tired her but the way in which she did it, and she listened eagerly to the directions that should teach her to do it with less fatigue, and, as an experiment, offered to go back and try the "lazy way" for a week. At the end of a week she reported that the "lazy way" had rested her remarkably, but she did not do her work so well.

Then she had to learn that she could keep more quietly and steadily concentrated upon her work, doing it accurately and well, without in the least interfering with the "lazy way." Indeed, the better concentrated we are, the more easily and restfully we can work, for concentration does not mean straining every nerve and muscle toward our work,--it means dropping everything that interferes, and strained nerves and muscles constitute a very bondage of interference.

The young woman went back to her work for another week's experiment, and this time returned with a smiling face, better color, and a new and more quiet life in her eyes. She had made the 'lazy way" work, and found a better power of concentration at the same time. She knew it was only a beginning, but she felt secure now in the certain knowledge that it was not her work that had been killing her, but the way in which she had done it; and she felt confident of her power to do it restfully and, at the same time, better than before. Moreover, in addition to practicing the new way of working, she planned to get regular exercise in the open air, even if it had to come in the evening, and to eat only nourishing food. She has been at work now for several years, and, at last accounts, was still busy, with no temptation to stop because of over- fatigue.

Care for Yourself

The more you are rushed, the more work you have to do, the more careful should you be in your eating, exercising, sleeping, relaxing, breathing and in the organization of your time.

The more work you have to do, the better reason you should take care of your body as religiously as the violinist does of his instrument. Wholesome care of the body and mind is necessary if you are to do the largest amount of work. Indifference and neglect mean steady decay for body and soul.

And the more work we have to do, the more careful should we be in properly preparing our minds before retiring, by charging the subconscious mind for rest, strength, efficiency and power in work.

But above everything else you should never attempt to fall asleep with mind or body in a state of complete fatigue. First practice the silence a few moments and then as you drop off to sleep you will partake of a refreshing invigoration that will cause your state of exhaustion slowly but surely to disappear.

Civilization is abnormal in this complex age in which we are living, man has been taken abruptly from his natural surroundings of the open (abruptly when the great length of time he had led a free life is considered) into offices, apartment houses, street cars, railway trains, books, ledgers, newspapers and periodicals. Since the invention of printing other inventions have followed so rapidly upon the heels of one another that we have fallen into the habit of using our eyes in a way which involves a tremendous amount of strain. We have not had time enough to evolve from the open, rugged life of our ancestors to a cooped up existence in pigeon holes of apartment houses for our eyes to become adjusted to small print, electric lights, long hours in the school room and a thousand" and one eye strains which man encounters day by day.

Hence we are constantly bringing a strain upon our eyes unconsciously, overworking these priceless organs when we are unaware of it. Many of the leading scientists believe that eye strain is the cause of neurasthenia which often includes insomnia, irritability, weariness, mental confusion, nervous dyspepsia, vertigo, car-sickness and sea sickness, restlessness, bad temper, inability to sit quietly even for a few moments, facial twitchings of school children, nervous prostration, cholera, epilepsy and some forms of insanity--all of which undermine the vitality of the nervous system.

Eye Strain

Eye strain even reacts upon the moral nature and if not relieved may result in perverted disposition. Thus we see that our character may be warped because of eye strain. This is easily understood when we recognize how irritable a person may become when he is overworked and jaded. Over tax the eyes habitually and there follows unconsciously a reaction upon the moral attitude of the individual, resulting in an abnormality of character.

When the mental therapeutist reaches the charitable and common sense mental plane of understanding that the physical affects the mental, to the same degree that the mental affects the physical and is willing to pay the price of good health in eating right and sleeping right and breathing right, and exercising right, we shall have made a great stride forward. We shall, moreover, have reached that happy medium where the power of mind over the body will achieve its maximum influence free from the taunts and criticisms of the man in the street who fancies "There is no matter --All is Mind--Sit down--Do nothing—Enjoy yourself."

After your healing you should be sure that you add to your daily exercises the exercising of the eyes, and that you take plenty of rest following the overstraining of the eyes.

It is as much of a sin against the natural laws of life as it is a sin against nature to overeat, overwork, under-exercise and under-relax.

Dr. Eisley cites an extreme case of a man who suffered excruciating headaches culminating "in loss of consciousness, convulsions, frothing at the mouth, and wounding of the tongue, after which he would fall into a profound sleep, often lasting for several hours, from which he could not be aroused." Dr. Eisley corrected his eyestrain, and when he saw him eight years later, found that the headaches and convulsions had entirely ceased since the treatment of his eyes.

The human eye has evolved under conditions that called for distant vision. Primitive man used his eyes preponderantly for objects remote or coarse. With the discovery of writing and printing all this suddenly changed. It is one of the fundamental principles of evolution that new conditions call for new adaptions, and the beginning of writing and printing is still very recent, when considered from the standpoint of adaptive requirements.

Some of man's organic diseases arise from the strain upon the organs that have not yet adapted themselves to the upright position, and yet man has been a biped very many times longer than he has been a reading and writing animal. With the change from rural to urban life the conditions requiring near vision again made rapid strides, with accompanying additional eyestrain, and the eye has not had time to adjust itself evolutionally to the new situation. In other words, an eye adapted chiefly to distant sight, with only short periods, if any, of near vision, is suddenly called upon to reverse its habits.-- Charles E. Swift.

Diet, hygiene, rest, exercise, sleep, are as important relatively as right thinking. It is true that we attend to them habitually and with little thought, but the forming of the habit of right living requires attention just as does right thinking.

One cannot expect to sleep in a closed room and be filled with the same degree of health and energy as when one sleeps in a well ventilated room. One cannot neglect cleanliness of the skin and have it perform its excretory functions as well as when it is kept clean and glowing with health. One cannot expect to neglect the daily functions of the body, and be filled with the same joyous health and energy as when prompt attention is given to nature's calls. One must not blame "providence" for disfiguring layers of blubber when one eats a preponderance of fats and sugars. In other words, if the body is treated intelligently it will return dividends in health and comfort, a hundred fold.--"Emmanuelism--The Christ Science," by Thomas Parker Boyd.

WORK – SERVICE – HOBBY

Many people are sick because they have nothing constructive to occupy their minds. Work is one of the greatest blessings to humanity.

Play at Your Work

All work should be play.

If a man plays at his work and lives in conformity to the laws of hygiene, right eating, exercise, breathing, sunshine, fresh air and right thinking, he never will be sick.

The soldier in battle does not feel the pain of his wound, and in an emergency everybody develops powers of which he was not aware. The same effect which religion produces may thus be secured by any other deep interest; service for a great human cause, enthusiasm for a gigantic plan, even the prospect of a great personal success.

If the invalid, semi-invalid or convalescent is engaged in no particular occupation, has, in fact no business connections, no special tasks to perform, he will find himself with time on his hands, more than sufficient for all the requirements of regular exercise, affirmations and due attention to proper diet. Let him then be up and doing work of some sort, paid or unpaid. Let him get busy let him bestir himself, let him acquire an object in life. Work is the natural condition of man. "With- out it he cannot be happy and certainly does not live long. This is evidenced by the statistics of successful men who retire from active business to have a good time for the rest of their lives. Records show that they retire only to die. There are certain metaphysicians who, in my opinion teach the most absurd doctrine imaginable namely that the way to get well is to do nothing; to enjoy yourself; to go on an extended vacation; to take life easy; to go to a "Do Nothing" heaven. But the first premise of such advice is false. Toil is not a curse but a blessing.

Man cannot be happy without some useful vocation or avocation.

To have had a healing, then to eat properly, to exercise regularly, to cultivate proper hours of sleep--all this is good, but not enough unless accompanied by some study and congenial occupation.

In the case of an individual who (because of the possession of great wealth or otherwise) has been raised in idleness, a pre-requisite to the accomplishment of any lasting cure is, in plain language, for the patient to go to work. Too much time on his hands gives him opportunity to think of his aches and pains, to brood over his real or fancied maladies, to ruminate upon his misfortunes.

The Non-Workers' Union

Some metaphysical, psychological and mental science dreamers, idealists and impracticalists have a very peculiar way of living in the flesh where certain economic conditions and natural laws exist, and treating the ills that flesh is heir to.

You hear them say "Sit down. Do nothing. Treat. Have a good time. Go on a vacation."

Dr. W. A. McKeever, widely known lecturer and author, as well as a national author on juvenile problems, says:

" Work levels all. Work as service elevates all. Teach your child to work as faithfully as you would teach him to say his prayers or his reading lesson.

"Show your boy that the man who retires during middle life--no matter how wealthy—thereby enters upon a period of decay. Only the compelling pressure of work, business or philanthropy can possibly hinder a slow acting dry rot.

"Explain to your boy or girl how work happily done acts like a medicine, clears his eye, hardens his muscle, aids digestion.

"Explain to your children how work which fits their age or grade is a wonderful stimulant to the mind, enabling one to think clearer, faster and with a sense of joy."

Take your choice. Do nothing or work. If you can do nothing and be happy, I believe you are a world beater. I have never known a single person to do it successfully.

I have never heard of anyone who has led an active life going on an extended vacation and being happy. We are not so constituted. We follow the example of the Creator himself. It is recorded in the first chapter of

Genesis "In six days the Lord made heaven and earth, and the seventh day he rested." The very people who quote the Scripture, who tell you to treat and do nothing, to go on an extended vacation and be happy, seem to have overlooked the fact that the name Scripture says "'work" and proves it by representing the Lord as taking an earned rest after His labors.

Those who accept the teachings of Jesus as a philosophy of life will remember that Jesus said: "My Father worked hitherto and I work." In fact, it seems to me that the gospel as well as practical common sense are punctuated by work. From a religious angle McKeever may not be right, but he is right from a common sense basis, and my own opinion is that any religion that has no common sense in it is a religion that ought to be put on the bargain counter, sold at auction, knocked down at half price and whoever gets it buys a dear article at that.

The time may come when work will not be necessary to our enjoyment of life, but we are going to be a long time "evolution' " to that stage. The most unhappy man in the world is the man who has no work. If you don't believe it, try going for a year or two without anything to do, just making an effort "to be happy" by doing nothing and see how unhappy you will be at the end of your "vacation."

But we are not dogmatic. We lay down no strict rule or pedantic principle that any one has to swallow. Each fellow ought to have the right to swallow whatever he wants to. So, far be it from us to tell any searcher after truth that he must do a thing because we think he ought to. But we believe it would be most interesting for somebody who can be happy without work to organize a lodge, an institution, a party or a Union to be called the "Non-workers of the World."

If he could get enough agriculturists to join his new-fangled institution, he soon would rid the world of all its ills that flesh is heir to by starving everybody to death. If the farmers were all to join the "Non-workers of the World," there would not be enough food to keep us alive twelve months. But if the farmers did not all join and the railroaders did, if the farmers had raised enough to half feed us, and the railroaders became members of this "Non-workers of the World," how would we get the food stuff to the cities? And should there be railroaders enough to get part of the vegetables, grain and eatables to the cities, what would happen if all of the store- keepers, clerks and merchants were to seek membership in the "Non-workers of the World?"

There would be no way of distributing the food, if all joined the " Non-workers," so most any way you take it, if all became "sit-downers, treaters, extended vacationists and have-a-good-time-bugs" could get enough of their "buggy bugs" to make their "buggy bugged" institution a real "buggy house," if we didn't all become "bugs" the world would soon starve to death, and there is not much difference between a dead bug and a live bug any more than the dead bug would probably be a better member of the "Non-workers of the World" "buggy outfit" inasmuch as he would be on an ex- tended sleeping excursion and would not even have to exert enough energy to wake up in the morning to dress to continue on his extended vacation or report at the N. W. O. W. Union headquarters.

But far be it from us to prevent the organization of the "Non-workers of the World." If anybody can be happy without work, let him go to it; as for me and mine, we are going to work for the next few years. That is, we are planning on it now. " Great men change their minds" (and fools also), and who knows what the future holds? I suppose a man can be happy though crazy. Some of them are. Maybe the "Non-workers of the World" are just as happy as though they had good sense.

Take your choice--the "Non-workers' Union" or McKeever's plan of work. As for myself, I believe McKeever is right. If I were to make a humble suggestion, I would put it something like this: Work and treat. Visualize and concentrate. Plan and labor—combine the two and be happy. Take your vacation when you want. Rest when you feel like it. Work between times. As for me and my house, we will work and treat. "Be good, sweet child. Let those who will be clever,

Do noble deeds, not dream them all day long, And so make life, death and the vast forever, One grand sweet song."

Fuel for Life

It is only when engaged in work which we like that we can attain the maximum amount of health and happiness in life. Carlyle was right when he said, "Blessed is the man who has found his work." Your work should be systematized and outlined, your goal staked out, and faith underlie your efforts if you would have the maximum of success. Every normal man or woman has a certain amount of ambition which needs to be realized. This is God-given. It's the dynamo which keeps the machinery in the human power house going.

Your subconscious mind when instructed for success, for prosperity in vocation or avocation, will work as many wonders towards accomplishment in your business affairs as in the realm of health and physical well-being.

If you find yourself becoming a slave to your work, if you are getting no play out of it then cultivate a hobby--an avocation. Find one that you can ride lickety split.

A barber who has been off his job for only three days in fifteen years says that he gets his recreation monkeying around his Ford. He would rather tinker with the Ford, oil it, paint it, take it apart, put it together, polish it up, wash it, play with it long hours on week days and nearly every Sunday morning until noon than drive it. Fifteen years steadily employed in a barber shop, working made endurable by monkeying around his Ford, riding his hobby!

Have a hobby. Ride your hobby. Talk your hobby. Live your hobby.

After healing what? Work! Have a hobby or avocation.

RIGHT "ATMOSPHERE"

Enthusiasm

Emerson says, "Enthusiasm will accomplish anything." When it comes to matters of health, it's a good thing to remember the Sage of Concord's wise admonition. For us to remain lukewarm about our health, about right surroundings or environment, about keeping well, after the healing has taken place, is to commit a sin against the laws of health.

Be sure to generate enthusiasm and wholesome thought, inoculated with fervor and pep, in relation to your health.

Why We "Revert"

F. W. Sears, who has had extended experience in healing others, writes:

Frequently a person says to me, "Why do I not get as good results today as I did when I first became a New Thoughter?" That is the history probably of almost every one. Why?

When we first become imbued with these truths; when we first learn these lessons, we are so enthusiastic, so vitalized, and so inspired with them, that we believe nothing is impossible for us. The result is our vibrations are raised, we are lifted up into the higher currents and nothing can withstand our enthusiasm.--In the old thought world this change is called "experiencing religion,'—As long as we continue in these higher currents we are all right, but like a child with a new toy, we get tired of living in them; they are too rapid for us, and so we begin to get down in our vibrations; we "backslide' as it were.

We try and expect to accomplish, the same things down in the lower currents, where we lack the interest, the enthusiasm and the vitality we did when we were in the higher ones; we cannot do it, because it is impossible to manipulate these heavier and slower vibrating currents in a way to get the constructive results to be obtained only in the more vital and rapidly vibrating ones.

This we must emphasize. The very first condition for most people, if they would maintain, restore or keep their health, is to live in a healthful mental atmosphere. This is one of the most important things we have to learn. Our thinking, our daily thinking, must be done along lines which are wholesome and aspiring and uplifting. And it must, just as far as possible, ignore and inhibit thought of disease and diseased conditions.

Here is the testimony of a physician:

In the maintenance of health and the cure of disease, cheerfulness is a most important factor. Its power does not treat like a medicine, is not an artificial stimulation of the tissues to be followed by reaction and greater waste, as is the case with many drugs; but the effect of cheerfulness is an actual life-giving influence through a normal channel the results of which reach every part of the system. It brightens the eye, makes ruddy the countenance, brings elasticity to the step, and promotes all the inner force by which life is sustained. The blood circulates more freely, the oxygen comes to its home in the tissues, health is promoted and disease is banished.--Dr. A. J. Sanderson.

The "Atmosphere"

"Cultivate the positive emotional states of Fearlessness, Calmness, Poise, Cheerfulness,

Hope, Faith, Confidence in the Powers-that-be in Nature, in, above and over Nature. Form the habit of expecting and looking forward to the normal, natural conditions of Health, not to the state of Disease. Trust the Life Forces and Nature to "pull you through," even when you may happen to 'slip'."

It has been proved that the mind can give tone to the various cells of the body, as we have elsewhere shown, so a cheerful, optimistic mental attitude filled with Enthusiasm about Mental Healing will form fixed habits in the subjective mind, which will produce in turn like character to the cells.

A man's physical health is largely a matter of his self-suggestion. If he maintains a mental attitude of health, strength and fearlessness, he manifests accordingly. And if he goes about with a mind filled with ideas and thoughts of a depressing nature his body will likewise respond.

"Think" Health

Christian D. Larson, who has spent a lifetime helping others be well and succeed, expresses it like this:

Learn to think health. Give every thought the idea of health, and impress your most perfect conception of health upon every thought or mental state that you entertain. Think of yourself constantly as perfectly well. Think of yourself as strong, and think of yourself as gaining in health and strength constantly.

Whenever you are reminded of pain, illness or disorder, turn your attention positively upon the highest and best thought of health, life and harmony that you can form in your mind.

Think Wholesome Thoughts:--Train the mind to think and entertain only such thoughts as are conducive to health, harmony and well-being. Think of the good, the true and the perfect; think of the larger, the greater and the better; think of the worthy, the strong and the superior; think of the pure, the beautiful and the ideal. Give attention to those things that build, that elevate, that make for a richer state of existence, and create only such thoughts as have a rising, growing and expanding tendency. Give health and wholeness to every thought, by thinking health into every thought. Use the power of thought to produce health and direct every mental action to add to the quality and the measure of health.

While Zimmer says:

The universe pays every man in his own coin; if you smile, it smiles upon you in return; if you frown, you will be frowned at; if you sing, you will be invited into gay company; if you think, you will be entertained by thinkers; if you love the world, and earnestly seek for the good therein, you will be surrounded by loving friends, and nature will pour into your lap the treasures of the earth.

Trouble Seekers

Look around you anywhere, and you will see there are specializers in trouble seeking. There are thousands of people regularly looking for disease. They keep on hand antidotes for all kinds of maladies under the heavens and medicine for every possible ailment. They are sure they are going to need these things almost any time. When they take a trip they carry a young drug-store with them. They are ready for every kind of a disease they are likely to bump into and, of course, they bump into lots of them. Possibly the only chance they have to use their medicine is just before the journey's over but they are always feeling ill, having colds and catching contagious diseases because they are expecting to.

Real trouble hunters and sickness detectives

Others, who don't anticipate sickness don't take any medicine along with them, and don't have any trouble.

Some people always have their nose in the air, scenting some impurity, sniffing sewer gas or foul air, looking for asthma or something worse. Their locality is too high, or too low, too wet or too dry, too hot or too cold, too sunny or too shady. If they have any kind of ache or pain, they are sure it is asthma. They are looking for it, and they get it.

Above everything else, make for yourself and surround yourself with the right "atmosphere."

"Poor Stomachs"

Others fix their attention upon their poor stomachs. It is their storm center for all kinds of ailments. They have charts to tell them what agrees with them, and what doesn't. . . How many calories of this, that and the other things they should take to make up a balanced meal. And while they are charting their stomach and "balancing" their food, they get all kinds of trouble with their stomach. All kinds of trouble everywhere. Gas in the sewer pipes, gas in the atmosphere, gas in their stomachs.

If you charge your whole nature with the health ideal; if you think health, dream health, talk health; if you believe that you are going to be strong and healthy, because this is your birthright, your very magnetism will be healing to others. You will be a living illustration of the power of divine mind over all sickness and disease.

The time is rapidly coming when disease, sickness, will not be mentioned in the home; when all physical defects and weaknesses will be tabooed; when, instead of being saturated with illness and disease thoughts, children's lives will be permeated with the health thought, the thought of wholeness, of completeness, physical and mental vigor, hearty, grace; when joy, gladness, optimism will take the place of the old discouraged, sickness and disease thought and conversation in the home.

The words of a famous writer who healed herself are very apropos here:

Do Something

Any condition is perpetuated by recognition--by continually thinking about it. If I had sat around after treating myself I would have held the old condition. But I got up and forgot it all in my effort to make up for lost time. This gave the health-statements a chance to work.

After treating myself for ANY condition, of mind or body, I get up and throw myself soul and body into some active, physical work. In proportion as I succeed in losing myself in that, in that proportion do I succeed in healing myself thoroughly and quickly.

We should think of health, not of disease; of life and not of death; of freedom, not of bondage; of physical strength, not weakness; of an ultimate achievement--never anything less. The mind should be kept even, steady, in repose that everything may be as favorable as possible for nature's restorative processes.

Lay aside all fear and doubt. Trust in fullest measure. Let yourself rest in the everlasting arms, in the bosom of that tender love, believe in its power, give all problems into its care. Believe that you will be perfectly well. Then give the new power an opportunity to work and be not concerned if there are fluctuations of consciousness. Your spiritual consciousness will triumph in the end.

Have faith that the same power which healed you can keep you well. Have faith that the same force and laws which healed you can keep you healed. Have faith in yourself, have faith in man, have faith in God.

It is well for a person who has been healed by mental therapeutics to continue taking treatments of some kind or to some extent for three or four weeks or months after the healing has been affected. It prevents relapses.

Every psycho-analyst and mental therapeutist who uses the analytical method, has, I am sure, noticed that certain patients after being completely healed, have almost periodical relapses accompanied by states of mental and spiritual depression. Sometimes the depressed state is not pronounced; sometimes the old idea of returning sickness may not recur until long after the usual interval has elapsed; sometimes this will be a period of three weeks, again it will lengthen out to months. This condition is what the psychologist refers to when he uses the word, "reflex." A patient who undergoes this or a like experience should, of course, visit the healer for a more or less prolonged mental training in order to combat successfully these unorganized and unconscious partial impulses.

As a matter of sensible precaution anyone who has been healed should continue to treat himself for three months at least after the healing—by suggestion, upon going to bed and during the day, as outlined in another section of this book.

How to Treat

The following treatment given as an example by F. W. Southworth, M. D., in his book on "True Metaphysical Science and its Practical Application through the Law of Suggestion," furnishes an excellent illustration of the form of suggestive treatment favored by this particular school. The patient is addressed as follows:

As thoughts are not only things, but forces and act upon our mental and physical life for good or ill, we must be careful to always keep ourselves in that condition of thought which builds up and strengthens, to constantly think thoughts of health, of happiness, of good, to be cheerful, hopeful, confident and fearless.

Each day look forward to the morrow for progress and advancement. Think health--talk it and nothing else. Be cheerful, hopeful, confident and fearless always, and you will be happy and healthy. Eat, drink, breathe and be merry.

After Healing What? Right mental atmosphere.

MENTAL INDOLENCE

I had taught that oft times the one little push that the mind needs to get it over the hill top for health, is a suggestion augmented by the pressure of the finger tips, palms of the hands, tips of the toes and feet.--"Hemisphere Therapy."

After this lesson had been given, a young lady, who had been brought into my healing class in a wheel chair, having no use of her legs or feet, was personally told by me, and her mother as well, to be sure to practice this treatment in order to help the girl's mind heal herself. Some three days after, I took the girl for a treatment. Her feet were encased in big, specially made leather shoes and were as cold as ice itself. I took off the shoes and began to give the healing demonstration. After I had worked like a Trojan for fifteen minutes the circulation began to manifest itself, and before the class, the girl raised her feet and used her legs which she had not been able to do before. I turned to the mother and said, "How many times a day have you given this girl "Hemisphere Therapy" treatment! to which the mother replied, "Not any."

Indeed, people want to be healed, but they want somebody else to do it, and that cannot always be done. The patient himself must manifest some interest, physical as well as mental, in many cases, to bring about the healing.

Therefore I should like to emphasize as the last reason why some people are not well the fact, that after they know what has brought about their sickness, mental indolence prevents their healing, or prevents them from keeping health gained.

An Example

In one of my classes was a woman who had suffered with rheumatism, for three years. She could hardly navigate. "When she did, each step was punctuated with shots of pain. She was instantly healed in my class demonstration. She walked up and down the platform, lifted her legs and walked away, as well as ever. The next night I could tell by the expression in her face that something was wrong. Trying to build up her mind to a psychological plane where there would be a permanent healing, I gave her no attention for the next three nights, hoping that when I did come back to her, she would be so desirous of a permanent healing, that she would do what I had suggested. I knew she had not followed instructions.

So in our healing class a few days later, I again treated her and she was healed for the second time. She walked easily, sprightly, free from pain, as well as before. The next day she had reverted again. I have so many to look after that seldom do I give personal attention to a patient more than once. That is enough. Oft times I only speak to them or just touch them gently, but I had twice administered to this woman my energetic, magnetic treatment. So the next day I turned her over to a man in the class whose talent for healing I had discovered. (I might add here that anyone can heal, provided he has the faith within himself, so that he can instill into the consciousness of others, the faith within THEMSELVES to be healed). He had as good result as I. For the third time the woman was healed.

After I had healed her the second time, I had given her direct instructions what to do; to continue to hold a mental attitude of peace, harmony, health, love, God; also to follow daily readings which I exact from all people who take my healing class. There are certain fundamental principles by which we are healed, and we should be in tune with these laws not only momentarily, when we are healed, but forever after, if we expect to retain our health. It is therefore very necessary that people set aside at least a few minutes each day to read, meditate, and concentrate for their continued health.

I asked this woman after I had healed her for the second time, if she would promise to go home and to follow the outline of our reading, "Meditation and Concentration" before the class meeting the next day. With tears in her eyes she said, "Indeed I will." But when she returned the next day, reverted again, I asked her if she had done as I had requested, and she said, "No." Then some excuses followed.

But really it was mental indolence. Psychology cannot give a permanent cure to people who are obsessed by mental indolence. The patient must help God to help the law of healing to help one's self.

Away with mental indolence if you would have health.

Give Health, Get Health

After we have our healing let us be sure to give out our health to others.

The more one gives of his energy, the more he has for himself. The more one shares the joys of life with others, the more capacity for enjoyment he has. The more one shows the spirit of friendship, the more friends he has. The more one loves, the more love is lavished upon him, so the more health we give out to others, the more we shall have ourselves.

To keep your health, tell others about the ways of living, the laws of nature and the healing power of mind. Not only tell but do--"faith without works is dead." Put a lot of work back of your faith and mental healing. Spread the health message wherever you can in every way possible. In short, go out of your way to bring healing to others and that which you give others you will surely get back again.

Helping Idea

I would suggest to and even urge the reader who is taking this course for health to re-read both this book and our other books on Applied Psychology, and as you do so take not only mental notes, but jot down the things which interest you the most. Turn them over in your mind and see what you can add to these thoughts and how you may apply them not only in your life, but also in the lives of others. Get such a fundamental knowledge of the power of thought that you will be well loaded, ready for double-barrel, rapid-fire answers to all doubts or questions that others may present from time to time.

Nearly everyone is so constituted that once in a while he needs to prove these things to himself all over again. It is necessary not only to build up a good foundation of faith in the virtue of mind healing, but to keep feeding that faith from time to time--growing in the grace of mental science.

Why is not every life cured of its disease? Simply because some lives are not sufficiently persistent in their development of a health consciousness. They want health, and they say they are ready and willing to do anything which will bring health to them, but when we put their statement to the test we find that they are only "ready and willing"' to do it their way, and that when they find "their way" will not do, they quit

Some Continue Treatments

We should not only read, study, attend lectures, clubs, and associate with those of like mind, to keep our healing but also to the advantage of our whole growth; namely, mental, spiritual and physical development.

Very frequently a patient who has been healed, been made perfectly well, and is enjoying complete health, desires treatment to continue for the sake of the spiritual benefits derived.

Therefore, many people who are of intuitional nature, of religious and moral types, and spiritually inclined, will be able to keep their healing and maintain their progress much better if they continue from time to time to receive treatments from those who have given them a spiritual up lift.

Of course, we now are speaking about spirituality in its deepest and most significant sense. As stated elsewhere we could emphasize this "spiritual" idea to an unreasonable degree. For to stress the "spiritual" in our healing unduly and to overlook the natural, material, physical laws, is to carry mental healing to what is called in logic a reduction and absurdism.

The spiritual is the biggest thing in man, but for a time at least, this spirit within man is here on a physical plane, earth-bound, if you please, so that the physical and the mental must be recognized and harmonized.

So I say it is most important, no matter what may have been our early religious training or belief, that we develop our spiritual natures, and cultivate religious aspirations and associations if we would attain to the loftiest spiritual plane. One of the aspects of the great Christian Science movement which is open to criticism is that everything is spiritual and religious to the Christian Scientist, so much so that he has overlooked the other important domain of man; the material. This has brought down upon the movement an avalanche of criticism which would have been avoided had the early leaders of the Christian Science cult, instead of denying "matter", recognized the material as well as the spiritual.

While, therefore, we affirm with all the emphasis at our command that we should live scientifically and think rightly, we assert that man is primarily a religious animal and thus to be a rounded out whole, his religious instinct must be developed.

Man is not material only, he is primarily spiritual and to develop this spiritual side to the full, man must recognize the divinity within, the source whence he came, that of which he is a part, the very essence of the divinity, in order to be, in the fullest sense of the word, a spiritual being--"now are we the sons of God."

The normal man and woman yearn for God "as the hart (male red deer) panteth after the water brooks."

It is hardly necessary for me, therefore, gently to admonish you, and direct your attention to the fact, that man has not yet come to the end of the rainbow of health, success and happiness. Indeed, we are only on the way to the crest, and are being swept onward to loftier heights by every gentle wind from the mental realm which touches the leaf on the calendar of time.

We shall know more about truth tomorrow than we know today. That means we shall know more about the natural laws of health and the natural laws of spirit tomorrow than we know today. That is as it ought to be. The wise student will ever be ready and open for the influx of the spirit to guide turn to a deeper knowledge of the laws of man, of nature and of God.

Look for truth everywhere!

Helping in the Future

As mentioned elsewhere not only may the subconscious mind be used for healing disease, but for warding off the encroachments of sickness. The method necessary to be followed is to hold oneself in the mental attitude of denying the power of disease and thus obtain the mastery over it. The instant the patient recognizes the first symptoms of any approaching sickness, he should vigorously begin auto-suggestions to the contrary, --affirming health, strength, power, harmony, denying that disease will have any power over him while he is in such a mental attitude.

Just as prevention of disease by materia medica has always been an important tenet of medical practice, so the prevention of disease by suggestion and auto-suggestion will in time become the most important phase of all mental healing. Indeed its chief value will eventually be found to consist in the almost unlimited power which the subconscious mind confers upon one to protect himself against contracting disease.

After the patient has persisted in his healing and it has been effected, should there ever be any inharmony a second time or should but one sickness out of many be healed, he will find that the next time he tries mental healing it will not take as long as the first. There will be less resistance of doubtful auto-suggestion to overcome, more strength of body and mind. The subconscious will take the suggestions of healing more easily the second time than the first.

In some instances irregular habits have to be corrected before the healing takes place. Remember, therefore, that after the healing the patient should not return to an irregular way of living--irregularity in eating, irregularity in drinking, excess in the use of tobacco, alcohol or stimulants, or abnormal sex practice.

Be sure that everything you do, you do with a purpose, using your mind continually. As you walk, you should take your health affirmations or formulae. You should breathe with the thought of health and life, strength, vitality, love, purity and growth. You should eat and drink with a purpose, bringing your mind to the attention of health and life and love and God.

Don't Talk About Your Sickness

It is not, however, enough in mental therapeutics to present good suggestions: we must also remove previous bad ones. Such a patient must therefore be isolated to avoid conversations about, and sympathy with the patient's sufferings, all of which keeps up the action or vibration of the diseased ideal centers.

Anyone who talks much of illness radiates a diseased consciousness.

One who regards soundness as normal and to be expected, sheds it broadcast, and his very presence will strengthen and uplift.

In "Self-Healing through Suggestion," Henry Harrison Brown gives a unique illustration:

Thought-conditions which have lam latent in the system make themselves known to consciousness, just as an imperfect stringer in a bridge will sometime manifest in an accident. When any unpleasant condition becomes apparent we can but say: "'It is an old condition coming to the surface. Let it come and I thus shall outgrow it!" With such thought there will be new nerve conditions instituted so that recurrence of the trouble becomes impossible.

You re-live in old conditions whenever you recall them. You recreate any condition by brooding upon it. Therefore memory is either a life-bringer or a life-destroyer.

When you "note the bright hours only" memory is one great source of health. Cultivate "the gentle art" of forgetting all that is not pleasant. Never recall, never talk about, never think about, the unpleasant past. The outline for right thoughts is given in previous pages. Any thought born in, or that will create, any morbid emotion, is to be avoided as you now avoid poison. Turn from it and affirm the opposite.

Think of yourself as perfect in spirit and as manifesting that perfection through your body, now.' This picture of perfection is your Ideal.

Exaggeration the Next Step

Many a person who allows himself to dwell upon his sickness and to tell others about it comes in time to exaggerate until his imagination leads him to believe that his pains and aches are much worse than those of any one else, notwithstanding the fact that thousands of other good, patient people have actually suffered more than he who talks the most about it. By recalling our sickness and telling others about it (unless we are so well grounded in our own healing and so fixed in the new attitude toward life that we see only the good, think only the good and live only the good), we are quite liable to effect a return of the old habit of thinking about sickness until the sickness may and often does return.

So you see common sense must be applied to psychology if nature is to be given a chance to do its part.

How It Reacts

Notice how this acts upon the dyspeptic, gloomy, pessimistic, downhearted and dreary. He enters the house and at once puts his wife on edge with the fear that he will lapse into another fit of temper or spasmodic tantrum, either because he does not like what is cooked, or because his morbid caprice demands something else that is not cooked. The good housewife seeing her dear hubby in the door-way cannot even wait for him to be seated at the table before beginning to admonish him to be careful what he eats. Hubby must eat this, and hubby must not eat that. This will hurt hubby's stomach, and that will clog hubby's liver. Hubby will start to eat something, only to be interrupted by a terrified wifely cry that it will be the death of him.

Now although this precautionary nagging is not maintained through any sinister motive it is none the less the very worst policy of suggestion which could possibly be followed. The solicitous wife thinks she is helping to prevent another attack of dyspepsia, whereas in reality she is merely giving her spouse a few pushes downward into the dyspeptic slough of despond. He takes up the suggestion that this thing or that thing is bad, that his stomach won't stand this or that, and more harm is done than as though he ate a real square meal of the right stuff. He goes about with insufficient nutrition, and what little he does eat is taken in an atmosphere of dread and fear.

The stomach begins to contract, the gastric juice secretion is curtailed, and the sufferer develops a sinking sensation inside. When he reaches the next meal he is as hungry as a bear and this time he overeats despite the fusi-lade of advice from his alarmed counselor across the table. He overeats partly to make up for the scantiness of his previous meals and partly in a spirit of resentment and contention; resentment toward his wife for telling him what he should and should not eat, and contention with himself for eating as scantily as he did.

Unhealthful Communities

This is what we mean by having the right atmosphere.

Watch all suggestions which reach you after you have been healed; discouraging the negative and pessimistic and clinging only to the positive and impressive.

We frequently see unhealthful atmosphere generated in communities through such mistaken but well-meaning devices as "cancer week," "tuberculosis week," and other "weeks" of similar nature, when people are advised to seek counsel from a family physician or someone else who is willing and able to give the advice and take the money for it.

Much harm is done in this way, because the indecisive and uncertain state of mind produced. The "what's-it-all-about" feeling engendered, and the naturally resultant dread of a thing so blatantly advertised, all combine to create a worse state of mind than before, not only in the actually sick, but likewise in those who are sensitive and susceptible to suggestion.

Create your own "atmosphere," if negative suggestions are all around.

If conversation about disease is forced upon you by other people, banish such thoughts and turn the discussion into happy and useful channels.

Keep your mind occupied by healthful, happy, bracing and pleasurable ideas. This will stimulate the bodily organs to perform their functions in a normal and vigorous way.

Cancer Talk

The power of mind to attract disease came most forcibly to me while writing "Fundamentals of Psychology" during a visit to the rural community in Pennsylvania where I was born.

The main conversation in that little town among people on the street corners, and visiting – and here they have the habit of most rural districts, of neighbors and relatives visiting a great deal, especially in the winter--the burden of the conversation was sickness, sickness, sickness. I heard more about cancer in the two months I was in that little town than I have heard in all of my life spent elsewhere. These conversations recalled my boyhood days and the many good people in that section who had died of cancer. It is such a horrible disease that it gives people who are so inclined occasion to talk about disease to their hearts' content.

And so doing, they deeply impress the cancer percept upon the subconscious, with the result that cancer is a very ordinary disease. I never saw anything to beat it. They talk about cancer as other people talk about colds and coughs. What they talk about they get. Members of the Ladies' Aid Society talk about sickness at their meetings, the fishermen talk about sickness, people on the streets and in the stores talk about sickness, punctured and staccatoed and pizzicatoed with cancer until the whole air is filled with cancer, cancer, cancer.

A real way to get cancer is to talk about it, and the safest way to get rid of it is to take mental treatments. Readers of this book will have done with the gossip of cancer before all the pages shall have been read.

What May Happen

If you continually give your cell minds the suggestions of cancer, the cell minds are going to respond to that suggestion. If you tell your cell minds that you are well, you will be well. If you think health, you are thinking health into your cell minds--if you think sickness, you are thinking sickness into your cell minds.

If you cannot get your mind off your own sickness and trouble, become interested in other people who are well and associate with them as much as possible. Study the laws of health and hygiene as a matter of private and necessary business; but seek the companionship of those who talk health success and happiness, rather than cultivating the sort of gossipers who spend their hours swapping stories of indigestion, rheumatism, hardening of the arteries and high blood pressure.

In "Suggestion and Autosuggestion," Baudouin comments very practically and enlighteningly on this line of health talk:

When we have occasion to refer to our habitual ailments, we should be careful always to employ the past tense, saying, "I have slept bade of late;" instead of the customary present, "I am a bad sleeper," which condenses the present and the future, and involves the future just as much as if we were to say, "I shall sleep badly tonight." Furthermore we should make it a rule to talk as little as possible about our ailments. When we are asked how we are, it is better to reply "Quite well, thank you"--better not only that we may avoid aggravating our own troubles, but in order that we may avoid disseminating suggestive contagion. Speaking generally, we should turn our minds away from "undesirable'" things.

The Greeks Were Right

The Greeks had the excellent sense not to talk very much about their ailments.

If you are not a Greek, in blood, at least be a good Greek in spirit when it comes to putting the soft pedal on the discussion of your troubles.

Get Your Health Stride

When one hits the true gait in talking health, and really gets his own stride in spreading the gospel of well-being, it is easier to talk health than ill-health.

Get your health stride!

We must talk about the things we want; the perfection of that which we hope to reach.

Suppose the artist were always to talk about imperfect models, or the architect always to look at bad plans. Where would they get ?

As the artist must think about perfect models, and the architect think about good plans, so must the health-seeker think about health rather than ill health, perfection rather than imperfection, and harmony and growth rather than sickness and disease.

Jesus gave good advice when he admonished the leper he had cured, "See thou tell no man." It was an injunction which he often repeated during his career as a healer of the sick.

We have had all kinds of exegetical comments on this passage from the Scriptures, but I believe the only correct interpretation is that Jesus understood how when a person is suddenly healed by any process he becomes avid to talk about it in public and private, and to sympathizer, believer, skeptic and scoffer alike.

The skeptical people who doubt the very principle of such things become argumentative, or ridicule the idea of healing by mental processes.

Jesus understood this and realized that skeptics might talk something like this to the patient:

"You have been cured by exciting your imagination. You think you are healed but you are not. Your disease will return as soon as the excitement has subsided. You are on a mental spree, ana when your mental drunkenness wears off you will be worse off than before."

"Watch Your Step"

If the one who is healed is not strong enough to maintain his own idea about the thing, and thus ward off such incredulous tirades, he may fall by the wayside, accept the negative suggestions, and by crediting the skeptical theory become worse than before.

Jesus gave no classes in mental therapeutics, but only exhorted his subjects to have faith.

It is essential that every person be thoroughly grounded in the process by which he is healed, if he would safely retain the results of the cure despite contact with negative and materialist minds. To this end one cannot too strongly urge that people who have been made well by the power of the mind refrain from talking about their past troubles.

Of course there is another side to this--a side arising out of the fact that one man's testimony will help to heal others. Testimony was one of the mainsprings whereby Christianity spread so rapidly in the first two centuries after Christ.

Testimony indeed is what helps many a cult to grow; but before you give your testimony (which everyone who has been healed should ultimately do) be sure that you are grounded and anchored and doubly anchored in the faith that you have been healed logically, scientifically and everlastingly. Then you may tell others, but not until then

Besides some who tell of their sufferings suffer again, and the reaction upon the consciousness of the sick man is commensurate with the responses which the sympathetic listener gives to the doleful sick tale.

Watch His Face

Along this line you will notice very often that when a patient begins to tell of his serious illness or the sufferings he has endured, he reflects his former symptoms in his actions and his facial expressions. Reciting his old troubles restores to the picture gallery of memory in the subconscious his past experiences and even if this does not bring the old pains back it will very often retard the patient's progress toward recovery.

So when you tell others about the wonderful power of mind for healing and explain that you have been healed, be sure that you hold uppermost in your mind your improvements. Concentrate not upon what you were, but upon what you are, and what you will be. Think only the thoughts that you desire to have manifested in your body.

If a person is always talking about his particular sickness, he conveys his unhappy thoughts to his subconscious mind and his body is affected accordingly--that is, provided he is not strong enough to speak about his sickness without dwelling upon the past. If his thinking concerns itself chiefly with his wholeness today and that which he desires tomorrow, no harm will come of it.

At all events it would be well for all who have just been healed to take positive affirmations after they have told others of their sickness and their healing, such as "I am well, whole and complete," "I am one in spirit, divine in life, whole in body, in tune with the Infinite. I am, therefore, harmonious, well and complete" "Health, Life, Love, God."

Never Mind Diagnosis

Here is another striking reason why it is not well to pay much attention to the cause or to the diagnosis of your disease: A person who is in- disposed, who doesn't know just what is the matter with him, who has perhaps over-eaten or is run down physically, goes to a physician. The good doctor being only human and liable to err, possibly misreads the symptoms and wrongly diagnoses the case. If now the patient is a highly sensitive person, a diagnosis, indicating a malignant or dreaded disease, may arouse in the patient (especially if he be a thoracic or a muscular) an emotional state such that the suggestion erected by the faulty diagnosis really causes a serious disease.

Many physicians will not state the results of a diagnosis in the presence of a person who is in an emotional state.

I should not be understood to assert that nothing but unfriendly suggestions may be readily accepted during emotionalism, for a person in a high state of emotionalism is just as impressionable to favorable as to unfavorable suggestions. How quickly a man in the heat of anger will change his attitude when a sympathetic third person gently speaks to him in terms of confidential and comprehending love. Therefore, all emotional states should be used to call up imagery of the beautiful, of the good, of the wonderful, the successful and the healthful.

We have been taught and have been maintaining certain attitudes toward life in terms of conventional theories of disease and suffering. Your attitude is now beginning to be that of a thoughtful soul, speaking the language of health, not the nomenclature of disease. Out of this attitude will spring new habits of life and better health. Out of this attitude physical changes will come. They are bound to come. They must come. They will come. The essential thing is to attain this serene attitude and enjoy its benefits.

Toward the close of the wonderful Sermon on the Mount Jesus admonished his hearers to be as modest in the matter of prayer as in all other aspects of deportment, in the following words:

And when thou prayest, thou shalt not be as the hypocrites are: for they love to pray standing in the synagogues and in the corners of the streets, that they may be seen of men. Verily I say unto you, they have their reward.

But thou, when thou prayest, enter into thy closet, and when thou hast shut thy door, pray to thy Father which is in secret; and thy Father which seeth in secret shall reward thee openly.-

-Matthew 6: 5-6.

Of course, Christ does not mean necessarily to go into a closet--he means to be by oneself in mind. This may be upon the street car as well as upon the desert sands. We may be surrounded by the multitudes and yet our mind be in the inner most recesses of the soul.

The injunction Christ gives means that what you desire you should ask for in secret, and it will be presented to you openly.

THE SILENCE:
WHAT IT IS AND HOW TO USE IT

Contents

Approach to the Silence

Wrong thinking produces inharmony in our body, which in turn produces sickness. Our bodies sometimes are instantly re-harmonized while in the Silence. In the Silence our minds become passive, open, free and loving, at which time the Infinite Master of harmony touches the mental chords of our being and we are well.

Just as the piano can be tuned, so can the mind. Man's body is made up of twelve octaves the same as in music. All matter is music. All matter is composed of twelve octaves. Wrong thinking brings inharmony in some of the octaves of our body. Right thinking tunes these organs, puts them back into their normal condition.

Boys have their little steel magnets by which they pick up small pieces of steel, pins and so forth. When overworked, these magnets no longer attract. Then the boys take their magnets, have them rubbed against strong magnets or remagnetized with an electric current and their power is quickly restored—so with our bodies. Mind is the re-electrifier and re-harmonizer of the octaves into all harmony.

Right thinking, therefore, is the most important thing in life. As a man thinketh in his heart so is he. Just as a tuning fork near a piano will respond with a vibration when a key of the same pitch is struck on the piano nearby, so likewise do the bodies of men respond to proper stimulus and become in tune. By right thinking man can re-harmonize himself, can achieve health, success and prosperity.

To enter the Silence one must first establish perfect relaxation in mind and body. Then as the consciousness is brought from one part of the body to another the tuning takes place.

If the leader in the Silence should be intoning, there will be many in the audience who will feel tinkling sensations—vibrations—and often are instantly healed. They have been instantly re-harmonized. Sometimes it may take several intonings in the Silence for a complete healing. Should you have a violent vibration, feel no fear, but thank God for your healing because the more violent the vibration perhaps the worse has been your condition and the more surely has the re-harmony begun. Some people will feel this vibration for hours, even days, throughout which there is always healing.

Others may not feel the vibration at all, yet if there has been any inharmony in the bodily organs, these organs are unconscious to the conscious intoning re-harmonization. Many people who have been healed of divers and many malignant diseases were at no time conscious of any vibration. Never be discouraged if you feel no sensation. If you do feel a vibration, know that you are susceptible and on the high road to a healing demonstration.

The one intoning may or may not be feeling vibrations. Religion is the life of God in the soul of Man. The Silence is the medium by which the life of God and the soul of man are brought into At-one-ment.

The Silence is a medium by which man comes in a closer touch with the Infinite; a medium by which man becomes conscious of his nearness to the Infinite. The Silence is the meeting place where man's spirit links with God's spirit; where spirit meets spirit and the marvel of His grace never ceases.

The Silence is another way of praying, which is another way of concentration. It is another way of visualization.

"As a man thinketh in his heart so is he." In the Silence a man can by his thoughts change his life, his conditions, his environment, his all. By right thinking man becomes harmonious. A harmonious man—in tune with the Infinite—is on the King's highway to health, success, abundance, prosperity, happiness, love and peace.

By means of wrong thinking our minds are put out of harmony with the great Infinite spirit of God. "As a man thinketh in his heart so is he." When wrong thinking becomes right thinking, then man's right relationship to God is restored. He becomes an open channel for the influx of the spirit so that whatever demonstration he may desire he may have.

In the Silence a man may change his thinking as in no other way, therefore, may change his heart, change his whole being, change his environment, change every condition to which he was subject.

The human body may be likened to a harp. When man thinks rightly his body is in tune; but wrong thinking creates inharmony in the body and produces sickness. Wrong thinking produces inharmony in the mind, which, of course, disconnects man from rightful association with the Divine. A man must, therefore, think right. Yet, because of centuries of erroneous conception of God and of the world, man has been a negative instead of a positive being, and his unwisdom has reacted upon the present generation.

We are mental sending and receiving stations. What we receive depends upon how we are thinking Now. For success, health and happiness we must in the silent chambers of the soul change our thinking if we are holding negative or inharmonious thoughts. In the Silence there is presented to man his greatest opportunity to change his thinking. Wrong thinking produces inharmony of the body which in turn produces sickness. If we change to right thinking we have health, success and happiness. Therefore the Silence when properly used re-harmonizes our bodies and minds through the simple agency of right thinking.

"There are steps of approach to the Silence. Stillness is one thing and the Silence is another. One may quiet himself physically and not be still, and he may be still without entering the Silence. When one becomes physically and mentally at rest, he is apt to become receptive to psychic influences; and when these are not desired it is advisable to protect oneself while mentally negative. One may affirm his Oneness with God, his being surrounded and protected by the divine Goodness, and may symbolize this by enveloping himself in thought with the white light of love or the mellowed tints of sunshine.

"With the senses calmed and unresponsive to the slower vibrations, but responsive to the quicker ones, a peace and calm pervade one's mind, and it becomes consciously receptive to higher vibrations of vital energy. Immune from the lesser harmonies, one opens himself to the greater ones, which are always seeking avenues of expression. With the greater influx of the One Life, a sense of power steals over one and he becomes conscious of increased vigor and vitality.

"In relinquishing specific thoughts, one opens inwardly rather than outwardly, and becomes receptive to subconscious impressions that are directed by his conscious affirmation of fundamental Truth. The subconscious responds by returning to the conscious the logical sequences of the Truths that have been consciously impressed upon it. The subconscious follows the lead given to it by the conscious affirmations of Truth, and it brings back the consciousness of those Truths in their various ramifications."

Health Silence

Select one or more of the affirmations or formulas below to hold in thought while in the Silence. You may change or vary these as you choose:

Soul is health, spirit is health, God is health, I am health. Since there is but one mind, there is but one mentality. This mind and mentality is God; God is health. I am health.

"I am whole, perfect, strong, powerful, loving, harmonious and happy and what I am myself I desire for everyone else."

"I am filled with the abundant, intelligent, ever-present life of Spirit. It flows through me freely, cleansing, healing, purifying and vitalizing every part. I am one with this life and in it I am every whit whole."

"The all-powerful Christ Mind in me dissolves and dissipates every adverse thought. My body is the pure and Holy Temple of the Living God, and every organ and every function is now in Divine Order and Harmony."

All the organs of my body are functioning normally and I am well, whole and complete.

All is mind, all is God, all is universal energy. I am part of creative force and I am health, abundance, joy and peace.

I am filled, I am thrilled with Life Eternal and I radiate that life within to me and without to all.

Every experience of my life has been for my good and I am happy in living.

God is Spirit. I (use your own name) am life. Life Spirit is now flowing through me freely and I am well, whole and complete.

"Be still and know that I am God."

USE THE FOLLOWING AS A BASIS FOR YOUR MEDITATION AS YOU DEMONSTRATE HEALTH. OF COURSE, YOU MAY USE OTHER THOUGHTS PROVIDED THEY ARE CONSTRUCTIVE HEALTH THOUGHTS.

You may practice the Silence sitting, reclining, or in bed.
There is no better way to learn how to relax than by going into the
Silence. Are you tense? Let go. Relax.
Then direct the mind to go from one part of the body to another. Take a deep breath between each change of your consciousness. Be sure to use the diaphragmatic or abdominal breathing—breathing through the nostrils, mouth closed until the muscles of the abdomen expand.

The best time to hold the Silence is as you retire at night, and just as you awaken in the morning.[1] But you should hold your thought at least three times a day, without stress or strain, without doubt or worry, passive in mind and body—perfectly relaxed.

Hold the Silence or thought upon retiring at night, awakening in the morning, and at noon day. Of course, you may take any other time that is convenient. You may concentrate on the roadway, street car, home or office, but it is well, if possible, to have one room for your Silence. Most people in that way will build up stronger vibrations. At noon now there are all over the world thousands of others holding Silence so that there is a great combined mental force working together at one time for success, health, prosperity and happiness, and we therefore get the benefit of this great vibration.

The more often you hold the Silence without stress or strain, as a rule, the quicker may be the demonstration.

The real part of me is Spirit, not matter. I believe that this body of mine is a Tabernacle for the Spirit. The real "I am" within me is therefore Spirit. The real "me" is Spirit.

This Spirit is the God Spirit. This is what Jesus meant when in the fourteenth chapter of John and again in the seventeenth chapter of the same Gospel, speaking to His Disciples He referred to "I in you, you in Me and We in God."

My Spirit is a part of the God Spirit. God is health, God is perfection, God is abundance, God is harmonious. Therefore, the real "I am" is God; the real "I am" is health, perfection, abundance and harmony.

When I am sick I know that it is the material of me that is sick, not the God Spirit; it is my physical being which is out of harmony, it is this Tabernacle of which Paul speaks, housing my spirit, which gives me pain and suffering. The real "me" is not sick, it is my body.

For centuries we have held to a wrong idea of life. We have thought that life is material; but life is spiritual, it is the invisible within me which is eternal, which is God. Many still believe that life is material and matter, instead of mind and spirit. I no longer hold that conception. I believe that all is mind and Spirit.

Just here is where the healing methods of drugs and the scientist's explanation of life is so limited. Not until we recognize that life is really a thing of spirit—not matter but mind—not material but spiritual—do we come into an understanding of Truth.

Jesus said, "God is Spirit," and on different occasions told His

Disciples that this Spirit was within them as well as within Himself.

Therefore, this same Spirit is within me and this same Spirit is the

God Spirit of health, abundance, happiness, harmony and perfection.

God is all health, all abundance, all harmony, peace and perfection. Therefore the God Spirit within me is the same. I am sick in body; not in mind, not in Spirit.

Inasmuch as I cannot conceive of God being sick neither can I conceive of my Spirit being sick. My spirit is health, perfection and harmony. My body may not be well, but since mind is all, since this material is subject to the spiritual, since matter is subject to mind, I believe and affirm that my health does not depend upon matter but upon the God Spirit within me. It depends not upon the material but the spiritual, upon the God mind within.

Just as wood when made into a violin and properly tuned, will give forth harmony, so my body, though made in the material, when properly tuned by mind will give forth harmonious living, perfect health.

As the tree standing in the forest may be made into the violin music box of harmony, so my body, the material in the forest of matter, may be put in tune, become harmonious and be raised to perfection by the Master Musician, God—His mind within me.

God is all health. No one could conceive of God as being sick. I can visualize only the eternal spirit of the Infinite Father. Perfection existing in everything and I being a child in Spirit, am well, whole and complete in Spirit. My real "I am" is well.

Science now asserts that matter is composed of twelve octaves, just as in music. My body is the composite of these twelve octaves. Science also says that every cell atom, every electron in my body is intelligent.

This spirit of mine is housed in the Tabernacle of the body which is composed of millions and millions of cells, all of which having intelligence respond in my body according to the way I think.

Every word I entertain, every thought I hold, influences every one of the millions of cells making up this Tabernacle.

My body is made whole and complete physically. That is, all the cells of my body are made over new every eleven months. The body I have today is not the body I had eleven months ago. I get a new body every eleven months and my body is today what my thinking was yesterday, the day before that and the months before that. My body in the future depends upon my thinking in the future. I am what I think I am.

When I affirm that I am well, whole and complete; that I am perfect, harmonious and strong, I am suggesting to every atom in my body perfection and every atom in turn begins to make my body over, new in health and in perfection.

I may or I may not have to wait for the element of time to make over every cell. That may be done spontaneously and instantly. There is no limitation to the power of God so I shall not set a time limit for my healing, knowing that all things are possible with the Father. I affirm that now I have that which I desire. I know that now the Spirit of divine health is surging through me, touching and reaching every atom of my body and that now the God Spirit within me is perfect and that Spirit makes my body perfect.

"Man is a Spiritual Being. Man expresses himself mentally and manifests himself physically. The One Life animates all that exists. Harmony of existence depends upon the polarities of the three aspects of life. The mind is at ease when open to the inflow of the Spirit. It is discordant when it follows sensory impressions. The body is healthy when responsive to the direction of the spiritualized mind. It becomes diseased when it accepts the physical as its guide. One achieves mental ease and physical health through his mental polarity. If open to the physical and closed to the spiritual, discord will prevail. If open to the spiritual and closed to the physical, he lives the One Life, in mental ease and physical health. I open my mind to the inflow of the Spirit. I place my body under the control of my spiritualized mind. I feel the One Life animate my mind and my body. I AM a Spiritual Being. I AM Perfect Health!"

Miscellaneous
Silence[2]

THOUGHT TO HOLD IN THE SILENCE FOR ABUNDANCE

(See also Abundance)

"The Universal Abundant Spirit Supplies All My Needs."

There is no want or limitation in the law. If, perchance, there should appear to be lack of, or need of, abundance in our lives, it is because of wrong thinking—not because there is a lack of abundance. Therefore, we should enter the Silence with the profound faith and conviction that the world is filled with plenty, and that all our needs are most bountifully supplied.

The mind should be saturated with the conviction that all life is filled with abundance—all space is overflowing with abundance—all living comes from an abundant source of supply.

In a Universe where this is true, there can be no want, no lack for you or yours (for me or mine).

As you take your exercises this month, take the affirmation above. As you walk on the street to your office, or place of business, continue this thought. As you go about your daily duties in the home or workshop, let the mind be saturated with a spirit, a feeling and thinking of abundance— "The opulence of the Universal Source of Supply now meets all my needs," "The Abundant Life Giving Spirit of Prosperity now leads and guides me into the paths of plenty, peace and power," "My mind is filled with prosperous thoughts, my being is pulsating in abundant rhythm, my soul is uplifted and sustained by a thousand thoughts of ever-present abundance, prosperity and opulence."

As these thoughts are maintained and repeated again and again, absorbed and sunk deep into the subconscious mind, know that all of your needs are this minute supplied. Know that you could not ask for anything from the Universal Spirit—Father, God—without that Spirit being most willing to supply, instantly, all your needs. The spirit and body are well, but the flesh is weak. Allow your flesh to be stimulated, and your body to respond by thoughts of abundance, prosperity and opulence.

"I am now rich in thought, rich in body and rich in spirit. I am now part of the abundant ever-present spirit of prosperity and opulence. All that I need is now mine, mine, mine."

The Universal Abundant Spirit supplies all my needs.

Thought To Hold
In Meditation In The Silence

FOR MISFORTUNES, GRIEF, MISTAKES, REVERSES, FAILURE, SORROW, LOSS AND DISAP-POINTMENT

"All is Good."

We are entering upon a new consciousness for the human race, a higher plane of mentality, and a greater development of the spiritual life.

In spirit, of course, there is no wrong, no sorrow, no grief, no misfortune, no losses, no reverses. In short all is perfection.

The age in which we are living has not yet developed this spiritual understanding. We are still of the earth—earthly—and we are still in that consciousness where the physical is affected by seeming misfortunes, reverses, sorrows, griefs, trouble, sickness, etc. We may be wise in not expecting that suddenly this generation of man will reach that spiritual plane where there will be no recognition of anything except good.

We are a part of the Infinite Spirit ourselves and, of course, in spirit, we are perfection. But this physical body of ours manifests imperfection from time to time, because of our past training and past thinking, because of our own consciousness. In time there is no doubt in my mind but that the spirit within will make a perfect body without. This perfection will be recognized in health and in peace of mind. It will be recognized so that there will be no such thing as misfortunes, sorrows, reverses, failures, griefs, disappointments or losses being able to affect our mentality or our body. In this state of consciousness, as we are emerging from the chrysalis, material stage of man into the greater life, into the deeper spiritual understanding, we are subject to certain conditions not conducive to peace of mind without an effort. In other words, we recognize, or feel the effects of losses, misfortunes, disappointments, sorrows, griefs, etc. We recognize now, that the time is coming when the spirit will be so completely in control of matter in the body, that we will not recognize any inharmony. To reach that Great Spirit is one of the big forward steps in this generation. To reach that spiritual plane also means the right kind of thinking now. We plan, today, for tomorrow. This is true in every walk of life.

We plan our home today—and build it tomorrow. We make our merchandise today and market it tomorrow. We sow our seed today and we reap the harvest tomorrow. We build our career today, little by little, and we reach the outcome tomorrow. Therefore, our thinking today will change our tomorrow. The thinking of this generation will change the condition of tomorrow's generation. If tomorrow's generation is going to be free from the recognition of sorrows, misfortunes, griefs, fears, pain, losses, failures, reverses, inharmony, discord, etc., it depends upon our seed sowing.

Our seed sowing today should be "All is Good." All is Good in spirit. You can say that and be honest with yourself. All is perfection in spirit. All is good for us in spirit. All is good for our lives here. Spirit transcends matter. When we recognize, affirm, and continue to hold the constructive thought that All is Good in spirit, we are changing our own mental attitude, our own bodies, all matter in general—getting ready for the greater realization of the spiritual manifestation in the next generation.

Therefore, for your own good here today in success, prosperity and happiness as well as in health, peace and harmony, begin to pronounce over everything in life, *All is Good*. If you have any misunderstandings, *All is Good*. If you have any losses, *All is Good*, any reverses, *All is Good*, any sorrow, *All is Good*, any inharmony, *All is Good*. In everything at all that is out of perfection you must recognize only the good. *ALL IS GOOD*.

Sending your thought energy by repeating All is Good, and thinking All is Good, and living All is Good, you will actually, in this day, overcome your difficulty, and turn all of your mistakes, blunders and misfortunes into stepping stones for your own success, health and happiness.

I enter the Silence this month, this day, this hour and this minute. My mind is obsessed and under control of the Divine Spirit, I recognize here and now only good. I see in my fellowmen only perfection and good. I see in nature all around me only perfection and good. I see in every transaction of life only the perfect good. I see in every activity of my experience, and in every form, color and thought, good. All is Good for me now, today and forever.

God is spirit; spirit is love; love is perfection; God's spirit is harmonious, I am perfect, I am love, perfection and harmonious.

ALL IS GOOD.

For Harmony, Peace, Comfort

Base your thought for this Silence upon the following. You may add any constructive thought you choose.

"My Subconscious Mind, I Desire and Command You to Have Peace, Harmony and Justice Reign in the Hearts of Men Everywhere."

I realize that there can be no negative thinking for my destruction, downfall or harm sent out by anyone else that can reach my consciousness, or do me ill, unless I am afraid that such negative thinking will produce the evil affects others are planning.

I know that Thought is Energy. This is scientifically demonstrated, and I realize that a constructive thought has much more energy than a destructive thought. I know, because it has been conclusively proven, that constructive thinking will blast away every negative thought-current sent out by one person, or by a thousand.

Therefore, if there should be any inharmonious thoughts anywhere in the world—any discordant thought-current by those who seek my downfall, or block my progress, or by those who would endeavor to hurt my reputation—I know that by holding a harmonious attitude of peace, love, joy and success for everyone, including those who would do me wrong that such constructive thought-currents will blast away all of the discordant and inharmonious mental currents of evil so that they will not even reach my conscious mind.

I also realize, when I hold my silent thought, "*my subconscious mind I desire and command you to have peace and harmony and justice reign,*" that I am sending out the energy of construction which is bound to turn all of the efforts for my embarrassment and destruction into a higher current for my greater achievement.

Therefore, I send out blessings and thanksgiving to the very ones who would work my downfall. I charge my subconscious mind to let peace, harmony and justice reign so that all things will work together for the good for me and for those who are thinking evil.

If I should think it hard to send out blessings to my enemies, I remember the affirmation of the Greatest Teacher of all ages Who said, "Forgive until seventy times seven." I remember that when He, Himself, was reviled, reviled not in turn. I remember that when His merciless enemies had nailed Him to the cross, had apparently crushed His fondest ambition, had scorned and reviled the Kingdom of which He had spoken, and had tortured Him as He hung on the cross, He uttered the immortal, lovable, constructive words which have rung throughout the centuries, and will continue to bless all mankind throughout eternity: "Father, forgive them, for they know not what they do."

So those who would try to block my way, curb my progress or put thorns in my crown are doing so "not knowing what they are doing." "Whatsoever a man soweth, that shall he also reap." Instead of hurting me, they are sowing weed seeds, which shall bring forth a harvest of weeds and tares in their own lives, and not in mine.

I, therefore, do not wish them harm, nor think that they should feel the reaction. I do not have to concern myself about the negative people in the world—for the law takes care of them.

I shall always think constructive thoughts, harmonious thoughts and loving thoughts. "My Subconscious Mind, I desire and command you to have peace, harmony and justice reign, and know that all things are now working together for the good of my would-be enemies and for myself."

I relax (here pause and wait), take time for meditation (here pause and rest relaxed) and I become happy in the silence—holding my thought of peace, harmony and justice reigning in the hearts of men everywhere—and, as I relax and wait, I feel my vibrations rise. I am resting at ease, in faith. (Pause.) I am perfectly calm and contented. (Pause.) I am sending out love, peace and harmonious thoughts, and, as they go, love, peace and harmony will come to me. These are now returning. They enter my being and uplift my soul.

I am, therefore, sending out a strong current of spiritual blessings, with such a spirit of helpfulness, that I am getting back the same which I send out. My harvest shall be peace, love, joy, harmony, justice and contentment, because I am sowing the seed of love, peace, harmony, joy, contentment and justice into the great subconscious soil of the universe.

"My Subconscious Mind, I desire and command you to have peace, harmony and justice reign everywhere throughout the world."

I wait—I rest—I am relaxed—I am at ease and filled with the spirit of harmony. I wait. I listen for the spirit within. I feel and hear the voice of infinite love sending back into my consciousness these thoughts which I send out.

I know that my every constructive thought blasts away a thousand destructive ones. Therefore, I think peace, joy, love, harmony and justice, and, as I utter these words slowly and prayerfully, I feel my vibration rising—I experience ease of mind and peace of soul. Harmony is now within and without.

I realize that I cannot send out my affirmation of peace, love, joy and harmony without peace, love, joy and harmony coming back to me. I, therefore, send out my affirmation: "My Subconscious Mind, I desire and command you to have peace, harmony and justice reign-in the hearts of men wherever they may be." I wait and listen—perfectly relaxed and at ease—and I feel the vibrations which I sent out coming back to me.

I, therefore, know that no harm can befall my dwelling place. I know that whatever evil thoughts have been sent out for my destruction have been counter-blasted, and that now everything is working for my good.

As I recognize, and realize, that all things work together for my good,

I am sending out love-thoughts that all things are working together for the good of those who would do me wrong. "They know not what they do."

They alone will have to reap the harvest of the weeds they are sowing.

My wish for them is that they may learn their lesson easily and early.

My blessings I send out to them.

Again I wait. Again I listen. Again I am at ease, happy, and at rest. Love and blessings, peace and harmony, I send out—love and blessings, peace and harmony, come back. "My Subconscious Mind, I desire and command you to have peace, harmony and justice reign. My blessings upon all mankind—my love to everyone!"

Thought to Hold to as a Basis for the Silence

FOR SUCCESS

"I Have Faith and Conviction in My Ultimate Success."

I believe the Scripture: "My ways are not your ways, saith the Lord; neither are my thoughts your thoughts, for as the heavens are higher than the earth, so are my thoughts higher than your thoughts."

I understand by this Scripture that the thoughts of the Infinite God are far above the understanding of finite me; that God's ways are higher than my ways. "God moves in a mysterious way His wonders to perform."

I also have faith and conviction in my ultimate success because I am a part of the Infinite Spirit, and in the Infinite Spirit, there can be no failure. I am harmonious, complete and successful in Spirit—in God.

I may not see my success today, or I may feel as though I have accomplished little, but I know that all my efforts and energies, in the past, present and future, are working together for my good.

Therefore, I shall hold the thought that my success has already been achieved. I am Success, I have success now and forever! Therefore, I think only success; I talk only success; I believe only in success; I am demonstrating success, and I know that success is mine.

The needed lessons I am having now, have had in the past, and may require in the future, are but necessary stepping stones to my greater success. The apparent delay of my greater success means that I am now demonstrating more success than I could otherwise have. Dreams that I have dreamed, visions that I have visualized, and the goal that I have mapped out, are all a part of my ultimate greater success. I have that now! I am successful now!

As Moses went into the land of Midian, and spent forty years of his life as a shepherd in the wilderness—(apparently with no future before him—which, however, was the great schooling necessary for his greater triumphant success in the future)—so I may be, in my land of Midian, apparently, only a sheep herder, but in reality getting the necessary training for my greater and ultimate success.

Therefore, I now rejoice in every experience I have—giving thanks for every apparent set back, and for every "seeming" blocking of my purposes and aspirations.

I believe that my past experiences, as well as present happenings, are for my benefit, and that I could not have been the great success I am, and shall be, had not the discouragements of yesterday, the perplexities of today and the drawbacks of tomorrow come into my life. I realize that I need to go into the land of Midian; that it is as necessary for me, as it was for Moses, to spend a few years in the wilderness of Life's experience. I am happy to know that I am in such company as that of the Great Leader of his people, and rejoice in the thought that the Lord has called me to spend my time in the land of Midian, getting the necessary training for the greater things the Lord has in store for me.

There is no place in the world where clouds do not gather, and storms do not rage; but when the storms abate, and the skies clear, then do we appreciate more fully the glories and beauties of God, the Universe and its natural laws, and Infinite Love.

However, I know by experience in the land of Midian, where clouds hover low, and where storms try the soul and body, that the dawn of a new day shall make life all the sweeter for me and mine.

Moses could not have enjoyed leading his people into the promised land, had he not been in the land of Midian. If he had stayed forever in the Court of Pharaoh, with its attendant luxuries, life would have taken on a dull, monotonous hue, and his experience would have seemed drab, wearisome and pale.

I am glad for the privilege accorded me to be in the land of Midian for a short time! I know that, as did Moses, I shall enjoy my promised land all the more when my greater success shall have been well worked out by the hand of Divinity.

Faith and conviction in my ultimate greater success is stronger today than ever! I hold such a strong thought, and such a deep and courageous faith in the workings of God's plan, that I know I now have that which has been intended for me, and nothing can take from me that which the Lord hath prepared for my success, health and happiness. I know, too, that I shall learn daily to enjoy, appreciate, and make better use of the success I now possess; that I shall unfold day by day into greater opportunities for more influence, power, friendship, charity, love, comradeship and service. I know that my present success is but a part of the greater success which the Lord has waiting for me—"just around the corner".

Therefore, I shall offer up prayers of thanksgiving and gratitude; I shall work harder, being more particular in the preparation for my greater work, than I have been in the past—never doubting but that every moment spent in this greater preparation will bring added interests, and a greater success in the future.

Even as Moses did not doubt the wisdom of the Lord for a greater future (when in the land of Midian for forty years), so shall I not doubt His ways today.

I claim, with a joyful heart and an attitude of thanksgiving, that my life could not have been as great in the future had I been denied my present experience. I know that greater things are in store for me, because God's thoughts are greater than my thoughts; because He is giving me that training now, in my land of Midian, which I most need. I trust the guiding Spirit of Infinite Love to lead me, at the right time, into my life's Promised Land.

The success today, in my land of Midian, is attracting unto me the greater influence and power in my Court of Pharaoh, and in my leadership, as I lead others into that promised land which the Lord has prepared for me and mine.

I smile—I sing—I rejoice, and offer thanksgiving and gratitude for my success now and forever. Surely I believe more and more: "My thoughts are not your thoughts, neither are my ways your ways, saith the Lord," and all things are now working together for my good.

Therefore, I have faith and conviction in my ultimate success—in my greater success—in my greatest success!

Abundance

"There is abundance in the world for me given by the bountiful hand of Omnipotence. I gratefully claim and accept all the supply for my needs."

The old idea of orthodox prayer was that of supplication and begging. I have spent a whole night at a time begging for a few pennies and supplicating for the salvation of others. What waste of energy. Each time that we send up such a weak supplication as the attitude of a beggar, with the timid, frightful thoughts that only a beggar's mind can have—this condition of mind, cross circuits the power to bring into our lives the very things we most desire.

When the beggar extends his hand for a copper, he knows that not everyone who passes is going to give him a coin. He, therefore, solicits more or less mechanically, with a mind not positive or sure. His hand is extended in timidity and weakness. Now and then he gets a coin from a sympathetic passer-by. The same principle holds true for the man who prays in the old orthodox fashion. He utters his petitions with doubts and misgivings, with timidity and wonderings. Some of his prayers are answered—just as the occasional coin is cast to the beggar. But most of the orthodox prayers sent up in the fashion of begging and supplicating are never answered. Of necessity, they cannot be, because the concentration is filled with fear and trembling.

Only by positive and courageous thinking do we attract to ourselves the answers to our prayers. When we are permeated with the spirit of doubt, our petitions are cross-circuited.

Therefore, in making your affirmation this time, rest assured that the abundant spirit of the Universal Supply has everything you need, and has it now. You have only to put your mind in a condition to receive.

You do not have to beg the sun for its rays, nor God for His love. It is there for the taking. Many of us keep the sunshine of abundance out of our lives by pulling down the curtain of doubt—just as we may go into a room, pull down a shade and keep out the sun. James Russell Lowell, seventy-five years ago, told us the same story in "The Vision of Sir Launfal," when he said that "Heaven is given away and God may be had for the asking".

By gratefully accepting all of the supply for your needs, you are running up the shade of positive faith and letting the sunlight of abundance in.

Send out the desire for your supply to the Universal Mind and then rest—feeling that it has been acquired. Of course, the stronger you concentrate, without stress and strain (as outlined in "Practical Psychology and Sex Life," by the author, under the chapter "How to get what you want," and chapters on "Concentration"), and the more positive and courageous your concentration, the stronger will be your mental thought currents and consequently the quicker your demonstration.

Omnipotence has provided for me and mine, I raise the shade of my faith and let in the Sunlight of Abundance. I know I do not have to beg for this, for it is mine now. When first I saw the light of day, the bountiful spirit of the Father made all preparations for my life's necessities and pleasures. They have been in the world since I was born. I now claim and accept my supply.

From now on the spirit goes before me—making easy and prosperous all my ways—and I have abundance for every need. From the bountiful hand of Omnipotence I have abundant health—I have abundant love—I have abundant prosperity—I have abundant peace. My Father careth for the grass of the field and the birds of the air—and He careth for me. I realize it.

Think it and live it now.

Abundance for all my needs is mine, now and forever.

Health, Success, Prosperity, Universal Peace and Brotherhood

"God Made From One Blood All the Nations of the World."

As I enter the Silence this time, expecting to get health, success, prosperity and happiness, I am going to have my mind filled with the Spirit of Divine Unity. Unity among the nations of the world, unity in abundance, unity in love, unity in prosperity, unity in health and unity in spirit.

There can be no separation in Spirit. All is Mind, all is God, all is Universal Energy. I am part of the creative force. I am a part and parcel of the Unity of Love, Nature and God. Therefore, where God is, I recognize a completeness. And I, being a part of God, a part of this spirit, a part of the power with Him, am, therefore, at one with God and all thought.

I am therefore at one with God and all spirit. Nothing can separate me from the love of God, but my own mental attitude. Nothing can separate me from abundance, happiness, success, prosperity and love, but my own wrong thinking. Love is dealt in the world in the spirit of God and, therefore, recognizing this unity of love, I am a part of it and have perfect love, success, prosperity, abundance and health.

The ocean is composed of water. If I take a bucket of water from the ocean, it still is the water of the ocean. I may take this water to an island in the sea. Though I have separated this water from the main body of the ocean, it still is the water from the sea. But, as the water is separated from the main body of the ocean, it loses its power, its strength and many of its cardinal properties. I am the same as the sea water when I, by wrong thinking:—whether it be jealousy, envy, hatred, misunderstanding, worry or fear—separate myself from the spirit of God. I am as one going upon an island of humanity. I am still of that same spirit; but it has been separated, so that within me, it has lost many of its cardinal virtues. These virtues are there, but I do not recognize them. Separation has lessened my strength, my vitality, my power, my health, my happiness, my prosperity and my joy.

Just as it is necessary for the bucket of water to remain in the ocean in order to contain all of its original power and to retain all of its original strength, to be intact, so is it necessary for man to keep in the spirit of at-one-ment with the Father, that we may manifest daily God's principle of Unity with God, man and nature.

When we have maintained that attitude of one-ness with the Father in all respects, we are then recognizing and expecting, in this act, the fullness of our spirit. This fullness of our spirit will, therefore, give us health, prosperity and happiness.

When I have a mind that is filled with negative, discordant or inharmonious thoughts, I am separating myself from the full expression of the Divine within me. I am the bucket of water going stale on a human island; but, when I make my spirit at one with the Father by harmonious thinking, by love, kindness, good will, fellowship and co-operation, I am not only maintaining all of my original properties, but I am in correspondence with the Infinite Spirit so that I can manifest and express His original spirit in every particular.

Where there is a unity of spirit, there is unity of all the good things of life. Perhaps I am not drawing from the bank of life's experience everything that I ought to have—because I have separated myself from the spiritual board of directors in this bank of life, and am not getting my dividends on time. My mental attitude is the cause; therefore, as I enter the Silence this time, I am going to maintain the faith and the love-spirit of my unity with all things. I maintain, therefore, my at-one-ment with God, with man and nature. I maintain that all of the original strength of spirit is mine. I hold that the manifestations of this original spirit will produce everything in my life for my ultimate good, because I am at one with the Father. All things are mine.

The Silence, this day, finds me at one with all. The Silence, this day, finds me at peace with God, Man and Nature. The Silence, this day, finds me in at-one-ment with God and all, in unity with every conceivable thing in the universe. Therefore, my unity, my at-one-ment with the Father, my wholeness of spirit with God brings into my life everything for my good.

All things work together for my good in my at-one-ment with Man, God and Nature—in my unity with all.

Hot to Have More

"I Am Unselfish in Action, Being and Motive."

The science of psychology as applied to everyday life is, strictly speaking, a new science. It is a matter of thousands of people in the world all of a sudden coming in contact with certain laws, which make them successful, healthy and prosperous.

It is quite natural, because man is interested more in himself than in any one else, that, when he finds these laws may be applied to give him more abundance, the tendency may be to use these laws for selfish purposes.

Nothing could be more unpsychological. The laws should be used for the individual, but should not stop there. Each individual who is profiting by the operation of the laws, or understanding of psychology, ought not only to get everything himself that psychology can give him, but he should pass these on to others; he should tell others about it; he should cry it from the housetops and megaphone it from the street corners. He should not want to get everything himself, but wish the same that he has to everyone else. By doing this, the law will rebound, and, instead of having less, he will have still more than he would have were he thinking about the laws for himself alone.

The human race is made up of a whole lot of selfishness, and the man, or the woman, who hopes to get the most out of life and out of psychology, must learn at the very beginning of his or her understanding of the laws. Then, only, will the best come to those who are absolutely unselfish.

If there is any selfish motive or selfish desire in your heart, you may operate the law and get a certain amount of benefit, nay, you may even become rich by it and have great power, but it should not end there. Your riches are for the use of others, as well as for yourselves, and the real psychologist, in getting his riches, will pass on to others that which he has. The real psychologist, in getting more power, will share it with others and will use it for the good of others, as well as for his own personal aggrandizement.

Therefore hold the thought: "I am unselfish in action, being and motive."

Many a person never will get the demonstrations he wants, because the channel of abundance and prosperity, happiness and joy, is clogged up with his own selfish attitude. The selfish person who does operate the laws, does so by overbalancing his selfishness with some other great virtue. But when he is extremely selfish, he may never have demonstrations as he wants; he may not have enough other virtues to outweigh his selfishness. He may live for years, and know what the laws are, and yet lack this one little thing, unselfishness, in operating the laws for his own abundance, prosperity or happiness.

If you are not having the demonstrations you want, it is because there is a kink in the mind somewhere. The kink may be selfishness, or it may be pride, haughtiness, duplicity, dishonesty, hatred, envy or jealousy.

This time we are going to hold the thought: "I am unselfish in action, being and motive," and each time we go into the Silence, this unselfish spirit shall be the guiding-star of our thoughts. It will be the personal touch with the Infinite Spirit itself.

The beginning of life's happiness, as well as the end thereof, is the spirit of unselfishness.

"I am unselfish in action, being and motive."

All Things are in Divine Order

"Divine Harmony and Peace Actuate Every Thought and Action of My Being."

I realize that all things are in Divine order for me and mine. There can be no disturbance in the world without or the world within my being but that is in perfect harmony with the Infinite.

The circumstances outside of my life are all for my good. My environment where I am now and the conditions in which I am living, I make harmonize for me by my attitude of mind. I think only peace, I breathe only love, I speak only harmony. My conditions and my environment, although outwardly inharmonious to my likes and tendencies, are changed by the alchemy of my thinking into a perfect symphony of happiness for me now.

"Divine Harmony and Peace actuate every thought and action of my being." This thought is energy, this thought is life, this thought is power. The energy, life and power of this thought weaves all of my diversified Life's experiences into a Divine pattern of perfection for me. There can be no trouble, disappointments, sorrow, reverses, loss or discord but that shall be changed for my good when I think Spirit and live the affirmation of today, namely, "Divine Harmony and Peace actuate every thought and action of my being." All things are in Divine order.

The Spirit of Divinity prompts my thinking. The Divine within me actuates my actions. The God Powers within, this minute are working all things together for my good. There can be no danger come nigh my dwelling for my body is the temple of the living God. Therefore, the God Spirit within me protects me from all harm, inspires me to high ideals, lifts me to heights of righteousness and fills my soul with love. Love for my circumstances, love for my present conditions, love for my environment, love for everyone in the world, love for all of the creation of God.

Therefore I have no enemies, for I love all. I recognize no misfortunes, for the love energy within turns all misfortunes and sorrows into stepping stones for my greater advancement and achievement. The God energy within transforms all inharmonious conditions without into a perfect harmony within. The Kingdom of God now reigns within me and I am at ease, at peace and at-one-ment with all nature and God. The harmony therefore within me in nature and in God gives me perfect peace within and perfect peace without. Divine thought and energy, love and blessing actuate every action of my being.

Where Divine Love reigns there can be no trouble, no discord, no inharmony, no lack, no limitation, no sorrow, no grief, no sickness, no failure. The energy of Divine Love transforms all things into my Good. The Love and Peace of the Father abideth within me and is manifested without so that my life is one harmonious whole touching the lives of all others who come in contact with me so that they, too, feel my vibrations of at-one-ment with the Father and they in turn become harmonious and complete in Spirit with man and God.

Divine Harmony and Peace actuate every thought and action of my being.

All things are in Divine order.

Thought to Hold in Silence and to Meditate upon During the Day

FOR JUSTICE

"There's a Spirit of Justice that Secures me in Which is My Own."

If we reach a consciousness of justice, we need have no doubts as to our care in every particular while journeying between the two peaks of eternity—from birth to the Great Divide.

There is nothing that can defeat justice; and the person who has a consciousness of justice will attract to himself every conceivable thing needed for this life, because it will be the logical objective of justice to supply to each individual that justice for which he thinks.

That is the reason why this affirmation is so complete in itself; namely, "There is a spirit of JUSTICE that secures me in which is my own, and this security is provided already for us by the Spirit of Justice."

It would be a psychological paradox to think that Justice could be defeated. That could not be. Perhaps it appears to you that your own has not yet been secured to you, but, remember that life is fleeting—that a year is as a tale that is told—and that a decade is but as "Ships that pass in the night"—when the years have vanished in the distance.

If you have lived a life of justice, and it appears now that your own is not coming to you, that someone else is having more of the good things of life than you, and that someone seems to have used the art of the man of injustice, be not deceived, God is not mocked, for "whatsoever a man soweth that shall he also reap." If you have sowed equity and justice in the days that are gone, be sure that the same equity and justice will be secured to you.

The Scriptures tell us not to think too much of the man who is nourishing like a green bay tree, for his efforts are soon cut off and he vanisheth away.

One who is astride the scales of justice, and who thinks that he can hold the balance, is gravely mistaken. He may have occupied his present position for many years, first putting his weight on one side and then on the other in an effort to keep his equilibrium. Perhaps today it appears that the scales of justice are being well manipulated by his insincerity, duplicity or trickery—but it is like the green bay tree. It will soon pass away.

Justice is as eternal as God Himself, and there is no more possibility of defeating it in the individual's life, in your own life, in the life of a nation or in the history of mankind, than there is likelihood that the sun can get away from its own rays. The justice of God is eternal, or, in other words, God always is Justice, personified. Where God rules, and where His laws and mandates have been given by His own fiat, "man, neither flesh nor the devil" can defeat the ultimate outcome of justice. Your own is secured to you.

Man himself is fashioned by the finger of Divinity. The crown of justice is placed upon his brow and no ruthless hand of greed, duplicity or evil dexterity can ever tear it away. It is there to stay, and the man who has been thus crowned because he has lived in this consciousness of justice—in the consciousness of God Himself—is bound to have come back to him that which he has thought, that which he has sowed—Justice. You are secured by this spirit of justice.

Perhaps already your life has had the law of compensation bring to you more than to others of whom you may think, and who, because of their bank account, get more out of life than you. A man may have a million dollars, and yet not be as happy as the laborer living in a thatched cottage. *Perhaps Justice has tipped the scales in your favor already—and you have failed to recognize it. Perhaps you have children, loved ones, family and fireside which bring more comfort to you than the land owner gets who lives in his palace on the hill.*

Half of Life, or the joys of Life, depend upon our ability to recognize and appreciate the blessings we already have. Therefore, in counting your blessings, or discounting your blessings, be sure that you use a moral standard, instead of a material standard, in gauging whether justice has been meted out to you or not.

The Justice of the Eternal secures me, the Spirit of Justice secures me in which is mine own. Believe it, think it, live it, claim it and Justice shall be yours.

––––––––––––––––

Question—In practicing the Silence, the mind seems to flutter all about and there is great nervous tension. What is wrong?

Answer—Lack of concentration. This person ought to follow some simple exercise of concentration, such as given below, until the mind has control over the body. By practicing a few of the simple exercises given below, fifteen minutes a day, and then taking the Silence a few hours after these exercises have been practiced, the mind will begin to be under control.

The nervous tension is caused because of this lack of control, and in the effort to bring the scattering mind into one focus the reaction comes upon the nervous system which, in turn, reacts upon the body.

Practice and exercises for lack of concentration follow.

Exercises

By Thos. Parker Boyd

(1) Select some part of the body, a foot or hand, with the idea of HEAT. While holding the mind in this attitude, breathe deeply and steadily, and, in from one to four minutes, you will feel the warm glow coming to the foot. In this way, you can soon master the entire body. Begin with the sense of feeling. If there is an itching of the body, make it stop by the force of your will. In from three days to three weeks, you can stop the itching sensation at will. Then try the habit of sneezing; stubbornly resist the inclination to sneeze, and you will soon have the mastery. Now try your will on coughing. When the tickling sensation comes, stop it by the exercise of your will. You can soon master it. Next try it on pain. When you feel a pain in the body, instead of rubbing on liniment, rub in a little will power; soon it will ease your pain as if by magic. With the fingers of one hand rub the skin on the back of the other hand, stroking toward the elbow, and will that all feeling shall disappear. In from one to three minutes, take a needle, and you can stick it through the skin on the back of the hand without pain. You may have to try it a dozen times, but persistence will bring success. Having mastered the sense of feeling, take up that of hearing.

(2) It may seem impossible at first thought, but you have seen people so absorbed in what they were reading or thinking that they heard nothing, although you addressed them directly. They are simply abstracted from all else, and are thinking of one thing—to the exclusion of everything else. They entered this state of abstractedness unconsciously. To do so intentionally, you go by the law of indirectness. For instance, take sight; concentrate your vision and your whole attention upon some object, real or imaginary, until soon the sense of HEARING becomes dormant. A little practice will enable you to study, think or sleep, regardless of noise.

(3) Having mastered hearing, begin on SIGHT. You have known people who walked on the street, looked at you and passed by without recognition, although they knew you well. A person deeply thinking on some subject, neither sees nor hears, but uses the mental sense entirely. The method is to let the eyes be open, but concentrate the thoughts on hearing or feeling.

(4) After getting control of your sight, take up the TASTE. Take some tasteless thing on the tongue, abstract the mind to something else until the taste becomes dormant. Then take something with more taste to it, abstracting the taste, until by this gradual process you can make the sourest pickle sweet.

(5) Finally take some light odor, and hold it before the nostrils, abstracting the attention from the sense of smell, by hearing or seeing, etc., until by practice you can pass through the foulest odor without inconvenience or notice.

Sit or stand absolutely motionless, except your breathing, for one to five minutes at a time. Do this often.

Practice closing each finger in rotation; then, when all are closed, open one at a time very slowly, keeping the attention fixed on what you are doing. Keep all the other fingers still, save the one you are exercising with.

Inhale gradually for ten seconds, and then exhale in the same way and time.

Look steadily at some point or object for a minute without winking the eye, keeping your attention fixed on the object.

Look at a picture critically, then close your eyes and mentally reconstruct it.

Close your eyes and construct the face of a friend, feature by feature.

Fix your attention on a hand or foot, hold on it the idea of heat and continue until the hand or foot feels warm. Then try cold; then try pain.

Will that the person in front of you shall turn around or put his hand on his head or neck.

Hold your hand on someone in pain and say, "I will the pain to depart." Repeat till the pain goes.

———————————

Note.—For a scientific understanding of positive and negative concentration, see "Practical Psychology and Sex Life," by the author.

Silent Treatment

Those at a distance or those who cannot attend my classes may have silent treatments—distance is no barrier—race or creed no bar to those who earnestly want to benefit from the Silent Treatment.

Many marvelous cures have been reported through Silent Treatment. Business has been increased, positions secured, bad habits broken, prosperity demonstrated, peace and harmony restored in home and business.

This is one of the strongest of Dr. Bush's study features. Use blank on opposite page for yourself, your friends or those whom you desire to help. You may begin it at any time.

You will get the vibration of the campaign and the power of thousands of minds working for you and with you for your health and happiness.

These silent treatments will help the sick rise above disease, overcome despair, and bring to themselves the positive healing vibration of Dr. Bush and his class.

USE BLANK ON NEXT PAGE AND BOLD THE THOUGHT OF THE DEMONSTRATION YOU DESIRE—THERE IS NO FEE. GIVE IN PROPORTION AS YOU HOPE TO SECURE. "FREELY YE HAVE RECEIVED, FREELY GIVE." THE LAW OF COMPENSATION DEMONSTRATES THIS TRUTH.

Notes

[1] For complete study of how to charge the subconscious mind, see chapters on the "Subconscious Mind," "How to Cleanse the Aura," "How to Get What You Want," "Concentration" and "Visualization," in "Practical Psychology and Sex Life" by the author.

[2] Scientific explanation of the Silence and How to enter the Silence and the benefits derived thereby, will be found in "Practical Psychology and Sex Life" by David V. Bush.

CPSIA information can be obtained
at www.ICGtesting.com
Printed in the USA
LVHW052040210222
711647LV00009B/200